A Life in the Struggle

A Life in the Struggle

Lawrence Hamm

As Told to Annette M. Alston

AFRICA WORLD PRESS
TRENTON | LONDON | CAPE TOWN | NAIROBI | ADDIS ABABA | ASMARA | IBADAN | NEW DELHI

AFRICA WORLD PRESS
541 West Ingham Avenue | Suite B
Trenton, New Jersey 08638

Copyright © 2024, Lawrence Hamm & Annette Alston

All rights reserved. No part of this publication may be reproduced, stored in a retrieval system or transmitted in any form or by any means electronic, mechanical, photocopying, recording or otherwise without the prior written permission of the publisher.

Book design: LiteBook Prepress Services
Cover Design: Ashraful Haque
Cover Photo: Courtesy of the Linden Public School system. The picture was taken at Linden High School in Linden, NJ by Gary Miller.

Cataloging-in-Publication Data may be obtained from the Library of Congress.

ISBNs: 978-1-56902-807-0 (HB)
        978-1-56902-808-7 (PB)

CONTENTS

Authors' Personal Note	ix
Foreword	x
1973: Prologue: Angry	1
1950s: Up South: My childhood in Newark	5
1960s-1971: Rebellion, Strikes, A Sit-In and Maybe Princeton	19
1971-1974: Kujichagulia: Board, Council Run and No Gun	37
1974-1980: Princeton Redux: Apartheid and The People's Front	81
1980s: Co-op to POP	111
1980s: Racing with the Rainbow	127
1990s: Perpetual Protest, Permanent Power	147
Interlude: Suddenly, Anthony	163
1990s-2000s: Police Forced: The Case of Earl Faison	167
A Luta Continua: 381 Days-Plus of Unwritten History	187
They Stole Us, They Sold Us, They Owe Us	199

A Life in the Struggle

2019 to 2022: Present Tense: Campaign, Pandemic, Uprisings	219
Coda: Chairman by Annette M. Alston	239
Post-Script: Adhimu Changa, A Man Devoted To Struggle Without Hate and Greatness Without Ego	253
Afterword: Adhimu, Always Laced Up	261
About the Authors	267
Annette Alston's Acknowledgements	269
People's Organization for Progress Preamble	271
Index	273

*For My Parents,
Grayce, Larry and Theresa*

AUTHORS' PERSONAL NOTE

It's important to thank God for preserving our lives long enough to bring this book to completion. This autobiography, probably like so many others, is conceived from a single thought, an idea that flows from a seed of divine purpose. Larry and I owe that little mustard seed to **Dr. Todd Steven Burroughs**, who recognized the need and handed it to us with a sense of urgency. Todd is a biographer, author, academic and most importantly, friend. His passion for documenting history, including even the history of characters in his beloved Marvel and DC comics, has proven to be contagious and I'm glad we listened to him.

Without his professional guidance, assistance and collaboration, this book may not have happened.

FOREWARD

By Dr. William Howard

Larry Hamm and I met in 1977, when he was a junior in college. He was also known as Adhimu Changa back then. Like virtually anyone who was just getting to know him, I wondered what on earth was the source of his passion, dedication, and discipline as he threw himself into causes that addressed the plight of people living on the margins of this society and in societies where he had never been.

When poor people in Newark couldn't afford fuel for cooking and heating, there was Larry helping to organize the Peoples' Energy Cooperative. When Black people in South Africa suffered under the crushing weight of apartheid, there was Larry in the forefront making his voice heard with others — "Free South Africa!"

Volumes can be filled with accounts of all the picket lines, all the marches, all the speeches and rallies where Larry participated and/or organized. These days, he may be without peer in New Jersey when it comes to prophetic, tireless, militant advocacy for people all-but-forgotten by others in leadership roles. A Princeton alumnus with a stellar academic record could presumably have ignored such a calling, but not Larry. He never considered it an option to not be out front in the demand for justice and fair play.

Foreward

That is why Annette Alston's accounting of his journey, and how he chose to use the considerable gifts he has inherited and developed on behalf of the people he loves - the people who appear voiceless, who appear powerless. What Ms. Alston has chronicled is vital to the next generation. Her work provides a kind of roadmap for people hungry for role models, and actual accounts of how a grassroots organization can ignite people power and cause people who might have suffered in silence to stand up for their rights.

The vehicle for so much of Larry's work for more than a generation has been the People's Organization for Progress (POP), a movement of citizens that is known throughout the Garden State and beyond. If you live in NJ and have not heard of POP or experienced its capacity to mobilize people "in a minute" in support of a righteous cause, your head must be buried in the sand.

Larry is POP's chairman, but more than that, he is its leader. Not all people with titles are leaders. He invites no one to go where he hasn't already been; to do what he hasn't already done; to risk what he hasn't already risked. What leadership is — past, present, and future — is revealed in the pages to follow in the story of a man who listens well, learns wherever good lessons are taught, then helps to convert bold ideas that others consider unlikely into a living reality.

Dr. M. William Howard is a renowned Ecumenical minister and former President of the National Council of Churches, former President of the New York Theological Seminary. He chaired the Death Penalty Study Commission in 2007 which led to the abolition of the death penalty in NJ. He served as pastor of Bethany Baptist Church in Newark from 2000 to 2015 and is the author of Black, Not Dutch, *published by* Africa *World Press.*

Newark Board of Education, circa 1971

1973:
PROLOGUE:
ANGRY

Tears filled my mother's eyes as she looked at me. "Larry, Larry, what are you doing with your life?"

Grayce Hamm, an everyday working woman, had had enough. She had become used to seeing me pictured and quoted in the newspapers, but this time it was a little different. The headline in *The New York Times* said it all: "Adhimu Changa, 19 and Angry." My mother was upset at me at various times in my life. She was deeply disappointed when I was suspended from elementary school. Years later, she would be annoyed when her soap operas were interrupted by a TV commentator editorializing against the red, black, and green flag in public schools.

In that moment, it was clear to me that the Newark mayor, Kenneth Gibson, was very disappointed with me, and I was stunned to read that comment in the newspaper. I wasn't stunned that he said it but surprised he said it publicly. Mayor Gibson was a hero in the Black community locally and nationally after becoming the first Black mayor of a Northeastern city. In another article, he said that naming me to the Newark Board of Education in 1971 was the worst mistake he had ever made. His appointment made me, at 17, the youngest board member in American history.

Me? The *worst?*

What made the article even more concerning was that *The Times* reporter said that I was the Black analogue of Anthony Imperiale, the Italian leader of Newark's North Ward who famously referred to Martin Luther King as "Martin Luther Coon." Imperiale had a kind of white-ethnic militia, comprised of Northern rednecks. He promised to keep his predominantly Italian ward safe from what they saw as the Planet of the Apes, and to Make Newark Great Again. *This* is who I was being compared to, believe it or not! The man back then was a combination of Theophilus Eugene Bull Connor, and the lead character in *The Godfather*. Bull Connor was the racist Birmingham sheriff who sicced dogs and attacked Black people with water sprayed from high velocity hoses. The protagonist in *The Godfather* was a ruthless Italian mobster.

I would say, at least *The Times* respected me enough to refer to me as "Adhimu Changa," the name Imamu Amiri Baraka had given me. However, I know that using my African name in their eyes only made me seem angrier. I didn't legally change my "slave name," but as one of my professors at Princeton would later tell me, it was my *nom de guerre*, which is French for "name of war."

What was my crime? Persuading the Newark Board of Education to pass a resolution that allowed students in Newark public schools to study and display the Black nationalist flag — the red, black and green standard popularized by Marcus Garvey's Universal Negro Improvement Association (UNIA).

Prologue: Angry

This Pan-African organization staged the largest mass mobilization of Black people in American history during the 1920s. Garvey believed that there was a commonality to the oppression that Black people faced globally.

I remember the night that the vote was taken very well. It was a volatile meeting in the North Ward. Police had to escort me off the stage as I came too close to a public fistfight with one or two of my white colleagues at the meeting.

Flags have always been a lightning rod in America, literally and figuratively. To put this in present context: This controversy *occurred eighteen years* before Colin Kaepernick was *born*. In 2016, NFL player Kaepernick was blackballed for taking a knee to protest police brutality against African Americans, while the American National Anthem played before the start of football games. But that's where the comparison ends: I understand he's a millionaire. Back then I was a college dropout just understanding how to navigate through my first real job.

My crime and subsequent trial in the court of public (white) opinion was based on my attempts to adequately represent the spirit of Newark's Black community. After the Newark Rebellion in 1967, and Martin Luther King's assassination the following year, all the Negroes in America had suddenly dropped dead - replaced with Black people.

Grayce Hamm transitioned from Negro to Black too, but she was worried about her only son, the radical college-drop out. "Larry, this militant stuff is going to get you killed!"

I knew it could: that was real. But I didn't think that I'd be taken out, not even by Imperiale and his goons. Of course, that was before the system I sought to change tried to frame me and almost put me in prison — before I was indicted and brought to trial on a phony gun charge.

For this I left Princeton? For this my mother anguished? But in my mind's eye, the revolution was right around the corner. The air was different then. It was charged with change, and I thought we'd look back one day laughing, recalling this stress-filled confrontation — after Africa is free from colonialism, and we have a Pan-African Front! Hell, even Gibson will laugh — and I might be in a good enough mood to forgive him for this bullshit!

Looking back like some sort of American Sankofa bird, I'll admit it now: the reporter had gotten a lot right. I was 19 and angry. I had every right to be angry. But rather quickly, I also had found my way to myself. Direction doesn't have to be fully formed or right always. My family had loved me into being — a phrase that Fred Rogers, just a few years on PBS as my mother cried for me, would decades later make famous. That love gave me a foundation in Newark, and the *Zeitgeist*, the spirit of *The times*, molded and directed me in New Ark, had given me a purpose. My spear may not have always been correctly thrown, but the edge was consistently sharp, and it always struck with conviction.

1950S: UP SOUTH: MY CHILDHOOD IN NEWARK

I was born on December 24, 1953, in Washington, DC., and was brought to Newark by my parents, Grayce Cobb Hamm and Lawrence Hamm Sr., before I was one-year-old.

I grew up in Newark's Central Ward, which back then was called the Third Ward. It was very Black, filled with people who came from the Great Migration. Later, I would learn that its dark monochrome came not from a positive nature, nor nurture; members of our community were prevented from buying homes in the white wards because of their race.

Our apartment was a cold-water flat at 5 Ridgewood Avenue, at the corner of Ridgewood and Avon avenues. Many people don't know what a cold-water flat is, and some of us have tried mightily to forget those days. Cold-water flats are apartments, or floors in two- and three-family homes, that had no hot running water. To take a bath or wash the dishes, people had to heat the cold water. (I didn't have access to a shower until college.) We had those old, pot-bellied stoves heated with coal. Everyone around us lived this way; I was one of the many Black Baby Boomers, *Up North*, who didn't know they were poor until they went to college.

The Central Ward was the heart of Newark's Black community. Consequently, by 1970, the year that Gibson was elected, I had heard a statistic that the Central Ward had more Black people per square mile than any other community in the United States. Now that might have to be verified but remember many of the major housing projects in Newark were in the Central Ward — Hayes Homes, Scudder Homes, and Stella Wright Homes. I remember Stella Wright because from 1970 to 1974, Stella Wright Homes had the longest public housing rent strike in U.S. history, led by Toby Henry.

My family lived in a six-family tenement, that was down the street from the projects. My mother was then a fulltime homemaker. She had worked at the Picatinny Arsenal in Morris County before I was born. My father drove Mack trucks for a living. I remembered how he sometimes pulled the truck up in front of the house and parked there. His truck was different from most because it had a bulldog on the hood. Sometimes, my father took me to the corner bar, the Ridgewood Bar, because we lived literally next door. He would buy me an orange soda from the bar's fountain. I loved those fountain sodas because you could taste the syrup. I slowly learned about adults who became addicted to alcohol quite early, from watching my neighbors at this bar.

He had a bunch of friends from the neighborhood that he saw there. Many had nicknames but the only one I remember was "Big Six." Maybe that's because I was learning my numbers then and that name stuck out. My family nicknamed me "Bootsy" because I liked cowboy boots. That was the rage for kids in the Fifties. One year I even got chaps - the sheepskin/leather-like coverings for your legs. My father was proud to show his friends that someone as young as I could pick out his truck key: "See, my boy is smart."

Up South: My childhood in Newark

My father died in 1958, when I was four. He was fifty-two. He had two strokes and was partially paralyzed from the second one. My mother and I went to live with her parents, Claude and Stella Cobb. There were five of us — my mother, my grandparents, Aunt Joan (my mother's sister), and my cousin Ralph and me. My grandparents lived near West Side Park, at 527 South Twelfth Street between Sixteenth and Eighteenth Avenues. My Mom went to work as a seamstress at the cleaners around the corner. We lived on Twelfth Street for twenty years, from 1958 to 1977. Eventually, My Mom would retire from being a teacher's aide at South Seventeenth Street School, where I went to elementary school.

During my childhood, people pretty much stayed in their ward. As a kid, it was a big deal to go into another of Newark's neighborhoods. My mother had a friend, Mr. Freddy, who I believe may have been a numbers runner. He always wore a suit — the best Italian knits! Mr. Freddy would take me in his shiny Cadillac to the White Castle at Elizabeth and Hawthorne Avenues, in the predominantly Jewish South Ward. In September 1962, that White Castle would be the site of what was perhaps the first civil rights demonstration in Newark. Although no one in Essex County would believe it now, that protest was about changing an all-white, White Castle. No Blacks could work there.

My grandfather worked with the boilers at a paper mill in Bloomfield. I think he did what today we call recycling: he and his coworkers collected paper and made it into cardboard. When he had enough to buy a car, he bought a '57 Chevy. But, interestingly enough, he didn't drive! No one in our family had a driver's license except for Cousin Ralph. So, Cousin Ralph drove him to and from work every day.

A Life in the Struggle

Although Newark was geographically Northeast, much of our experience in Newark could be described as Southern rural. For example, a couple of neighbors kept chickens in their backyards. Here's another one: my career as a watermelon salesman. After my father's death, my mother had a boyfriend, Jake Hughes. My first job was working for him, helping him sell watermelons out of a truck at Belmont Avenue. We'd be one truck of many, selling fruits and vegetables. We would shout "Watermelon!" to passersby. People would stop and I would have to carry the watermelon to their cars. The watermelon was as big as I was, but I would handle it. If people in the projects called down for watermelon, I had to climb flights of stairs with it. I liked watermelon, and I liked riding in the back of Jake's truck because he had hay back there. Jake taught me how to "plug" a watermelon: how to cut a small part out of it to show a customer it was ripe. He also taught me how to count change. Jake would roll up in the morning and pick me up. We would sell the watermelons, then he'd drop me off at home and take the truck somewhere.

Jake sold watermelons in the summer and coal in the winter. (To this day, you can see old Newark buildings with little windows close to the ground: that was where the coal, on a chute from the truck, would be sent into a coal bin in the basement of the home.)

I worked for Jake for maybe a couple of summers until he and my mother parted ways. Unfortunately, he was an alcoholic. His drinking aggravated me because he would want to grab me and hug me. He'd be sobbing and smelling like liquor. There'd be tears and the feel of his unshaven face up against me. But he was a good man. He took care of my mother and me. However, his issues with alcohol impacted their relationship to the point My Mom determined that he had to go.

Up South: My childhood in Newark

I lived in Newark during a time when the city still had a large white population. Large numbers of whites lived in what are now called the North and West wards. There were no whites on Ridgewood Avenue, but some white people did live on Twelfth Street. Back then, I understood skin color as just a fact; then I didn't think of race as a factor in human interactions. But the whites in my neighborhood did, and they acted on it by posting for-sale signs on their homes. Many think that Newark's white flight happened after 1967, but much of it happened after World War II, when the Great Migration hadn't yet peaked. By 1973, every remaining white house was for sale.

Between 1957 and the 1967 Rebellion, everything was in reach in my neighborhood. The candy store, the sandwich shop across the street, that vegetable store across the street, that grocery store across the street from that gas station. Next to the grocery store was another candy store and ice cream store. Then there was the Livshitz Pharmacy and Mindy's Italian Hot Dogs between Eleventh and Tenth Street(s). The Polish laundry wash-dry-and-fold place was between Twelfth and Eleventh Street(s) on Sixteenth Avenue. Fannie and Charlie's candy store was across the street from that, on the same block as the drycleaners where my mother worked. Next to the Hoffmanizing cleaners was a laundromat. For two summers I would work in the Hoffmanizing cleaners. Dr. Morano was on Sixteenth Avenue between Tenth and Eleventh Street(s). In my neighborhood, you could literally walk to the doctor, and the doctor would come to your house. You really didn't leave the community unless you wanted to go do serious shopping on Springfield Avenue or the other thoroughfares. Massive white flight, followed by the Rebellion, destroyed the strong sense of neighborhood community, of neighborhood safety and the rhythm of day-to-day life. On the other hand, when the whites left, Black people were no longer restricted to sitting in the balcony in a downtown Newark theater. Employment for Blacks opened up in the downtown stores that were previously not hiring and half serving them. They no longer ran the risk of getting beaten up like I almost was when I tried to use the Boylan Street (public) Pool in the city's Vailsburg section. The *Up South* reference to Newark was finally beginning to dissipate.

There were a lot of white kids at South Seventeenth Street School when my mother first enrolled me. My kindergarten class was very integrated. And it's interesting because I did not have a real concept of racism as a kid. I mean, I knew I was different, but to me it was just like how the Irish kid was different, with red hair and freckles. Another kid had blonde hair and blue eyes, and I just happened to have brown skin. I didn't really understand racism at that age. It was just incidental. I remember my kindergarten picture, where the Black kids were the class's minorities. We had one Black teacher, Mrs. Green. Some years later she became the principal. We had a Black speech teacher who rotated from school to school. She helped me with my speech impediment from second grade through part of my seventh grade. Eventually she started teaching me Spanish after my impediment cleared up. I had very few Black teachers growing up. I remember my speech teacher, and later at Arts High School, Mr. Robert Howard, my chorus teacher. Mr. Robert Howard became a legend at that school among music majors at that magnet school.

I used to walk to my elementary school by myself. Because I didn't have brothers and sisters, I tried to get along with the other students. I wasn't a loner, but I wasn't the most popular kid, either. I was an asthmatic who spent many a day at St. Michael's Hospital when I would have attacks. I'm not sure what brought on the attacks. It could have been the coal from the furnace heating the building and/or my grandfather's smoking. But I have vibrant memories of having to drink this terrible tasting beef broth the hospital regularly served. As a child, I was also overweight, so you know how kids can be. I was tagged "Fat Hamm." The nickname stuck for years until I thinned out as a pre-teen. In fact, I lost about sixty pounds by the time I was in seventh grade. The loss of weight was so dramatic, that my mother took me to the hospital where they did tests. But they didn't find anything wrong.

I grew up during the "Doo-Wop" days. "Doo Wop" is now thought of as a Black male music style that is performed on America's streets. Think of it as "Soul music" through the lens of Be-Bop. The Doo-Wop group I remember is the Hightower Brothers. The group was crazy about Jeanette, our next-door neighbor. The Hightowers used to stand outside her house and serenade her on a Friday night. You couldn't help but hear the free concert on the block. The Hightower Brothers cut a couple of Gospel records but remained only local celebrities.

Doo-wop was just a part of the post-World War II jazz-to-rock cool. You acted cool. You dressed cool. I hit the scene every fall with new school clothes. Bamberger's downtown was the place to be to get hooked up for school. We sported the latest Teardrops, iridescent suits and sharkskin suits from the Universal Army and Navy store. Mom was able to save money and still make sure I looked sharp. When we got to eighth grade, folks were rolling with Italian knits, cardigans, Italian sweaters, cashmere sweaters and Panama hats.

I wanted to look sharp. I wanted to dress like Mr. Freddy. I even had the shoe-shine kit you screwed into the wall. I tried to dress well in elementary and high school. When teachers met Mom, they always said, "Oh, your son is so well-dressed. He comes to school so neat." I think some students thought I was spoiled.

My Mom and, to a certain extent, my grandparents were all working class. When they weren't at work, they were at home. They always made sure ends met. My mother and her sister, Aunt Gladys, supplemented their work income by hosting Tupperware parties and jewelry parties. My mother didn't go out a lot. And occasionally, the social club she was involved in would have a little dance or some kind of event, but that was it. I remember her making onion dip for those gatherings. I now realize that my mother sacrificed a lot for me. I was her life.

Our family unit was me, Mom, my two grandparents, Claude and Stella, Aunt Joan, my grandmother's sister, and Cousin Ralph, Aunt Joan's son. Five adults and one kid, all on the second-floor apartment of a three-family home. There was never a time when I was unsupervised. After my grandparents passed away, it was just Aunt Joan, Mom, William Counts and me. William Counts was Mom's friend since 1968 and he was kind of a stepfather to me. I'm not sure how Mom and William Counts met since she did not get out much. But she did meet plenty of people at the cleaners where she worked. Maybe that's how they met. He courted her for sometime before moving in.

Aunt Joan lived with us until she went into a nursing home. Ralph got sick, and later died. He was so sick he could only drink buttermilk and eat rice. He couldn't drink a soda. He couldn't drink coffee. He couldn't even drink liquor. My grandfather was a smoker and died in 1968 from lung cancer. Claude was a World War I veteran who remembered his bad treatment during the time he served abroad. The white Southern soldiers told the French that Black men had tails. He hated the racism of the South; he told us, "If you put my body on a train to be buried down South, I'm going to get up, come back and beat your behind." A year after my grandfather passed, my grandmother died, I believe from loneliness.

Race consciousness began to trickle in around fifth grade, when I played Crispus Attucks, the first man to die in the American Revolution, in a school play. I don't think I ever thought of myself as a Negro until then. Fifth grade was also when school started to click for me. My grades improved to the extent where one semester I received straight As.

My eighth-grade scores started to slip a bit but my eighth-grade teacher, a white woman named Mrs. Ryerson took an interest in me. One day, she did something that would have gotten her suspended or fired in today's public-school culture. Without asking permission of my mother, or having any official permission from the district, she took me downtown, to Bamberger's department store, to a book signing. She pushed her way to the front, dragging me along, making sure I got the book and the author's signature. I had no idea who this Jesse Owens dude was, but I assumed it was important if Mrs. Ryerson went through all that trouble. She basically demanded that I take the admissions test for Arts High School. Later, when I became a track star at the school, I would learn about Owens and his struggle as an Olympian. The "field trip" was both an interesting experience and, because of my youth and ignorance, a missed opportunity. But I now appreciate Mrs. Ryerson and her efforts to push me past the world of my Newark neighborhood, into excellence, and into history itself.

A Life in the Struggle

Newark has been a very Christian and Muslim city since the 1970s. As a kid, I didn't go to church often. But I remember following several of my friends into Way of the Cross Pentecostal Church. It was then on Camden and Bergen Streets. Nowadays, it is the site of Camden Street School. I liked it, and I think the pastor, Elder Harris, took a liking to me but I could never get the Holy Ghost. One day Elder Harris called me up and anointed me with oil.

Maybe the closest I came to feeling the Holy Spirit was when I was with my Aunt Joan. We were in the kitchen, and she had a white Bible. I opened it up and it came to the Beatitudes, Matthew 5:1-12. I read it for the first time.

"Blessed are the poor in spirit, for theirs is the kingdom of heaven/ Blessed are those who mourn, for they will be comforted/Blessed are the meek, for they will inherit the earth/Blessed are those who hunger and thirst for righteousness, for they shall be filled."

Don't ask me what happened next because I can't, to this day, explain why. I was reading it, and tears came out of my eyes. That was the closest thing to a deeply religious experience that I had had.

That real story is important for me because of the ideals imbued which help shape the political ideals that I would formulate or adopt later. Those ideals may have, in fact, pushed me in a direction to be more political.

Later, in study and in the streets, I would see the extraordinary power of Black church oratory. I saw that, for example, Adam Clayton Powell and Malcolm X touched people personally and politically. Dr. Martin Luther King did the entire trifecta:

he could touch people personally and politically, convert them and send them out into action all at the same time. The Black church is the transforming agent of our communities. It is not surprising that in 2018, almost fifty years to the day, Rev. William Barber used the Black church to revive King's 1968 Poor People's Campaign.

I love the Black church, and if you asked me what I identify with, I would say my family is basically Christian and I would say I am Christian, but I don't belong to any church. I don't want to be constrained to a specific set of beliefs. I don't want to be put in a position where I must see any other people as less than because they don't practice the religion I practice or see our shared religion the way I see it. Fundamentally what torments humanity is this idea that some group of humans is less than another group of people. Ethnic and or religious conflict are a constant around the world, be it between people of color or white. If you go to Thailand, it's Buddhists vs Muslims. You go to India, it's Hindus vs Muslim. And then there is the continual strife between Israel and Palestine. Religion can and does unite people but under other circumstances, religion divides people.

So, my childhood was a normal one. I knew my neighborhood, including its streets, and they knew me. I was a Boy Scout, but the gang and I liked scouting because of our scoutmaster, Richard Crooms. Mr. Crooms was a third-degree black belt and taught us Goshi-Shun style karate. I was so into the idea of fight-training, that I actually considered going to military school.

But even karate wasn't enough to exhaust my Black-boy energy. I ran around with some knuckleheads, trying to get a rep. You would think I would have learned my lesson from a few years back when I was about eight and some kids were talking about what they had stolen from the variety store. They turned to me and asked me what I had ever stolen. I said, "nothing." They then dared me to steal something from the variety store. It was owned by Fannie and Charlie, a nice white couple that had owned the store for years. I went in there and came out with a Devil Dogs. Then what did the "friend" that dared me to steal do? He told my mother that I stole a Devil Dogs. My grandfather was still alive then. And he was someone I definitely did not want to be angry with me. My grandfather was the one who used to protect me when my mother was getting ready to put a real whooping on me. My grandfather would often go to the candy store and buy me what I wanted. I would never want to be on his bad side. But on that day, he found out I stole that Devil Dogs, he grabbed me up and walked me across the street to that store and made me tell them what I did and apologize. Then granddad paid for the Devil Dogs I had stolen. I should have learned my lesson about hanging with a bad crowd from that experience, but here I was in eighth grade being expelled by Mr. King, the principal. When running with a bad crowd, you did what the bad crowd did: we threw rocks at the school and broke several front windows.

My mother acted as if the world had ended. And Mr. Freddy — man, *he saved my life* when my mother found out I had been expelled. My mother used to whip me with a barbershop strap — the ones that were used to sharpen straight razors. One hit with that strap was like being hit three times with a regular belt! Mr. Freddy knew my mother was about to commit murder or come damn near close to it. He pleaded with her to not hit me, because we all knew how sorry I was for getting kicked out of school.

Up South: My childhood in Newark

The next week, Grayce Hamm went to the school on a mission: to save her child and get him back in school so he could graduate. I have *never* seen my mother cry as much as she did in front of Mr. King to get me back in school. She cried harder than she did when my father died! But it worked, and I was given a second chance. I would try to make the most of it and conform to what my family wanted. But the conformity of the 1950s was long gone by 1967.

It was replaced with something new, energetic, dangerous. Much more unconventional than my old Boy Scout troop or karate class. And I would be among many young people my age who would gradually be drawn in the middle of it.

1960S-1971: REBELLION, STRIKES, A SIT-IN AND MAYBE PRINCETON

People who know me as an adult are shocked when they find out that I was neither born an activist nor was the scion of an activist family. Far from it. From my childhood through my adolescence, I was not political at all. Until 1967, I did not hear my family speak about in-depth race and racial issues. From time to time, I would catch snatches of conversation from my grandfather, who would say things like "The Black cop will beat you worse than the white cop," and, when Martin Luther King caused outrage around the nation when he spoke out against the Vietnam War, "King should stick to civil rights." The Sixties was a transforming decade for the world.

I can only guess that my grandparents who were both dead by 1969, were very upset with the behavior of rebelling Newarkers in 1967. They knew and frequented many of the stores that were torn apart, and my family could see the violence from our porch.

I was kept out of the rebellious activities by fate and circumstance. Not only was a National Guard outpost just two doors down from our house, but I had promised my mother after I got expelled from eighth grade that I would stay out of trouble. When the Rebellion happened, just before I entered Arts High

School. I kept that promise to my mother as long as I could, but being a troublemaker was about to become not only normal for me, but for young people worldwide.

So where was Lawrence Hamm when John Smith, a Black Newark cab driver, was beaten by police and thought dead? Where was Hamm when Newark rebelled as a result?

Thanks to Willy C., I was near home. Willy C was a friend from North Carolina visiting his family for the summer and he hosted a party July 12th across the street from my house. Somebody ran upstairs to where we were and said, "Man, Springfield Avenue is on fire!" We ran down the stairs, because Springfield Avenue was only a few blocks from where we were and I started to follow the kids down the street, but my mother wasn't having it. My mother, who was on the porch, was able to see me as I walked out of the house party. She called me and ordered me to come home and go upstairs, and that probably saved my life.

Twenty-six dead.

One thousand, five-hundred injured.

One thousand one-hundred arrested.

Riot? No. It was an insurgency. Martial law was declared. A riot can be put down by the police. When you must call in the Army and declare martial law, that's an insurgency.

Initially, from the view of my window, it looked almost festive. But it didn't stay that way. People had broken into stores taking whatever they could carry. I remember boxes of corn-

Rebellion, Strikes, A Sit-In and Maybe Princeton

flakes everywhere and seeing women carrying big bags of flour. But later there would be rock throwing, police sirens and gunfire. The intensity increased as the evening and days wore on.

I remember trying to walk to Good Deal, which was the first supermarket I went to as a child and the closest to my home. It was on the corner of Springfield and South Tenth Street, and you couldn't walk anywhere without stepping on broken glass. There was nowhere you could go and not smell the burned buildings. So many shop windows were broken. Destruction surrounded us.

Based on written coverage of the events and my analysis, I concluded that the Newark Rebellion would have probably faded out if the State Police and National Guard had not shown up. Resistance creates rebellion, and oppression creates and feeds rebellions.

The destruction of neighborhoods was never seen as a good thing in Newark, and the destruction is not remembered that way. But the reality is that the Rebellion helped spur the Black Power Movement that resulted in Kenneth Gibson being elected as Newark's first Black mayor three years later. It was the Civil Rights Movement that dealt with the mechanics of civic life: where you could shop, whether you could vote. But it was the Black Power Movement that changed the consciousness of the people: that promotes the idea that Black and Brown people should control their cities.

Since the founding of the organization, the People's Organization for Progress has conducted a ceremony in remembrance of the Rebellion. The families of the Black victims have spoken at many of these events.

A Life in the Struggle

It is September 1967 and my first day at Arts High School. I didn't know it at the time, but this magnet school was the first public high school in the United States to specialize in visual and performing arts. I played the guitar, so I auditioned, took the academic test, and was accepted in. I was turning a new leaf. Between Mom and Mrs. Ryerson, this freshman music major was ready to start over. I was ready for the proving ground of high school, which would lead to the proving ground of work, which would lead to a middle-class life.

It was time to put the past behind me. Thanks to Mom's tearful intervention, I had returned to eighth grade and graduated. The Rebellion had happened, and now was the time for the city to rebuild itself. The first national Black Power Conference had been held in the city, at the Robert Treat Hotel, two weeks after the Rebellion. The Black Power Convention, a local one, would be a year later, in 1968 at the West Kinney Junior High School.

But I didn't know about any of that then. It was time for me to face front and move on.

During the freshmen class-orientation school assembly, the entire direction of my life changed. I don't remember what the principal said, but I remember he was there. What I will always remember was that the student "Mayor" (as in, Student Body President) of Arts High — David Hammond — got up and started denouncing the Vietnam War. The principal told him to be silent, and he refused. They had a scuffle on the stage. Arts High was still integrated in those days, so the fact that both the student and the principal were white were not lost on me.

Later, sociologists and others would talk and write about how Vietnam was the focal point of the "Generation Gap" — the divide between the Baby Boomers, born between 1945 and 1964, and their parents. In my seat in the Arts High auditorium, I had not only seen the Generation Gap play itself out, but I had seen the future of post-Rebellion Newark and the larger world.

Until that moment, I never knew that you could use the post of student leader to critique the establishment. (Hell, at South Seventeenth Street School, we learned *The Ballad of the Green Berets*, back then a recent hit! Because of the song and the martial arts training, I wanted to *be* one! And this was *before* the John Wayne movie was released!)

In his writings, imprisoned journalist Mumia Abu-Jamal discussed his encounter with a Philadelphia police officer at a George Wallace rally. Abu-Jamal stated that the police officer basically "kicked him" into joining the Black Panther Party. David's boldness shook me, because it showed new, powerful options for life outside of post-World War II conformity. It was at that point, that I decided that I wanted to be the head of Arts High's student government. The seed was planted.

High school allowed for a new interest: running track.

Arts High didn't have a football team and though I had played softball in elementary as a left-handed pitcher, I wasn't coordinated enough for its baseball team, or tall enough for its basketball squad. So, I had to choose something else.

I started running around what was, before the Rebellion, a lake in West Side Park. (For some reason, it was filled in after July.) "Fat Hamm" had become a distant memory. I applied myself to school and to track. Both were challenging, but it was on the field where I publicly excelled.

It didn't happen overnight. Not even close. I joined the Arts High track team in the spring of 1968. I was so slow the coach put me in the two-mile meets because I couldn't run anything else. My first meet was against West Side High. My girlfriend, a love that went all the way back to fifth grade, was in the stands, ready to support her man.

Ready.

Bang!

A two-mile run is an eight-lap race. To be lapped once was humiliating. I got lapped *twice*. Oh my God! It was so embarrassing, my girlfriend left me. *That day.* I came in last in every race of my freshman year; I was lapped every time.

There was no way for me to recognize all the benefits of continuing track at that point. Though I did notice one major difference. I could breathe better than I could before. Running had allowed me to outgrow my asthma and the regular trips to St. Michaels.

The only reason I got a varsity letter in my sophomore year was because there were so few people running the two-mile meet, I could reach third place by just showing up. So, I showed up.

By my junior year, sucking the taste of defeat in my mouth like a lozenge, I applied myself. I became a beast, training three times a day.

Morning: West Side Park. Easy to do since I lived across the street.

Lunch break: I ran around the block of High Street where the school was located, since Arts High didn't have a gym or playground, much less a track.

After-school: Track practice at Riverbank Park in the East Ward.

I did this for two years.

Arts didn't have a cross-country or indoor track team. So, I hooked up with the Leaguers, a nonprofit social agency for African Americans. James Harris ran the Leaguers Track Club. Harris, who would later become a dean at Montclair State University, the State President of the New Jersey National Association for the Advancement of Colored People (NAACP) and President of the New Jersey Association of Black Educators, was quite an athlete in his day. More importantly, he and Jerome Marcus, my Arts High coach, took the slowest runner on the track team and turned him into a star. I say this not to draw any accolades toward myself but to recall the immense task that Marcus and Harris undertook to take someone with no significant athletic ability and limited resources and make him into a state champion.

By the end of my junior year, I was a record-holder: the first in Newark to break ten minutes in the two-mile run. What's interesting is that I was unable to repeat that time after that. I attribute that possibly to the fact that the field was smaller, a fifth of a mile. Five laps instead of four made it easier to calibrate the minutes. Every time I came around, the coaches would give the time. Mr. Marcus was getting so excited. He knew I was on the way because when you're a good two-miler, you can run a mile in five minutes. It's after that first mile that you can really see that you can make it happen. By the seventh lap and then the ninth lap, then hitting the last lap in under sixty seconds, I was on my way. But I knew I had not arrived. I was faster and winning meets, yet I was not undefeated. Barry Mason made sure of that. He was from Weequahic and those who ran against him expected to be humiliated. His event was the mile. He won that handily and then crossed over and ran in my event, the two-mile. He won that too. That ended my winning streak for my junior year.

It was in my junior year that I decided to go to the Outward Bound Program for the summer. It was really a survival-training program at fifteen thousand feet altitude in the Oregon Cascade Mountains. But the reason I decided to participate was because I thought it would be good complimentary training or what people think of today as cross-training for my long-distance running. One of the features that stuck out for me was that on the next to the last day of the twenty-eight-day Outward Bound program, there was a twenty-mile run or race. Now I was a two-miler in high school. I wanted to see if I could run these twenty miles. I figured whatever I was doing up until that day would only strengthen me and make me a better runner. Tommie Smith and John Carlos had just won the Olympics in 1968 for track and field while holding a deeper win in my heart for their Black Power salute. But my drive in the direction of Oregon stemmed from an earlier track and field Olympic I remember watching in 1960 and 1964. Abebe Bikila of Ethiopia won the gold both of those years. I was listening to commentary about how the high altitude of Ethiopia gave Bikila an advantage in training. I was just in high school and therefore, no expert but, I had a hunch that the Oregon mountains could work to my advantage.

Off I went to Outward Bound in July of 1970. What an adventure was ahead of me. Flying for the first time and in Oregon, seeing the stars-really seeing the stars. It was a blanket covering the sky like a billion diamonds. You can't see this in the city. But there I was high in the mountains, looking down at the ocean touching the warm setting sun one moment and then the next moment trudging through waist-high snow- shirtless. While it was beautiful, it was a little more dangerous back then than it is now. There were a lot of accidental deaths. There were possibly two when I was on tour. Two were mountain climbing and one fell into a crater of an inactive volcano. They had to get a helicopter to get him out. Two people that were in my group had mental breakdowns. In twenty-eight days, we covered two hundred and six miles. Every eleven days, we would come to a camp where we would be re-supplied with dry goods and food. The first time we came into a camp after the first eleven days, it looked like a scene from the Civil War. It was dark and we were coming out of the woods on foot into this camp with campfires going. People were sitting around the campfires all bandaged up, arms in slings.

I completed the twenty-eight-day tour and the final twenty-mile race in one piece. I returned to New Jersey still hungry for more. I convinced my mother to send me to Roaring Valley Track and Field Camping the next month in August.

In competitive track, if you want to get better, you need to run against people who are better than you. You are forced to condition yourself to the pain that comes with training at a higher level. It's not like someone stabs you with a knife but it becomes uncomfortable. Breathing becomes difficult. Yet I learned to push through and embrace the stress knowing in the end, I would be that much stronger.

By senior year, Arts High School had formed its first cross-country team. The race was held at West Side Park. We never really saw crowds of spectators at the cross-country races. Spectators would come out to the city-meets. But the cross-country races were not on a track. They were up and down hills and paths and it just wasn't a spectator sport. There was a field house at the park where the team would always change. However, because I lived directly across the street from the park, I changed at home and started over to the park. As I approached, I noticed a large crowd of people around the entrance. And of course, I thought it must be a fight. That was not the case. As I drew closer, I saw three or four yellow buses parked in front. All of the students were from Weequahic High School. Lenny Moore, the Weequahic coach, had brought up busloads of students so that they could see Barry Mason beat me.

I began shaking my head. "Oh my God, Barry Mason is going to beat my ass again!" Even though I had experienced a mostly successful junior year; and even though I had trained with absolute abandon, I still approached the starting line with a sense of dread-some might have called that feeling the "starting-line blues."

I should have reminded myself at that moment that I knew something that Barry and Lenny didn't know. I had learned a few tricks over the summer at Rough Valley and I intended to implement them. I stayed right behind Mason for most of that race. I was so close on him he could hear me breathing.

Rebellion, Strikes, A Sit-In and Maybe Princeton

The race was for two and a half miles, and I let him lead it – right up until we got to the last hill in the last half mile. Then taking Mason totally by surprise, I passed him, summoning all my energy to speed up that hill and I stayed ahead of him. The throngs of people who constituted the four busloads were lined up for a quarter of a mile along-side the bridle path leading to the finish line. All that could be heard was silence. It was a glorious day. It was the day that my starting-line blues were finally and decisively trampled, never to be seen again.

That year, I was Arts High's state champion two-miler and a state record-holder. I took City and that victory was really sweet because the girl who had left me was in the stands, supporting her new man, who I *whupped*. He made third place.

I am reminded of a scene in the Hollywood film *Conan, the Barbarian*, where James Earl Jones, is the villain Thulsa Doom, who beheaded Conan's mother and destroys the village. Doom captures Conan, played by Arnold Schwarzenegger, as Conan seeks to avenge the death of his mother and destruction of his village. Doom looks the hero in the eye and tells him he made Conan what he became. That bitter taste of defeat from the humiliating laps of my freshmen year brought out a stubbornness that taught me how to become more.

That year I won everything but the Meet of Champions — a big-time state meet among the high schools. But the more I stuck to running, the more it rewarded me. It got to the point where I would overhear people say, "If Larry Hamm is in this race, I'm getting out." My self-confidence was developing, and the person who broke his mother's heart in eighth grade was long gone.

A Life in the Struggle

While I was studying and running, racial tensions in Newark had significantly increased. In addition to the increased poverty and incessant police brutality, there was Newark City Hospital, later named Martland 1967 and 1968, a butcher shop you tried to stay away from. It would be replaced, urban-renewal style, with the Newark College of Medicine and Dentistry. The problem was that its proposed site was in the heart of the Central Ward, which prompted complaints from ward residents that they were the victims of Negro removal. That complex is now known as the Rutgers New Jersey Medical School. Another public controversy was the repeated refusal of the Newark Board of Education to name Wilbur Parker, a Black man with a master's degree in accounting and the first Black CPA in the state of New Jersey, to the post of board secretary. The man nominated for the position by Mayor Hugh Addonizio was James Callaghan, a white man who only had a high school diploma. This controversy turned out to be one of the matches that lit the fuse to the Newark Rebellion. Addonizio was determined not to give the position to a Black man despite the fury from Black Newarkers. Addonizio rescinded the appointment of Callaghan, created a deputy secretary post position for Parker and told Arnold Hess, the incumbent, that he could not retire.

There were sixteen thousand students in Newark's public high schools, and an estimated seventy-five percent of them were Black. Addonizio had become mayor just six years earlier by creating a Negro and Italian coalition, but a combination of Italian racism, Mafia corruption and Black Power crushed that connection. Addonizio's crumbs in the form of scant Black appointments were not enough. An attempt in 1968, led by Amiri Baraka's United Brothers had fizzled. In 1969, that effort expanded when Amiri Baraka's Committee for a Unified

Rebellion, Strikes, A Sit-In and Maybe Princeton

Newark (CFUN) connected to the Newark Young Lords to form the Black and Puerto Rican Convention. It was this event in combination with another convention in 1970, led by activist and historian Bob Curvin, that pushed Ken Gibson, a city engineer on his second run for mayor, as the candidate.

Gibson and Amiri Baraka's CFUN, an outgrowth of the second convention, won and much of the power of the city changed complexion. The Mafia no longer openly ran Newark. The people had a taste of real democracy. In Newark back then, democracy meant not just voting, but standing your ground. It was a place in which working-class people of all types had to try to understand each other. In 1970 and 1971, Newark's teachers decided to strike for better working conditions. The responses to those strikes set me in the direction that I had seen glimpses of in that first high school assembly.

During the first Newark teachers' strike, I was Deputy Mayor at Arts High, but my mind was set on track. Here's how conscious I was: In my senior year, I read *The Communist Manifesto* in my humanities class. It said that a specter was haunting Europe. I thought Marx and Engels were speaking about a ghost. I really couldn't understand it at the time. I had yet to read *The Autobiography of Malcolm X* or what, just a couple of years later, would become my personal favorite, *Malcolm X Speaks*. I purchased the latter book from *Nyumbya Ujamaa*, The House of Cooperative Economics, which was the name of Baraka's bookstore. I passed by something called The *Hekalu Umoja*, The House of Unity (the headquarters for CFUN) every day, walking past what we students called "The 'Habari Gani' People," because we knew no Swahili. I had no dashikis and no political consciousness. I didn't even know what *As-salāmu alaykum* meant and I had no heavy "rap", but I did have a small afro.

This is what we knew in 1970. We knew that our classes were overcrowded and that we didn't have a real gym, playground, or cafeteria. We didn't have adequate art or music supplies.

The complexion of the school system had changed in the four years I attended high school and probably even before that. Arts High was integrated during most of my four years there. However, by the time I graduated, there were only a handful of white kids in its student population. So, even a non-political person like me was getting the message about Black Power and community control.

In my private thoughts, I sometimes wonder why our teachers, who clearly understood what we were doing, did not teach us how the assigned readings some of us snored through, like Thoreau, Marx and Engels, actually applied to our exact situation. Why did I have to wait until I went to Princeton — an elite, capitalist university — to learn about socialism? And even there, we had independent study groups! Thinking back on it now, I think that many of these public-school teachers, working-class Americans, and proud members of the Newark Teachers Union (NTU) who had to fight very hard to get a college education, were afraid to rock the boat and lose full-time jobs with great benefits. After all, the Newark public school teachers' strikes were about making sure that teachers had the resources and time they needed to teach, not *what* to teach.

Two things helped me tremendously. The first was what influenced so many of us in our age group — the constant student walkouts across the nation, including in New Jersey, in protest of the Vietnam War. The Vietnam War energized students as much as the Civil Rights and Black Power movements. Students were feeling empowered and would walk out over issues

Rebellion, Strikes, A Sit-In and Maybe Princeton

as varied as the need for more Black teachers and the quality of the food in the cafeteria. People forget that between 1960 to 1972, there were one thousand violent uprisings in America's urban areas. With mass media exposure, public resistance to the status quo could no longer be isolated. Many of these high school and college students chose non-violence, not as the result of some great ideological debate, but because they wanted the ear of people in authority to accomplish their goals.

The second influence was that of Amiri Baraka. He came to our school during the first strike in 1970.

I wondered, *Who is this man?*

I never saw anyone at Arts High speak this way. It was as if a foreign power had invaded the school. This guy in African clothes — the first such clothing I ever saw — came with these two big brothers as his bodyguards. The principal, Ms. Theresa David, didn't let him address an entire assembly, just the student council.

I was in awe of him. He was talking about things I had never heard of; ideas that I never had. I had a cousin who was in the Nation of Islam, and I knew how Black preachers sounded because I had gone to church, but this man was different. He was preaching Black Power—community control. He wanted to convert the slave ship of Newark into a New Ark, one responsive to the needs of the 1970s Black revolution.

Since the Rebellion, the 1969 Black and Puerto Rican Convention and Gibson's election, Newark had become a center for Black Power. Baraka, with his CFUN, had become one of the foremost spokespersons for Black Power.

In 1970, by virtue of being a student government leader at my school, I was involved in the Newark Federation of High School Student Councils. In 1971, I was being drawn into the world of political activism because of what was happening inside Newark. The second teacher strike happened in my senior year when I was the Mayor of Arts High.

The students at the city's still predominantly white high schools — Vailsburg, East Side and Barringer — had left the coalition. The city's predominantly Black high schools were Weequahic, Central, West Side, Arts and South Side. At that time, the Black community supported Baraka more than the predominately white teachers' union. I regretted the conflict because I didn't see the whites as the enemy. So, it is with mixed feelings that I point out, however, that the Student Federation's fight had become a Black student fight. As Mayor of Arts High, I was mayor of all the students, Black and white. In time, I would realize the value and strength of purpose in working together for a common cause.

Yes, the *Zeitgeist* of the movement played its part, but the main catalyst was the threat to our graduation imposed by the 1971 teachers strike. We were warned by school staff that under state law high school students who were absent from school for thirty-five consecutive days were ineligible for graduation. We were having none of that! I was a National Honors Society member and had been accepted into Harvard, Princeton, and Yale. I thought to myself, *And you tell me I'm not graduating, because you adults can't get your act together? Are you out of your minds?* So, the Arts High walkout was planned to take place in March of 1971.

Ms. David, who, by the way, was Arts High's first Black principal, had gotten wind of our planned walkout. No revolution was going to happen on her watch. She stopped me in the hallway the day before our planned action. "Larry," she said, "If you take these students out of here tomorrow, you're going to get suspended. You're not going to graduate, and you won't go to college."

Oh, shit. But it was too late! I couldn't call it back!

The day arrived. As did the bell separating second and third period — 10:35 a.m. Our zero hour. Time to meet out in front of the building. I'm out, ready to lead. Nobody.

At 10:45, tears begin to well up in my eyes. *Nobody is coming* and *I'm not going to college. How will I ever tell my mother this?* At 10:50, the doors flung open, and about ninety-nine percent of the students left the building.

We marched downtown to the Downtowner Motor Inn, where the Newark Board of Education and the teachers were negotiating. We barged in, not on anybody's side but ours. We took over two floors of the hotel. "Look, you guys got to get this thing together and end this strike so we can graduate," I demanded of those in the meeting.

I had never led a sit-in before. Some reporters were there with cameras. They were taking pictures and there was a lot of pressure. It was like two hundred of us. People were worried and coming to us talking about we were all going to get arrested. I was upset with tears forming in my eyes again because, I didn't want to get people locked up. Reporters tried to take a picture of me, and two sisters got between them and me. The sisters told them that they couldn't take any pictures and they had to leave. I'll never forget that. That's why there are no pictures from the actual sit-in. I kind of regret that now. But my fear then was that published photographs of the students who participated in the sit-in could result in those students being arrested and/or suspended from school.

Mayor Gibson arrived. He told us that a very nervous public safety office had stationed police officers and fire engines outside the hotel, ready for any new rebellion. He continued: "Look, I know what you guys are doing. You're doing the right thing. I am proud of you. If you let me handle it, I believe I can get this strike over. I don't want anybody to get hurt or arrested. I believe in what you are doing."

We huddled. I was already won over because of what Gibson said to us. We left.

A few weeks later, in April of 1971, the strike was over. The Newark Federation of High School Student Councils continued to negotiate with the board. The Black students favored negotiating with the board, while the city's white students favored the NTU. Some of the Black students would later regret this decision, when they learned that Blacks in office and progress for Black people did not have to be synonymous.

We had presented a list of one-hundred actions we wanted to see accomplished including: 1) the completion of contract negotiations by September 1; 2) the revision of the school curriculum and student involvement in those revisions; and 3) more Black and Puerto Rican Studies courses. It was hard to understand that, for now, we were being stonewalled via talk. But I had gone through the fire with no smoke on my clothes. My first sit-in was successful and I was accepted to Princeton, Harvard, and Yale. However, Princeton offered a more adequate financial aid package. So, I was on my way to Princeton. But not entirely.

1971-1974:
KUJICHAGULIA:
BOARD, COUNCIL RUN
AND NO GUN

Opportunity did what most people say it never does: it knocked on my Twelfth Street door one summer day and asked for me by name. Pete Curtin, an aide to the mayor, came to my house one Saturday and asked me if I wanted to be appointed to the Newark Board of Education. I said I don't know, then said to ask my mother. Mom said, "It's up to my son," and then I accepted.

I was on the way to college — Princeton University, in weeks — and I had to focus on that. The plan: Princeton, then law school, then hopefully a successful career. Curtin said that meetings were only once a month and that the board would provide me transportation and anything else I needed to make it work.

Normally, turning points don't announce themselves. But mine did. That's really the beginning because if I hadn't accepted the appointment, my whole life would have been very different. I would have probably been some Political Science professor or an African-American Studies professor. But the turning point beckoned, and the arrow was pointing to Newark, not Princeton.

My appointment on July 1, 1971, made national headlines. Here's what Gibson said, according to the press: "The first time

I had a chance to meet Larry, I said to myself, 'it would be great to have a mind like his on the Board of Education. He has a clear mind, a desire to be fair, a commitment to better education and a sense of inter-group dynamics which is hard to find anywhere."

And here's what I said: "I realize that the appointment of someone my age to a post on the Board of Education is a new occurrence. Because of my age, some may consider me inexperienced and incapable of handling the job. There will be others who will resent my appointment not only because of my age but because I'm Black. But for me, the biggest challenge ahead does not lie within these matters. The greatest challenge is within the educational system of Newark. Our school system must be transformed from one of the nation's worst to one that will give a useful, meaningful, and relevant education to the children of Newark."

So why did it happen? My guess is Gibson wanted to shore up support by appointing someone who would give the board a Black majority. Gibson did not fare well with Black activists during the teachers strike. By appointing me he would appear innovative.

Someone was paying attention. Weeks later, the Southern Christian Leadership Conference would give me the SCLC's Youth Leadership Award at its annual convention in New Orleans. I got to meet all the pillars of the Civil Rights Movement: Rosa Parks and the Revs. Jesse Jackson, Hosea Williams, Ralph Abernathy, and Andrew Young. Mrs. Coretta Scott King personally handed me the award.

In August of 1971, fresh from the SCLC convention, I moved onto Princeton's campus. I felt like I was on another planet, but I attempted to adjust. It didn't work.

Kujichagulia: Board, Council Run and No Gun

By the beginning of November, I had dropped out, making national headlines again. It was also one of the final, *"why-are-you-throwing-away-your-life?"* sad moments for my mom. Then I tried to be a board member and a student at Rutgers-Newark. I dropped out *again*. I tried a "University Without Walls" program at the University of Massachusetts at Amherst. *Strike three.*

Why? Well, my first answer is that I couldn't balance the academic workload because folks were raising hell in Newark and the board started meeting multiple times a week.

But there was another, deeper answer. In 1971, the Black and Left movements peaked in American society. We thought we were on the edge of victory — what Amiri Baraka called *around-the-corner-ism*. To achieve that practical victory of a Black and brown people running a city, you had to actually be on the ground *running* it.

People my age were in the streets demonstrating all around the world. The Student Nonviolent Coordinating Committee. The Black Panther Party. The Young Lords. The Brown Berets. The American Indian Movement. All wanting change *now*. Even the incarcerated wanted change. The Attica uprising was happening during my first weeks at Princeton. And though I wasn't fully aware of all of that at the time with my slowly burgeoning consciousness, the wind was blowing in the direction of a real democracy, true freedom. I had set sail. So, I could not, would not, abandon Newark for Princeton because the liberation of the oppressed seemed so close as to be irrepressible.

I wasn't a martyr, but societal change requires hands-on work. I accepted that I would try to do it all. But, with the demands

A Life in the Struggle

of the time resulting in so many board meetings almost every other day, I ultimately decided to fulfill and devote my full time to my term on the board.

In reality, I was a kid trying to navigate the situation as best I could. As I recalled of the experience seven years later in my Princeton University undergraduate thesis:

I served on the Board of Education for three years, from 1971 to 1974. During that time, I was chairman of the Committee on Student Affairs and served one term as second vice president. As a board member, I was made aware of the educational aspirations of the Black community and also of the wretched condition of the Newark public schools, particularly those attended by Black children. But my role as a board member was not limited to educational affairs. I was expected by community people and activists to play a definite political role. Beyond being a board member, I was viewed as a community leader and was expected to participate in community struggles in other areas besides those concerned with education. This increased my awareness of the political awareness of Black people, and with their disillusionment with the political process...

By the time the [second teacher] strike had ended in 1971, this is how I viewed the situation: the main reason Black people were oppressed was because of white racism, and it was white racists who controlled the institutions and its distribution of goods and services in the Black community. To rectify this situation, Black people had to be put in posts of power to bring the institutions under Black control; by doing so, these institutions would then function in the best interests of the masses of Afro-Americans. With Blacks in control of city government, we could rectify the problems that plagued the Black community because we would be in control of the distribution of municipal goods and services. With Black control of the Board of

Kujichagulia: Board, Council Run and No Gun

Education: more Black teachers and administrators could be hired that would be sensitive to the needs of Black students; we would appropriate more funds to have new schools built in the Black community, and, finally, the curriculum could be made relevant to the needs of Black students. I believed that when these types of things were done, education in Newark would improve...

When I was appointed to the Newark Board of Education, I knew almost nothing about politics, electoral or otherwise, but now both my feet were planted firmly in the city's political arena. Although board members are appointed and not elected, they are politicians, nonetheless, formulating policies which affect the lives of Newark public school students. In fact, the Board of Education's annual budget for the entire school system, well over $100 million a year, is one of the city's biggest political issues (for the politicians, that is) every year. For more than a decade, the majority of the students in the Newark public schools have been Afro-American. Because of this, the Board has been a major focus of Black people's striving for political power in Newark. The belief was that once the city had a Black Board of Education, then something could be done about the inferior education Black students were receiving. Faced with these factors — including the use of confrontation politics, defined as bringing out angry crowds to disrupt business as usual until an issue was heard — how would I function as a political actor?

For some more cynical observers of local politics, the question was this: Would I be Gibson's puppet, or Baraka's?

U nder Gibson, the board now had a new Black majority. Gibson had appointed Jesse Jacob, Charles Bell, Mrs. Helen Fullilove and Fernando Zambrana, a Puerto Rican. The only remaining Black person already on the board from the

Addonizio administration was Mrs. Gladys Churchman, wife of the founder of the Churchman's Funeral Home. John Cervase, Michael Petti, and Thomas Malanga, all white, made up the remaining remnants of the Addonizio administration.

On my swearing-in day, before the swearing-in ceremony, all the Board members were called into the mayor's office. The mayor sat at his desk with all of us facing him from the other side. Gibson proceeded to give his "suggestions" as to who would run the Board. It was understood that these "suggestions" were not to be taken lightly. Not-so-subtle pressure would and could be applied when and if necessary. His suggestions: Fullilove to be elected president and Petti to be elected vice-president.

Looking back, I now know that Gibson placed pressure on us because he wanted to diminish the power of Jacob, whom the mayor found he could not control. As a result, Jacob was maneuvered out of the presidency. Gibson would have suggested Bell-who voted to approve Gibson's settlement with the NTU, after waffling-but he knew that wouldn't fly with the Black community. I never forgot hearing Elayne Brodie's rebuke of Bell. Ms. Brodie was a Black woman who, at the time, was head of the powerful Title I Parent's Council. She was happy about Fullilove's election. She was not at all happy about Bell. In that July 1 meeting, Brodie set off the warning shots. "I am not going to play games about it... Be he Black or white, when you are a misfit in this community, the New Ark community rises up!" Brodie's sentiments represented that of The New Ark community — the Black and Hispanic community. They were diametrically opposed to the appointment of Mr. Bell. I am thankful that the mayor had the political expedience to recognize the powder keg he was sitting on. Although Fullilove did vote against the teacher's demands, Gibson thought he could still work with her. He thought that since she was an advocate for the Black community and would be the first female president of the school board, such a move would repair his tarnished image as a racial accommodationist. Ironically, it was the more conservative Bell and not Fullilove, who I went with to the Angela Davis' trial in 1972 when we were at a National School Board Convention in San Francisco.

When it was officially time for Fullilove's nomination for president, everyone followed Gibson's lead. It was interesting to see Jacob as first in line to support Fullilove for the board presidency, then Bell, then Churchman. The final vote tally was eight in favor, none opposed. Fullilove abstained. But it would only take a few Board meetings for the olive branches to be forgotten and those who applauded her to become her vocal, public opposition.

The motion to nominate Petti as vice-president was made by Malanga and seconded by Zambrana. Many in the audience were upset and made that known. This was because during the second strike, Petti had voted in favor of yielding to the teachers in the face of Black community opposition. Jacob, in gamesmanship mode, seconded the nomination. The final vote was eight in favor, none opposed. Petti abstained.

The only way Gibson could have gotten a better script was to write it himself. Between Fullilove and myself, the mayor got a lot of political mileage logged that day.

Fullilove would only be in the president's chair a year before the non-white majority asserted its Black Power and independence from Gibson by appointing Jacob back into the seat. I was happy with this. Yet there was some irony. When

I was a student fighting for direct representation in contract negotiations between the Board and the union, Jacob was one of the main opponents of this move. He wanted the students to play a more advisory role. As we started negotiating student demands with the board, I began to develop a personal connection with Jacob. He treated me with respect and made sure no retaliation was taken against us when we had the sit-ins. At that first board meeting when I was sworn in, Jacob said he didn't know whether to extend his congratulations or his condolences. "I wouldn't sit here and try to tell you that you're going to have an easy task," he continued. "You'll make mistakes, but I'll be right beside you to help you make them and help you correct them." Indeed, he did.

Black Power was also exercised in the hiring and upgrading of personnel. Deputy Secretary of the Board of Education Wilbur Parker would be vindicated; he would finally be awarded the Secretary position that was denied him by the Addonizio administration because he was Black. Hess would finally be able to retire. Callaghan, the high school graduate initially awarded the position, was enroute to prison for embezzlement, with Addonizio not far behind.

But I have to point out that some of the white teachers — particularly the labor union activists — had a radical class consciousness. Perhaps some of them saw days as college campus radicals. I don't think they were characteristic of the average public-school teacher in Newark. Yet, in 1971, the board was Black and the NTU was still predominantly white even though Carole Graves, the newly-elected NTU president, was Black. The demographics had shifted, not the power. Over the years, the power would still prove to be white, as in Italian.

Kujichagulia: Board, Council Run and No Gun

Black Power had its various shades. As a board member, I had a good relationship with both Jacob and Bell. However, I wasn't as close to Bell because he came out of a labor organizing background and he wasn't as consistent as Jacob was in advocating for Black community control. Bell had a little more critical consciousness and took some different positions often enough to let me know that he might not be as reliable as Jacob. Bell was a wheeler-dealer. He would straddle a bit, but never strayed too far from Gibson. But I had an effective working relationship with Bell, Jacob, and most of the Black members. When I presented matters for consideration by the Board, most of them supported my positions. If no one else seconded a motion of mine, Jacob would. Even the issue concerning the liberation flag, they all voted for it. I, however, got the heat. More on that later.

I saw the people organized, at least some of them. There was an organization called ONE, the Organization of Negro Educators. It was run by a fellow named Fred Means. The goal of ONE was to get the board to hire more Black teachers and administrators. Many Black and white people saw teaching as a job that was reserved for white people. Most of the teachers were white. Fred made clear that though teachers' working conditions weren't what they wanted them to be, they were still much better than the jobs held by the Black people whose children they taught.

From the beginning, my appointment to the Board was a political hot potato. Unfavorable responses came from, among other places, the Newark City Council. "This is highly impractical, unfair to the student, and not in the best interest of the community-at-large," retorted South Ward Councilman Sharpe James, one of the United Brothers. "It is not the time to experiment with token appointments. There are many 17-year-olds who, by virtue of their residency and community involvement, would have the time to serve. But Hamm will be a full-time resident at Princeton University, and a possible member of the Princeton track and cross-country teams." James continued: "The Board of Education, facing an educational crisis, needs individuals who can meet the rigor of regular, special, and emergency meetings. To suggest that Hamm will be able to properly commute between classes and assignments at Princeton University and the Newark Board of Education is insane."

I had to admit a few months later when I quit Princeton, that he was more right than I wanted him to be. Apart from my fellow Board member Cervase, who many Blacks often accused of racism, most officeholders appeared to be mute about my appointment. Did they not have an opinion, or were they biding their time? I didn't know but Cervase was very clear when he said, "The city's schools are like a company with $1 billion in assets and a budget of $100 million a year…Can you conceive of an 18-year-old child effectively administrating General Motors?"

I knew what I was up against, but I couldn't pass up an opportunity to steer this ship in the right direction. During the first two weeks that I started to go down to the Board's administration building at 31 Green Street, one of the first things I noticed were long lines of mostly Black and Puerto Rican students waiting to get working papers and applying for jobs. There were working papers available, but no jobs. I was struck immediately by the contrast I witnessed in the Board offices upstairs. There were many students with summer jobs in the building. However, most of them were white.

Kujichagulia: Board, Council Run and No Gun

This bothered me and I began to inquire. I found out that the students working there were not even Newark residents: they were the sons and daughters, nieces, and nephews, and even friends of the Board's white administrators.

For the first time, I was positioned to directly affect the change I wanted to see. I knew that a proposal that was directed at Black students would be rejected by the Board. At a July 15, 1971 special Board meeting, I proposed that the Board hire Newark public school students and graduates for student jobs. After some discussion on the matter, the Board put it to a vote in conference and then again in public. Five in favor, one opposed, one abstention. Cervase was absent from the meeting, and Petti, had left before the final vote was taken a well-known political tactic. The "no vote" was cast by Fullilove, who said the measure excluded Newark residents who attended parochial and private schools, making it unfair for them and their city taxpaying parents.

Before the week was out, I was assailed by every white politician in the city. First, City Council President Louis M. Turco and Councilman Anthony J. Giuliano stated their public opposition to the new policy. In addition to echoing Fullilove's complaint, they said it was morally wrong. Next Councilman Michael P. Bottone added to the opposition, saying it would cause an exodus of city's non-public schools and overcrowding in the public schools. Following Bottone was State Assemblyman Anthony Imperiale, the man who called Martin Luther King "Martin Luther Coon." He went so far as to file a complaint with the US Labor Department charging that the new policy was discriminatory. By the next meeting, the resolution was rescinded and replaced with one that required student employees to be city residents. The vote to rescind was led by Zambrana, who

47

had voted "yes" the first-time round. The final vote was five to three. Jacob and Bell joined me in opposing the resolution. Cervase was absent. Malanga then proposed that students under twenty-one years of age hired by the Board of Education, be Newark residents. Zambrana proposed that two-thirds of the summer jobs offered by the Board be given to past or present public-school students. I speculate that Zambrana sympathized with what we're trying to do, but he was alone. His motion received no second. I believe that Imperiale, et.al. were more concerned with political capital than equal opportunity for Newark students.

The public criticism stung. I was being blasted in both local newspapers and elsewhere. Little did I know this was merely a mosquito bite. The hornet's nest was yet to come.

I began to realize the power the Board wielded to index Black history publicly by naming schools. After meeting Rosa Parks at that SCLC convention, I started an effort to name a city elementary school after her. That's how Waverly Avenue School became Rosa Parks School and Robert Treat School became Marcus Garvey School. The Summer Avenue School was renamed Roberto Clemente in honor of the Puerto Rican Major League Baseball player who called for a daylong strike after Martin Luther King was assassinated. The South Tenth Street School became the Harriet Tubman School, and the South Eighth Street School became Martin Luther King School.

I'm glad we weren't intimidated, because when we voted to change the name of South Side High, a beloved South Ward institution, to Malcolm X Shabazz High School, it caused such

Kujichagulia: Board, Council Run and No Gun

a tumult that the board had to post a security detail at the school. Teachers were telling their children they would never get into college with Malcolm X's name on their high school diploma. Some students were planning to physically attack the young brother, Norman "Akili" Buchanon, who had started the petition signed by one thousand students. Nobody but the youth and segments of the community had taken it seriously until the resolution passed.

All hell broke out at the former South Side High the day after the resolution was passed to change its name. Some of the teachers were actively agitated and wanted the board to change the name back. I had to go to the school and speak to a whole auditorium full of students, explaining the justifications and the importance of the name change. I believe that perceptions of Malcolm X were based solely on his involvement with the Nation of Islam. I think that my address to the school helped, but South Side alumni still want their old name back. And it's important to note that, to this day, most people, in informal speech, only call it "Shabazz High School" or "Shabazz" for some reason, while the full names are used for the other renamed schools.

The Black nationalist symbolism felt good, yet, I slowly began to realize, this symbolism didn't deal with the root of the problem. Throughout the country, Black people were finally defining themselves and finding themselves in the annals of history, but the school curriculum had not caught up with the times. Curriculum revision was necessary in light of ample evidence that the content of many of the textbooks that were used in schools was biased, racist and distorted. Distortions included the exclusion of African Americans from national and world history. Biases were also extended on gender, class, ideological and political lines as well. I had learned by then that denying the oppressed and exploited their own history and the knowledge of how they can change their position in society was a way of perpetuating the status quo. As a result, they became unknowing accomplices in their own victimization. Civics courses were not offered in all the public secondary schools, but students enrolled in them where they were given. So, I had four resolutions passed at the public board meeting held on August 31, 1971.

The first resolution dealt with voter education and registration. It stated that the Board, as of September 1, 1971, would set aside one or more school days, between September 9 and September 23, for voter education in the public schools. The second was that, as of September 2, 1971, the Newark Board of Education petition William Yeomans, Commissioner of the Essex County Board of Elections, to have all eight public high schools designated for the taking of voter registrations on the dates submitted by the Newark Board of Education. The third called for the formulation of voter education curriculum requiring visual and audio aids and lectures that provided an understanding of the voting process. This was to be a permanent part of the high school curriculum.

Finally, I proposed that the Board, as of September 1, 1972, offer in all secondary Newark public schools a one-year Civics course. It would pay particular attention to Newark and be so constructed as to present the present-day structure of urban cities, their governments, administrative organizations, civil matters, etc. This would also include students attending, as a class, Board meetings, city council meetings, court sessions, et cetera.

The Board passed all of them. As I began to understand my power, I began to reflect on my purpose — the reason I thought this was important enough to sideline my college education. It was the obligation to ensure that the student demands we had negotiated in the heat of the second teacher strike were brought to the floor, voted on and implemented, if passed. I hoped to see the fervor rekindled. It was time for students to be directly included in the decision-making processes. So, I had three resolutions passed at a special September Board meeting.

- That the Board resume negotiations no later than October 4, 1971, with the Student Federation.

- That students participating in negotiations between the Board and the Student Federation be given official recognition on the Board's agenda; and

- That the Administration direct that in all secondary schools where Parent and Community Advisory Committees are established, students in those schools be included on such committees.

All three were passed. My next lesson pointed me to the long road between the formulation of a policy and its implementation. By October, the Board had not resumed the negotiations and there was no major effort on the students' part to have them do so. One of the reasons for this was that many of the student leaders and activists who were involved in organizing efforts during the strike had graduated and gone on to work or college. I found that student demands would only be dealt with seriously if pressured to do so. It was only after leaving Princeton that I was able to invest in reviving the charge. My new job as an aide to Central Ward Councilman Dennis Westbrooks and my Board duties allowed for that time.

Early in November, a meeting of about seventy-five student representatives from public secondary schools throughout the city was held at Central High School. At this meeting, the original student demands were reviewed and discussed, and new ones were added to them. I took the list raised verbally by the students and later elaborated on each one of them in written form.

One of the reasons given by the Board for rejecting the demands the first time they were negotiated was that they were vague and needed to be more explicit. Not only were these demands more explicit, but they were expanded from twenty-seven to one hundred and one. The demands basically covered four areas: teacher accountability, curriculum revision, upgrading of facilities, and student and community representation. Unlike other Board members who may have been unclear as to what the students' objectives were, beyond providing the public-school students of Newark with a "quality education," the demands gave me a clearly, defined program to attempt to implement.

Aware that the Board would not act on the demands just because we asked it (or on account of a student being one of its members), it was necessary for students to be mobilized to press for their demands. This effort led to the establishment of the New Ark Student Federation, a city-wide organization. It was clear that without this pressure, the students' demands and other proposals that I put forth would never have moved forward with the Board. Chuck Stone, founder of the National Association of Black Journalists, once pointed out that organizations, not individuals, wield power. It was clear: the Federation was the source of any real influence I held as a Board member.

At its peak, the Federation had close to 500 members dispersed in over twenty schools throughout the city. These schools included the eight senior high schools, five junior high schools, three vocational technical schools, three elementary schools, one Catholic school, Rutgers-Newark, and Essex County College, then a brand-new community college. While Baraka and the Committee for a Unified Newark were influential in the establishment of the organization, the Federation developed its own constitution which embodied its own ideological perspectives.

The members of the New Ark Student Federation may have been influenced by the times, but we were not into personality cults. We believed in democratic leadership and mass mobilization. I was never in CFUN. I was a fellow traveler. In fact, when I told Baraka I was thinking about joining, he advised me that I would be of greater use outside the organization. But it's funny because the student federation was more of a hybrid between the Black nationalism that Baraka was advocating and the politics of the Black Panther Party. In contrast, we were more democratic. The ethos of the Black Panthers and the Student Nonviolent Coordinating Committee appealed to us, so we wore jeans and jean jackets instead of dashikis. We believed that African dress was appropriate for celebrating Kwanzaa, but not for organizing. In New Ark, everyone got a say and a vote. But we did respect and embrace Black Power.

The group's slogan was "Education for liberation." There were ten aims and purposes that focused on unifying students while making them aware of their community's needs and building them up to address those needs. The major thrust was directed toward changing the schools, putting them under the control of and making them more relevant to the needs of the Black community.

Racist ideas and practices were challenged and authorities and administrators who wanted to preserve the status quo were defied. When meaningful change was not effectuated, students organized protests, demonstrations, and walkouts. Some demonstrations took the form of marches to the offices of the Superintendent, the Board President and or board members, as well as mass attendance at Board meetings on Tuesday nights. Of course, there were many who felt that this activism on the part of students was creating chaos and anarchy in the schools. But having tried the proper channels and finding that they did not work, the students believed that such activities were the necessary next courses of action. I wrote in my undergraduate thesis that: *The demands and actions of the Black students confront the racism that has always been present in the schools and is finally being unmasked. The view of many administrators and teachers that student revolts are deleterious is refuted by others who see the efforts to attack and destroy racism as a positive force that will benefit both Blacks and whites.*

The themes of my first few months on the Board had been established, and I took the cues that Black people were giving across the nation: It's about providing members of our community a political education in line with revolutionary struggles and community control over local electoral politics. These demands met with some resistance, even though research demonstrated, for example, that Black students did benefit from a political education curriculum. My constant Board adversary, John Cervase, used this demand as a rationale to oppose all the rest. In voicing his opposition to funding the programs outlined by the demands he stated, "The programs Hamm talks about are infected with a philosophy which goes against Black and white people. One of the demands is geared toward Third World peoples. I think if we want to do anything tonight, I say we should cut the things Hamm talks about out of the budget."

Student demands deemed "radical" were progressive, and relative to what had been happening in the schools. Perhaps they did appear to some to be extreme measures. But that was because we assumed that the changes called for could be made within the framework of the existing social system. We called for revolution rhetorically, but we really meant radical reform.

The student demands were presented to the Board at its November 30th public meeting. Four hundred students, most of them from Arts High, Central and Malcolm X Shabazz turned out to confront the Board with their demands. The pressure the Board was under that night was apparent when the meeting had to be moved from the Board to the Newark Municipal Council chambers. But even there, the number of persons was beyond the room's seating capacity. The students had learned well from the second teachers' strike; numbers do count. Students were unrelenting for the next four months. They spoke at public Board meetings until the Board approved a combination of proposals. What the Board called the "negotiated agreement" was ultimately approved on March 28, 1972. The problem now was in the implementation.

The vote victories we had were hard-won and gave us a deserved sense of satisfaction. But I quickly learned that it was the job of administrators to carry out the mandates. If the Board sends down a new policy that a principal doesn't like or believes will be unpopular in his or her school and or community, he or she might ignore it or implement it half-heartedly. In big city school systems with large bureaucracies, it is difficult to conduct a thorough check on every administrator. If the Board discovered that a principal failed to implement its policy and decided to take action against the administrator, then it may also have to deal with an angry community that believes that person is acting in its best interest. On the other hand, if that principal chooses to fully implement that policy against the communities' wishes, then he or she might have to deal with angry parents demanding that the Board transfer the principal to another school.

Newark's first African Liberation Week in 1972 is a clear example of the difficulty in implementing a new board policy. From 1972 to 1974, I championed the passage of resolutions declaring May 19 to May 26 be observed in Newark public schools as African Liberation Week. The birthdate of Malcolm X was May 19 and May 26 was proclaimed African Liberation Day by African liberation support groups in the United States. During the observance, the current progress, development, movements and problems of African people and their descendants in the Diaspora were to be studied and discussed. The topics to which particular attention was to be paid were the life of Malcolm X, politics, economics, human development, international policy, and the role of youth in the struggle for social justice. The legislation mandated that the Board's Curriculum Department develop special materials to be used during the observance. In addition to this, school assembly programs were to be held featuring speakers, films, cultural arts performances, and other activities. In Newark, the city that had celebrated Kwanzaa since its inception in 1966, the Black Consciousness Movement that was dominating the early 1970s — spurred by Black Power movements and the creation of Black Studies nationwide and African Liberation movements worldwide — finally made Black history and a liberation consciousness public school policy. At least as long as I was on the Board.

But on the ground, the implementation varied widely, and sadly, not surprisingly. In most schools located in Black communities there was some observance of African Liberation Week. The administrators of some schools put more effort into it than did others. Schools under Black administrators and that had active Black parent organizations, such as Weequahic and Malcolm X Shabazz high schools, had elaborate programs that took up the entire week. In my visits, I found other schools where the materials prepared by the Board's curriculum writers had gotten no farther than the school office or a shelf in the storage room of the Social Studies Department. It goes without saying that most of these schools were in white communities and under white administrative supervision. This was unfortunate to me not just because I understood that Black students at those schools were missing out, but that I knew white students also could benefit from such "progressive," "radical" subject matter. I came to understand the hyperlocal political reality: if some of these principals had tried to organize activities related to the observance they would have probably been harshly criticized by whites in their schools' communities.

Social movements are an interesting combination of nature (spontaneous actions) and nurture (a planned strategy). For example, Rosa Parks' refusal to give up her seat to a white man appeared to be "spontaneous," but she and the Movement in Montgomery, Alabama had been well-prepped for the resulting bus boycott. Mrs. Parks was the secretary to the local NAACP and played an active part in the Movement. Movement's ebb and flow; they seemingly pop out of nowhere, created by random and maybe not-so-random acts. But they always come from a foundation, created by conditions, and guided organically into political ideals.

Stuff just happens sometimes. Particularly when Movement members are young. Movements are flexible, so mistakes can be made and corrected. But Movements *move* — and spontaneity is the lifeblood of motion. Activism is, by definition, taking action.

The New Ark Student Federation and its fellow travelers, including myself, the 17-year-old Board member, were no exception on November 30, 1971. We were all relatively new to political activity, and impatience was the order of the day. Under such conditions, the unexpected can happen.

How I handled the Black Liberation Movement flag issue — the one that opened up the tear-filled well of concern within my mother, the one that had me mentioned in newspapers worldwide — was one such occurrence. As a result of the international attention this achievement received in the media; it is probably the only one people can remember — if they remember anything at all —about my Board tenure. That is truly sad, because the policies we passed — with the active support and input from organized and committed Newark students — had *real,* not symbolic, impact on the city and its education system. But existing racial tension plus spontaneity equals sensationalism.

The brouhaha happened during the same meeting the students presented the Board with their original demands. Sadly, these demands — which did not include the flag — were overshadowed by the flag controversy.

It happened this way: after nearly three hours of listening to grievances from the city's high school students, the Board then heard a set of demands from Glenn Thomas, president of the Area Board Three Youth Council. Thomas was a student at Rutgers University in Newark, and Area Board Three was a division of the United Community Corporation, Newark's anti-poverty agency. One of his many demands was to have the Black Liberation flag in each public-school classroom, "along with the American flag, because we know that y'all not gonna change your Old Glory out of there."

Superintendent Franklin Titus talked to Thomas about the state requirements of American History versus the new Black History courses, and then the flag issue. He explained that to have the flag in Newark schools would be a "policy decision by the Board of Education, and it is susceptible to administrative fiat." "Now wait a minute. Y'all got this rule, right? As the board, y'all could change this rule?" Thomas continued, "If somebody could make a motion to change this rule, would somebody make it PLEASE?"

Fullilove asked if there was a quorum for such a vote. Was I a fool for what I did next?

"Will you accept this?" I asked. "I so move that a Black Liberation flag be placed in all schools where there are over fifty percent Black enrollment."

I mean, why not?

Fullilove quickly countered: "As you know, I'm very conscious of money. I would rather see how many flags we need and how much money it would cost. If I seconded it now and there's no money...."

Thomas wasn't hearing it. Neither was Jacob, who seconded my motion. While Jacob and Fullilove were trying to figure out how many flags were needed, Thomas continued, throwing the other demands to the wind. "You got an American flag in every class. Why not a Liberation flag in every class?"

Bell and Fullilove and Hess —who had been board secretary since 1945, wanted to talk about the cost first but relented. (Remember: the students were putting intense pressure on the Board.) Jacob thought the Board could worry about the cost later. He and I stood firm.

The resulting votes were Bell, yes; Churchman, yes; Hamm, yes; Jacob, yes; Zambrana, yes; Fullilove: "If we find the money, yes.... money, yes." (Malanga did not vote, according to the transcript, and Cervase was MIA.) The motion was carried by a majority vote of the non-white Board members. *Ungawa.*

Public policy for tens of thousands of students, done on the fly. No prior discussion of the motion between Board members, either in private, in committee meetings, or in the closed conference that preceded every public meeting. No prior discussions between Board members who supported the motion and those persons calling for it from the floor. Just spontaneous motion and a vote to pass it.

So why did I take this seemingly reckless action? I proposed the motion because I supported the idea. I was also onboard because it was requested, by The People. To not do so might have brought my own credibility into question. Even though the flag demand had not been part of the original student demands, there appeared to be an enthusiastic response from the students there when Thomas asked for it and I took up the flag, as it were. In addition, at the time I actually believed the Board would *not* pass this motion! I believed this not only because of what was being asked, but how the Board dealt with floor requests: they usually went to administrators or board members to be handled or simply ignored.

What was ignored were the other students' demands to improve reading and other learning skills, upgrading of school facilities, changes in curriculum, and a larger role in decision-making. I remembered my mother reacting badly to an editorial commentary on the topic on WABC-TV, New York's local ABC affiliate and flagship station for the entire network. It was delivered by the station's vice president of public affairs, who attacked me by name. The flag was flying through the airwaves and in the newspapers, and it sat atop a political lightning pole.

State Assemblyman George C. Richardson said the decision was Gibson's fault, since he had appointed the five members of the board who voted for it. To his credit, Gibson publicly came out against the decision but did not blast the Board. He said that although he respected the intent of the action — to imbue Black students with a positive Black identity, the flag was a potentially divisive symbol and would not, in the end, teach children to read.

Cervase, who missed the vote that night, well made up for it. He petitioned the State Department of Education to ban the flag in all the state's public schools. When flags started to appear not only in Newark schools but those in other municipalities in the state, Cervase obtained a restraining order in State Superior Court. The State Assembly passed a bill outlawing all flags in state public schools other than the American flag, but the Senate killed the bill. And, not surprisingly, white civic and community groups opposed the decision, and the city's white councilmen clamored for an elected Board.

Black community reaction in Newark was mixed. Black nationalist-oriented community and student groups supported it, while more traditional organizations were opposed. A Newark Urban League spokesman decried the decision, while Roy Wilkins of the National NAACP labeled it "transparent tommyrot." A Black newspaper columnist, Claude Lewis in Philadelphia, stated the flag's presence might spur pride and knowledge. Dr. Nathan Wright, a Newark civil rights leader who would later go into academia, approved the decision, saying it reminded Black youth "that their primary purpose is liberation from an unhappy and inequitable past and present, and from a hopeless future."

The issue was finally settled on January 26, 1972, when State Commissioner of Education Carl Marburger released his ruling on the matter. He said that he ruled against the Board's resolution was "so divisive on its face that it impedes, rather than advances, the task of improving" education. But he said his ruling did not mean that flags couldn't be displayed "for educational purposes." Cervase, who petitioned for this ruling, was unsatisfied. He understood that Black people would indeed find those purposes, and he was right.

So why do I call a victory an error? Because we didn't think through how to present the issue in such a way where it would have maximized the historical and educational importance of it. In this case, a Board of Education eschewed education for activist symbolism, thoughtful policy for a response to mass pressure. The People deserve their own symbols, picked by themselves, but they also deserve policy discussion. The Newark/Larry Hamm flag controversy was so well reported that Amiri Baraka later told me he heard about it when he was in *Tanzania*.

By the way, did I mention that the Board post *had no salary*? I received an allotment of $3000 for necessary expenses. I was being publicly attacked for a nonpaying job. My day job was working for Councilman Westbrooks.

Getting the heat from that flag controversy and the renaming of South Side High was part of being militant. At that time, I was definitely a Black militant. Baraka gave me the name Adhimu Changa (Kiswahili for "Important Youth") in 1972, after one of the most significant Black political meetings of the twentieth century — the National Black Political Convention in Gary, Indiana. I took that name not even a full year after I was named to the board.

The Gary convention was a transformational experience for me. It was a nodal point in my political development. I had never seen Black people organizing and moving like that before. When the convention ended, I knew we were on our way to the revolution. I thought Gary would start us on the pathway.

One of the best parts of Gary happened before we got to the gymnasium: The Black Liberation flag was flying all over the city, including lampposts. I wept openly because I had caught so much hell in Newark over that flag, and now I was seeing that it was possible to literally have a symbol of Black revolution as a public banner.

While the Black Nation rose in Gary, New Ark's Black community started to fragment. White people had moved out of the city after the Rebellion. So had many educated Black people who now finally had access to the suburbs in Essex County and other counties in Northern New Jersey. Additionally, a reverse Great Migration started as Black people began to move back South. This migration lasted for several decades. It's important to point out that many Blacks who did not leave the city, began to spread out into the fleeing-white West and South wards. Black Power was not consolidating but stretching out like a rubber band that would eventually break.

It appeared that Gibson and Baraka were going in different directions by 1972. Gibson was becoming disappointed with me as well, because of my controversial proposals and votes on the board. Gibson had appointed John Redden, an Irishman, as his police director. Baraka was not shy about pointing to the Prudential building and saying that the corporation had taken over the city. My feeling then was that Gibson had relied on a lot of people outside the Black community — like Pete Curtin, the white man that he sent to the heart of the Black community, the Central Ward's South Seventeenth Street, to invite me to join the board.

Up until the National Black Political Convention in Gary, Indiana in 1972, Baraka and his Committee for a Unified Newark/Congress of African People were seen at the center of the political movement in the city. But after 1973, Baraka's influence began to wane, and Gibson was left in power by virtue of his four-year term as mayor.

Kujichagulia: Board, Council Run and No Gun

In those early days of his administration, it felt sometimes like he had turned on the movement that had gotten him elected. Time allowed for a wider perspective.

Gibson died in 2019, and at his public memorial, I called him a symbol of the Black Power movement the same way King was of the Civil Rights movement. Before he passed, we joked about his public statement of regret of appointing that wild-eyed revolutionary Adhimu Changa on the board. I was glad I had the opportunity to honor him. I said he was one of the major male figures who shaped my young life.

As my first year on the Board was coming to a close, I waited for calls from its other members for my resignation. Instead, at its annual reorganization meeting on July 5, 1972, the board members elected me to a new post, second vice-president. The new office was proposed by Charles Bell, who was elected president during the same meeting. Dr. Petti, a resident of the East Ward, had been re-elected as vice-president. His connections with East Ward Councilman and Council President Louis M. Turco helped Gibson's relationship with the majority-white city council. Bell also named me chairman of the newly formed Committee on Student Affairs.

My election and appointment served as another example of how the mayor influenced the actions of the Board. A few days before the reorganization meeting, Bell, who had by now counted the votes that would make him president, came to me, and said that he would nominate me as vice-president if he won. I was astonished. Because of the flag controversy, the national and local media had projected the image of me either as a dumb kid or "Black racist," one who had single-handedly put Black Liberation flags in all the city's public schools. I didn't think the other members wanted my name even associated with the Board; I half expected them to run me up the pole with the flag!

Because Bell never gave me a detailed explanation of why he asked me to be vice-president, I can only speculate. He and I had no close working relationship, and on several issues, we ended up voting in opposite ways. On one occasion, he did say he thought I was doing very positive work with the Student Federation. Perhaps he saw my independence as an obstacle to his goals as president. At this time, I had the vocal support of many parents and students, at least those who attended Board meetings. Maybe he felt alienated by the action he took during the second teachers' strike, and that by working closer with me he would seem more legitimate in the community's eyes. I also could have been the swing vote for him to be elected president. There is also the possibility he actually thought I'd make a good vice-president.

Whatever Bell's reasons might have been, did not sit well with Mayor Gibson, the man who jump-started my political career just a year before. On the morning of July 5th, Bell phoned me and said that Gibson felt I shouldn't be vice-president, but would accept me holding a new office, second vice-president. Politically, I understood Gibson's position. In addition to an overall sense of humanitarianism, there are many reasons why a majority Black, two-thirds nonwhite Board should have a Black president and a white vice-president. Newark still had a white, taxpaying, home-owning population large enough to mean something to a mayor of a city stricken by urban blight on Election Day. When a Black mayor appoints whites to boards, commissions, and agencies, he reassures the white electorate that it is not powerless and that its interests are being protected. By placing whites in executive and administrative positions on these bodies, particularly those in the public eye, he reinforces that feeling. The Black mayor then establishes a reputation among whites as a man who gives fair and equitable treatment to all.

My new title was an attempt at co-optation. When a major conflict broke out at Vailsburg High in 1973, I got directly involved with this new tactic.

Black students at Vailsburg High were being harassed by white students. This was nothing new. What was different is that Vailsburg High had a Black teacher, James Mosselle, who oversaw discipline at the majority white high school. Black students demanded Mosselle's transfer out of the school, because they charged, he was lenient with white students but penalty-heavy with Black students. Ironically, white students complained that Mosselle was more active in dealing with the problems with Black students.

The high school's Swahili Club asked me to visit the school. I listened to their grievances about the problems the members had getting Black-oriented extracurricular activities approved, as well as their complaints about Moselle. After the office of the Superintendent intervened, Moselle was transferred.

The white parents were so enraged by Moselle's transfer, they organized a boycott of the high school which eventually escalated to all schools in the West Ward. Black students ignored the boycott and were attacked by whites as they went to and from school. The white parents demanded the disbanding of the Swahili Club and the transfer of Mrs. Judith Stewart, its advisor; Moselle's reinstatement; the outlawing of any flag but the American one in school, and...on and on. And guess who the target was of their wrath? I was branded as a radical and preacher of race hatred.

I had to go up to the school and rescue the club's leaders, Joann Dorsaw and Debi Hall, when a mob of white students threatened them. They had to leave the school from the back door and jump into the Board van I had driven to the school. It was intense but we quickly drove away. This was the event that would eventually have me in court on gun charges even though I never had one. Someone in the mob said they saw me with one.

Gibson was eventually pressured to respond to what was happening. Instead of the problems that the Black students articulated, he publicly blamed me as a disruptive influence. Why? Re-election Day was one year away, and Gibson had won election in 1970 with twenty percent of the white vote. I was now a political liability, and the city's first Black mayor gave license for whites in the public sphere to attack my character.

City Council President Louis Turco declared: "The members of the Board of Education should state openly what I'm sure they all realize – that Hamm is the culprit of this controversy." State Assemblyman Anthony Imperiale, Newark's white nationalist leader stated, "If the mayor will inform me of what he wants to do, I, as a state legislator, will prepare the necessary laws." State law prevented him from taking direct action to remove me from the Board.

Newark Councilman-at-Large Michael A. Bontempo added: "Hamm is immature and a troublemaker who is constantly bellowing about racism and racists, when, as a matter of fact, he tops both categories." NTU President Graves, declared: "His actions in the various schools are criminal."

During the Vailsburg conflict, whites actually tried to intimidate me at a February 27, 1973 Board meeting. They attempted to force me to stand and pledge to the American flag at the meeting's beginning. The white mob got the rest of the Board to stand but I remained seated. West Ward Councilman Michael T. Bottone, whose district Vailsburg High, was in, filed a Municipal Court suit against me, charging that I was instructing students not to pledge the American flag at that meeting. Judge Emil E. Mascia threw out the case. But Essex County Prosecutor Joseph P. Lordi ignored that and sent the case to a grand jury. Two friends and I were already under investigation by the grand jury because we were charged with having illegal weapons when we went to rescue the club leaders.

Both the flag and gun charges were dismissed for lack of evidence. But the character assassination attempts didn't end there. Gregory Knoll, the lawyer who defended me during this period, was contacted by the State Attorney General, who informed Knoll that there were people trying to get into his office to find out if I was a draft dodger. Some people don't think political prisoners really exist in America. I know better, because if I had had a bad lawyer or a corrupt judge, there would have been more than a good chance I would have been one. After all of this and more, Mosselle was permanently transferred to East Side High School. He later became Vice-Principal. And Vailsburg High is now a memory, thanks to the West Ward's 1970s white flight.

Another part of Black Power was creating public spaces to study and absorb Black culture. CFUN was a church that wasn't a church. As a fellow traveler, I would come by to Baraka's Sunday "Soul Sessions." Like Jesse Jackson's Operation Breadbasket/Operation PUSH Saturday morning meetings, there would be a guest speaker who would talk about a particular issue. The high point of the program, not surprisingly, was when Baraka spoke. He would talk about what was happening locally, nationally, and globally. It was very galvanizing, like having Black History Month every Sunday. It made you feel that you were part of a movement.

This gathering was important to me, because my family wasn't into "that radical stuff, that Muslim stuff." My first Malcolm X record was a compilation of twenty-four bits of speeches titled *By Any Means Necessary*. I had to listen to it in secret so my mother wouldn't hear and get upset. I got the *verboten* record from Baraka's store, *Nyumbya Ujamaa*.

Baraka always believed in keeping that kind of public space alive. In the 1980s, he would hold concerts and poetry readings in his basement once a month, on Saturday nights, for the public. He called the space *Kamako's Blues People*, after his sister, who had been brutally murdered. There would be live music, and live poetry by Amiri or his wife, Amina, and others. He kept this up well into the 1990s.

I always have appreciated allies because they keep my spirit up. Working for Councilman Westbrooks, a progressive guy out of CFUN, was valuable to me politically because I was not accountable to Mayor Gibson. Westbrooks, whose African name — Mjumbe means "Voice of the People" in Kiswahili, took a liking to me because my politics on the Board mirrored his on the Council.

Kujichagulia: Board, Council Run and No Gun

Two major community campaigns I worked on with Westbrooks were the drive to recall three white Councilmen and the Central Ward Garbage March. The recall effort against Ralph Villani, Michael Bontempo and Anthony J. Giuliano started in December of 1972, after the white council majority rescinded a tax abatement for Kawaida Towers — a planned housing development envisioned by Amiri Baraka — and refused to confirm a Black police officer, Lt. Edward Kerr, as the city's police director. Although it generated the support of hundreds of Black citizens, the recall effort was unsuccessful. In August of 1973, Westbrooks led a small army of demonstrators down to City Hall to dump their garbage on the mayor's doorstep in protest of living conditions in the Central Ward. When they got there, police, dressed in riot gear and on the orders of the city's first Black mayor, dispersed them. Garbage was strewn among injuries and three arrests. But militant activity was ever in the air, always a threat under the surface; in Newark, protest — mass action, people power — had become normalized.

Ironically, I believe the appointment of the first Black superintendent, Stanley Taylor, marked the beginning of the end of Black Power in Newark education. By the middle of 1973, Baraka's influence had begun to wane; too many of his candidates were losing elections. The education organizations built up by CFUN were beginning to diminish. Meanwhile, some parent activists had begun to cool out because they had jobs at the Board or City Hall. And the students had gone on to college and/or to work. Gibson did not reappoint Jesse Jacob, thereby compromising my effectiveness.

After the flag controversy, the Board seemed to be moving away from community input in the decision-making process. In the fall of 1972, the Board, without the input of PTAs and community groups, started rotating the meetings from the central building to different schools. Although Bell said the move was to involve parents who didn't normally attend board meetings, I and other Board members felt the action was really designed to water-down accountability. The selection of the superintendent was done without community input. The candidate Jacob and I wanted was not supported. Taylor was Black (as were all the finalists) but was a more conventional administrator. And Gibson got Jacob to vote for Taylor with a promise that he would be reappointed. Gibson reneged, and appointed Vicki Donaldson. Jacob's loss stopped any grassroots change coming from the Board. I learned, Black presence in political office is important but not enough.

My term as a Board member expired in June of 1974. I had no illusions of being re-appointed. In his third annual report, Gibson appeared to be more critical of my leaving Princeton than of my performance as a Board member. (That I had left Princeton had become a recurring public theme during my Board days.) He wrote: "I think young people should be on Boards of Education. Hamm was, in my opinion, an ideal young appointee. He was a student leader, a track star, and the recipient of a four-year scholarship at Princeton University. The boy has made some very bad decisions, not the least of which was quitting school."

Um, thank you, Mr. Mayor.

In my place, Gibson appointed George Branch, then an unsuccessful Central Ward Councilman candidate who was a recreational trainer at the Newark Housing Authority. Branch would later become a mainstay of the Newark City Council from 1982 until 1998, when he lost in a close and contentious runoff election with a young man named Cory Booker. Gibson told the press that it was obvious why I hadn't been reappointed and that Branch was the personification of grassroots work and community development.

In this period, I was still deeply influenced by Amiri Baraka, the Black Power movement and Black nationalism. Because I was serving and leading, I thought I could get an elected office. So, in 1974, my Board days about to be behind me, I ran for Newark City Council.

I ran for city council because I wanted to stay in Newark and help it develop. I was rather popular as a board member. I had name recognition and I wanted to get elected. I also saw myself as continuing the evolving position of using electoral politics for the Black struggle. I was heavily involved in the Essex County Black Political Convention and the New Jersey Black Political Convention, both outgrowths of Gary. I was elected to the New Jersey delegation of the National Black Political Assembly, the organization that grew directly out of the Gary convention. I sat on the Assembly's National Black Political Council. I saw myself as a local activist committed to implementing Gary's national Black agenda.

There were four at-large seats. I was cocky enough to run for an at-large seat, which meant that the whole city had to vote you in, not just one ward. I now think that was a mistake. Running for the Central Ward position would have given me a much better chance of winning, but it would have put me in conflict with my team member and employer, Westbrooks. I didn't win the at-large seat, but I did pretty well for someone who was twenty years old.

I was on the second "Community's Choice" team slate. (Gibson had been on the first, in 1970.) The slate was me, Ralph Grant, Jim Nance, Julie Grant and Westbrooks. Some of the elements of our platform included: 1) Establishment of a civilian complaint review board to monitor the actions of the police; 2) Free transportation for seniors to hospitals, doctors, and shopping centers; and 3) The creation of neighborhood health centers.

I placed twelfth in a field of twenty-five at-large candidates, and fourth among eleven Blacks seeking office. Westbrooks and Grant made it to the runoff election, but they both lost. Why didn't we win? Why didn't at least Westbrooks, who was an incumbent, win?

There were complex reasons: political infighting among Blacks, lack of money and experienced campaign workers were just a few. But the simplest answer is that we were endorsed by Baraka, and Gibson's forces had to crush us to prevent a so-called "takeover" of city government by Baraka. It sounds ludicrous now, but it wasn't then. There was no support from the Black establishment. Gibson was elected by a broad coalition of different constituencies — including white people who lived in Newark who weren't down with Imperiale. When Baraka enabled three district leaders to be elected, there was significant backlash, even to, and perhaps especially to, a "Community's Choice" ticket.

The Black community had been divided into camps led by former and current candidates for office — Gibson, Sharpe James, Earl Harris, Dennis Westbrooks, who, like Grant, had no problem with publicly disagreeing with Mayor Gibson. Then there was a whole group of Black people that were like Democratic Party functionaries. Democratic elections in Newark are nonpartisan. They're neither Democrat nor Republican. But they were all united on one agenda: crush Amiri Baraka, who had that time declared himself a Communist, or a Third World Marxist. They were against (Black) radicalism, against African modes of being, against Baraka and the whole thing.

In American popular culture, including popular media, the 1970s have now been flattened out to a time in which Black people joined American society uncritically: that we all wanted to be Black capitalists and be "Movin' On Up," like the show that premiered on CBS then, *The Jeffersons*. That was not the case. This was a period in which *thousands* of people of various ideologies, faiths and goals would show up to a meeting of the Board of Education or the city council. In 1974, arguing over ideology—which path forward? — was a normal occurrence among leaders and activists.

What was breaking out in Black communities nationwide by 1974 was this whole struggle between the race and class analysis: between people who were continuing to advocate for Black nationalism and Pan-Africanism versus people who were supporting some version of Marxism. You would go to a major conference, and it would be like an ideological shootout at the OK Corral.

Baraka had become a Communist by 1974. But before him Durham, North Carolina had Howard Fuller — also known as Owusu Sadaukai, founder and director of Malcolm X Liberation University in 1969. He also organized African Liberation Day. Tens of thousands of people showed up to the event held in Washington, DC in 1972, including citizens of countries that were still colonized under the Portuguese, French or British.

It was one of the events that really propelled the anti-apartheid movement among the Black community in this country, because the centerpiece of African Liberation Day was how to liberate South Africa and destroy the apartheid system.

Sadaukai was one of the first major people to make that change to Marxism and a whole group of people followed him. Initially he was opposed by the Black nationalists. Sadaukai tried to explain the political economy of how white supremacy came about. To be anti-capitalist, he and others argued, was to also be anti-imperialist, but a lot of the Black nationalists rejected Marxism- Leninism because they said Marxists were just another group of white people trying to manage Black liberation. Ultimately the class analysis gained currency in discussions about race in America.

What pushed the class analysis forward was that African liberation leaders were openly socialist. Many African nations had scientific socialist leaders or revolutionaries fighting to lead. China was anti-imperialist. Vietnam was anti-imperialist. Cuba was anti-imperialist. So Black revolutionaries in America thought that to be a revolutionary, you had to be a socialist. This is the path that Baraka chose. Many people in Newark were upset when he started tearing down Black nationalist imagery and replacing it with the images of the workers' revolution.

Around 1973, CFUN had made a poster that showed the "three cutting edges of revolution," which were listed as Black nationalism, Pan-Africanism, and Socialism. It wasn't hard to see how they came to that point. How could you read Julius Nyerere and Kwame Nkrumah and not come up with that conclusion? These ideas, and the apartheid struggle that propelled them, would consume me intellectually when I returned to Princeton.

Kujichagulia: Board, Council Run and No Gun

In the early Seventies, Newark was a hub of the Black Power movement. Things that were embraced then — Afros, Malcolm X and Huey Newton on posters (and now, Tweets), Kwanzaa, dashikis —are not as controversial today as they once were. An Afro was a sign to many you were a militant. Back in the Seventies, if you celebrated Kwanzaa, some people said you are against Christmas and Jesus, although that was not true. That revolutionary edge has smoothed out like a dull knife now.

I remember when I adopted — but not legally changed — my African name. I used it all the time. I told the board to replace the Lawrence Hamm name plate with Adhimu Changa. Newspapers would refer to me as — and inadvertently misspell — my African name, putting "Larry Hamm" in parentheses. Now we've had a Black president with an African/Muslim name and background, and the United States and the world did not end.

Contradictions were rife in the New Ark 1974. For instance, when Earl Harris, the Black city council president, called for my arrest during a city council meeting. Baraka, who had been blocked by the council to build Kawaida Towers in the North Ward, tried to have a housing complex built on Belmont Avenue. The location of the complex would start at West Kinney proceed toward Muhammad Ali Avenue. CFUN wanted people to come back to the city council and speak in favor of it and condemn the councilmen who were against it. And so, I got up there. I was much like the folks who go down to cuss out the city council now. I went down there, and I voiced some criticisms of Harris and others. The next thing I heard was Harris saying, "Arrest him." And two big cops promptly grabbed me, dragged me from the podium, took me through a connecting dungeon-like tunnel between City Hall and Newark's police headquarters at 31 Green Street. They didn't even have to take me outside of the City Hall. Junius Williams, the lawyer for the people, came and obtained my release from custody. Eventually the judge threw out the case as a violation of my First Amendment rights.

There was plenty of promise and much disappointment during that time, overlapping into the next phase of my life. Yes, I was pained that I did not win a seat on the Newark City Council, but I must be more honest now than I would have been then. The election loss was good for me because I was ready to finish my education. I was worn out from three years of nonstop board work and a failed run for council. I was ready to return to Princeton to embrace a new life there.

Then Fate decided college life would not be enough of a challenge. My girlfriend, Charlene, was pregnant. I found out in June when my term on the board ended. In July of 1974, post-board, post-election loss, Charlene and I were married. Amiri Baraka performed the wedding ceremony. I was only twenty years-old, and Charlene was seventeen years-old. A new life came into view as my new life began. My first daughter, Laini, was born on January 17, 1975.

Though I was four when my father died, I grieved for many years to come over that loss. Growing up, seeing other kids with their fathers, would fill me with envy. I cried real tears over this. I said to myself that if I had kids, I would be the father I didn't have. I was always determined to be a father living in the household with my wife and children. So, I married her. Baraka married us. We used our African names, Adhimu and Kipenzi, during the ceremony and I wore an African suit he gave me for the ceremony. At that time, we wore the same clothes size.

Now I had to balance Princeton and a new family. I came home on the weekends, and sometimes during the week. At the time all the traveling back and forth was rough. I worked as a Princeton student security guard — the graveyard shift, from 11 p.m. to 7 a.m., about twenty hours of week- sometimes more. I did this and still graduated *cum laude*.

However, balancing my love of family, passion for education and activism would prove to be a costly juggling act. Starting Princeton at twenty-years-old, I had no illusion that this would be smooth sailing, but I was driven. In the mid-70s, the Zeitgeist was still driving.

1974-1980: PRINCETON REDUX: APARTHEID AND THE PEOPLE'S FRONT

I had fought for the people's movement, but now it was time for *me* to move on. I was *bone tired*. I returned to Princeton, more grounded and more mature, a new family man excited by the prospects of my life ahead of me.

But *they* were waiting for me.

Who were they?

They were the younger students, who had read about my misadventures trying to create revolution in Newark. They had heard about me from older students that struggled alongside me in Newark, Akili and Mfalme. They were already there, and they wanted my involvement in the Harambee Club. The club was a forum for education and a venue for fighting against tuition increases.

The activist work I did at Princeton was another turning point for me. I was looking, searching, trying to find an explanation for what was going on in this post-Sixties phase of the Black struggle. Prior to returning to Princeton, I read Amilcar Cabral's *Revolution in Guinea*. ("Always bear in mind that the people are *not* fighting for *ideas*, for the things in anyone's head. They are fighting to win material benefits, to live better and in peace, to see their lives go forward, to guarantee the future of their children.") His essay "Tell No Lies, Claim No Easy Victories" had a profound effect on me. Cabral and Nkrumah helped me get a better understanding of class struggle. I finally dug into Marx while I was back in school. But if you read people like Nkrumah, Cabral, and others, you find they were fully engaged in revolution. At Princeton, I became acquainted with Marx, Engels, Lenin, Mao, and other revolutionary writers. Much of this study was done in study groups apart from my assigned classes.

Thinking revolution and practicing revolution is a dangerous combination. The life of Walter Rodney, who was assassinated in 1980, at the end of my Princeton tenure, proved that. We brought Rodney to campus to speak at the Third World Center a couple of years before his assassination. Stokely Carmichael (Kwame Ture), was also brought in to speak.

As a university student, I was pulling myself in an intellectual direction, while the *Zeitgeist* wanted something else. But this time, I was surrounded and befriended by radicals of all races and colors. For a moment, I had the balance. But it came at great personal cost — of peace, of my life going forward as I wanted with my family. There were no easy victories in my life's struggles.

Princeton afforded me the time, place and conditions for serious reading and reflection. The summer before I returned to Princeton, I read George Jackson's books *Soledad Brother* and *Blood In My Eye*. I was really moved by him. Once at Princeton, I was finally introduced to Martin Luther King, Jr., W.E.B. Du Bois, and Paul Robeson in depth. For instance,

Princeton Redux: Apartheid and The People's Front

I read Philip Foner's two volume, *The Selected Writings of W.E.B. Du Bois* as well as Du Bois' book, *Black Reconstruction*. It's important to remember that *Souls of Black Folk* — is the *beginning* of his analysis, not the end. Du Bois was a liberal who slowly evolved to a radical Marxist scholar and activist. In his nineties renounced his American citizenship and officially joined the Communist Party before living out his last days in Ghana.

We also read periodicals. Black intellectual magazines such as *Black World*, *Black Scholar* and *Freedomways* played major roles in our theoretical thinking. We had a study group, the Student Association for the Study of Scientific Socialism, that was devoted to reading articles, books, essays, and speeches from a variety of sources.

We were not studying for study's sake. We were trying to figure out how to make social change here in America. We wanted to change the system, although being at Princeton made that more than a little paradoxical.

I read socialist writers and thinkers, including Marx, Lenin, and Mao Tse-Tung; mostly in the study group but some in a few Princeton classes. I read much of what Mao wrote that was translated into English. Mao made several statements on the African American struggle around the time of the March on Washington. This was soon after Cuba gave asylum to Robert Williams, the former NAACP leader in North Carolina who had become a Marxist and expatriate:

"The speedy development of the struggle of the American Negroes is a manifestation of sharpening class struggle and sharpening national struggle within the United States; it has been causing increasing

A Life in the Struggle

anxiety among U.S. ruling circles... The evil system of colonialism and imperialism grew along with the enslavement of the Negroes and the trade in Negroes; it will surely come to its end with the thorough emancipation of the Black people."

In America in the early 1970s, this was an actual goal for many still-radicalized Black activists.

I also read the writings of revolutionaries from Asia, Africa, and Latin America—what we called at that time the Third World. These included writings and speeches of Fidel Castro of Cuba, Kwame Nkrumah of Ghana, Julius Nyerere of Tanzania, Agostinho Neto of Angola, Samora Machel in Mozambique, Amilcar Cabral of Guinea Bissau, and Sékou Touré of Guinea. The African radical world was now open to me. Though I read some of these before returning to Princeton, it was during my tenure at the university that I had time to reflect upon and discuss these writings. I became familiar with foreign periodicals, including the *Peking Review*. It was a periodical that came out of China. It was printed on rice paper — white and real thin. I found editions of it in Firestone Library that documented W.E.B. Du Bois' visit to China. In another edition, I read and saw pictures of a demonstration of a million Chinese people in support of Black Liberation. I was inspired by Mao and the Chinese Revolution, Fidel and the Cuban Revolution as well as other third world revolutions. At this point I'm trying to understand how to fundamentally change the American socio-economic system.

The experience was as powerful as it was painful. I gained a better grasp of how "the system" works than I did when I was 17. (Although it would have been helpful if Princeton's Political Science department, gave more weight to practical politics

Princeton Redux: Apartheid and The People's Front

as well as political theory. Maybe things have changed since then.) Back then, the solution to the problem was simple: put Black people in power, and Black people would be fine. What I learned from these books, which I re-read before returning to Princeton, was the complexity and promise of the world. I learned I had to re-read favorite books, like *Malcolm X Speaks*, because my understanding in 1974 was different than in 1971. I still have that paperback copy I purchased from *Nyumbya Ujamaa* in 1971. That book, not *The Autobiography*, had a profound impact on me: *Malcolm X Speaks* targeted the lack of Black Power as an obstacle to fully realizing Black self-determination. But we were in contradiction in Newark, because we had that to a certain extent. We had a Black mayor. We had a Black city council and I think Baraka had as many problems with them as he had with Addonizio. I was trying to find an intellectual home amongst constant, nagging contradictions. Like the African revolutionaries before us, we were beginning to see that revolution was complex. Black Nationalism, Pan Africanism and Black Politics were useful in the struggle against the American apartheid known as Jim Crow: de jure and de facto radical segregation. However, when that layer of oppression was removed, the economic underpinnings of racism were revealed, and it became clear that additional tools were needed.

So many Black activists adopted a class-based anti-capitalist, anti-imperialist analysis. They became radicals, socialists, internationalists, and Marxists of different stripes. For them, it was not enough to replace white people in positions of power with Black people. For them, the entire capitalist system had to be changed.

What was happening to me between 1971 and 1974 was an evolution of my own ideology, which in fact was influenced by what I was experiencing. When I started out as a youth in the Black

Power movement, we essentially believed that if Black people got control over the political institutions, we could essentially change the condition of Black people. And after three years of being at the center of Black power in Newark, New Jersey, we saw that wasn't happening. In fact, it seemed worse: and we struggled against the Black people who were in power. So, I was asking new questions, seeking new paths to freedom.

I kept seeing that Blacks in Cuba, Latin America, and all over Africa had attempted or were attempting socialist revolution. I thought back to the CFUN poster, the three cutting edges of revolution, Baraka's trio: Black nationalism, Pan-Africanism, and Socialism. This triangle — particularly the socialist part — dominated my intellectual world in those days. One book that I read cover to cover was *The Autobiography of Kwame Nkrumah*. I was impressed that he actually had the constitution of the party that he led in the book. When I was trying to form the New Ark Student Federation, there was a whole bunch of constitutions I had collected to try to put together as one. I was inspired by the example of Nkrumah's Convention People's Party.

In 1974, I and other Princeton student activists, continued to study the social movements of the world, Pan-Africanism — then defined as the immediate removal of white colonialist governments from Africa by any means necessary, including armed struggle. This became the dominant socio-political paradigm among students of African descent. With Pan-Africanism merged with socialist ideology, there was more than significant ideological common ground with Black and Third World student activists and white radicals.

Princeton Redux: Apartheid and The People's Front

The center of our ideological and geographical gravity was racist South Africa. I used my African name Adhimu Changa during my Princeton years. In my sophomore year, I worked with other activists on campus to form The People's Front for the Liberation of Southern Africa.

Black communities were beginning to learn about South Africa in the 1970s due to the intensification of the African Liberation struggle in South Africa. One thing that propelled the anti-apartheid movement among the Black community in this country was African Liberation Day in 1972, held several months after the National Black Political Convention in Gary, Indiana. Everything I had fought for as a Board member of the Newark Board of Education was in line with organizers in cities around the nation. Focus on African Liberation Day prepared students to educate Black people on how to assist in liberating South Africa by destroying the apartheid system.

It's hard to explain now, in the third decade of the twenty-first century, but publicly fighting against the white minority apartheid government in the 1970s was a very controversial political act. The racist white regime of South Africa was an important ally to the United States against the worldwide spread of Communism. The nation had nuclear weapons that could be pointed against the Soviet Union if the Cold War came to that. The African National Congress, then an outlawed political party with a significant armed wing, unapologetically had Marxists as its members. Opponents and supporters of the ANC saw its publicly stated goal for a multiracial South Africa as a call for South Africa to join the Marxist revolutionary governments of Africa and the rest of the Third World. Nelson Mandela was considered a terrorist to the right, a freedom fighter to the left.

We were trying to make a strong connection between the struggles against racism here in America and apartheid in South Africa. The strategy was to identify and boycott corporations that did business with the apartheid regime. In the late 1960s, Princeton student activists mounted a campaign to boycott Gulf oil and Gulf oil products, gasoline and so forth. And that was in connection with the struggle in nearby Angola, which was still under Portuguese rule. That struggle was part and parcel of the overall struggle to liberate southern Africa, which included Angola. Dr King called for an economic boycott of South Africa in 1965. We were fighting the fight that Dr. King would have continued if he were still alive.

So, we attempted to program connections. At Princeton, I met the Reverend Ben Chavis, who had then successfully fought his "Wilmington Ten" case. His was the most prominent American political prisoner case after the acquittal of Angela Davis. Chavis was one of ten people, nine men and one woman, who were wrongfully convicted of arson and conspiracy in Wilmington, North Carolina in 1971. Most were sentenced to 29 years but served 10 years before they won on appeal. We brought the Wilmington Ten, USA Ten Case film and Chavis spoke. It was important for us to have Chavis on campus because we wanted to show other Black students that it was possible to equally fight white supremacy on both continents. We brought radical activist Seton Hall Afro-American Studies professor Bill Sales to campus because he, together with Sam Anderson, the first chair of a Black Studies department at Sarah Lawrence College, had written the pamphlet *Black America, Southern Africa: Same Struggle, Same Fight*. It was like manna from Heaven. It showed how the same corporations that would give economic aid to South Africa were the same corporations that were discriminating against Black people here in the

Princeton Redux: Apartheid and The People's Front

United States. It oriented us in such a way that enabled us to go back, research more in depth and make connections that were not in that pamphlet.

One of the first projects of The People's Front was to try to get the banks in Princeton to stop dealing with apartheid by refusing to sell the Krugerrand, the South African currency. Then, we switched gears to college divestment after contacting a group called the American Committee on Africa (ACoA). That group used to create pamphlets on various topics related to South Africa, *e.g.*, education, labor, political parties, and the vote. These pamphlets were so good that I went to New York to ACoA's office on Riverside Drive in New York City regularly to get more.

I met a brother there named Prexy Nesbitt. We brought him to speak at Princeton several times. His presentations helped get students involved that weren't involved. He was extraordinarily informed about the situation in southern Africa.

In the beginning of our South Africa struggle, we had very small turnouts for our campaign. We'd have protests and forums and get between twenty-five and fifty people. Fifty people was a big turnout. Then we showed the film *Last Grave at Dimbaza*. We showed it at the Third World Center in the fall of 1976. We had a crowd of almost two hundred.

The lights went dim. My God, that film! It opens with a man digging small holes. Then there's some talk about apartheid. It's an excellent film about how everyday life in South Africa unfolds and how apartheid manifests itself. They talk about the effects of apartheid on the health of the children. By the end of the film, everyone realizes what these holes for. The holes are for babies that die. The death rate of babies was so high that they knew the number of graves that had to be dug every day.

There wasn't a dry eye in the house when we showed that film. They saw an evil that was without compromise. That event occurred forty-three years ago, and I can still remember the drone of sobbing students in the Multipurpose Room of the Third World Center.

Showing that movie marked a turning point for the Princeton anti-apartheid movement. Participation in our events increased. More showed up to protest. Our workers doubled.

I already knew about the power of film. When I was on the board, I used to show documentary films about issues that impacted Black people every week in my Green Street office. There was a sign over the door of my office that said, *Education for Liberation.*

At Princeton, we continued to draw connections. Another film we watched that same year that had a powerful impact on the Princeton students was *Harlan County, USA*, about poor whites in the Appalachian coal mines.

We also showed a documentary on Vietnam, *Hearts, and Minds*. There's a scene where Gen. William Westmoreland, the supreme commander of the US armed forces in Vietnam, begins his dehumanization of the Vietnamese by declaring that they are not like Americans, who see family as important. Then the scene switches to a funeral for a Vietnamese soldier killed fighting against the US soldiers. The woman is trying to climb into the grave and be buried with him. She jumps in the

Princeton Redux: Apartheid and The People's Front

grave with him while Westmoreland is saying, "Oh, they don't have the same kind of emotional family ties that we have." This woman is holding onto the grave so hard that it took a group of people to pry her loose. She wanted to be buried alive with him.

Films can be very powerful. But I never saw a film have the impact on a political struggle like *Last Graves at Dimbaza*.

In 1977, we decided that next semester we would have protests daily at Nassau Hall. Our operational unity around apartheid superseded our individual or collective ideological issues. We started on February 1, 1978, and we picketed every day for sixty-six days. We started on February 1 on purpose to connect the anti-apartheid struggle to the Black struggle. That was the date when, in 1960, the four students from North Carolina sat in at a Woolworth's lunch counter; the event that officially started the student civil rights movement.

The daily pickets, which included members using overturned garbage cans as drums, never got more than fifteen people the first month. But we were encouraged because anti-apartheid movements at Stanford and Harvard were successful.

Princeton di-vest!

Oh yeah

Just like the rest!

Oh yeah

And if you don't!

Oh yeah

We will not rest!

Oh yeah

We gonna fight.

And fight

And keep on fightin' some more.

Princeton di-vest!

Some of the public responses were not encouraging. People hurled sodas and racist epithets at us.

Then we got a snowstorm. A *big* one. Everyone thought, *Okay, that's it. We're done.* I went up to Nassau Hall, expecting to see just snow. There weren't even lights on by the building. It was snowing, and I'm by myself. *(Shades of Arts High walkout?)* I took a nearby garbage can and turned it over. I pulled out my drumsticks, and I'm beating on the can. One person showed up. Then another. And suddenly, these groups start showing up in the snow. More than one-hundred students came out that day. Remember, this is before emailing, before mass phone calls, cell phones, before .com anything.

From that day on, we never had fewer than one hundred students. The protests grew every day. By the beginning of April, we had about four hundred show up each day. Princeton officials were saying that they hadn't seen anything like this since the Vietnam era. When we got to six hundred, we said that it was time to take over Nassau Hall.

Princeton Redux: Apartheid and The People's Front

The People's Front was multiracial. When we decided that we were going to sit-in, we developed a cell-based system of communication. Our cells were formed based on the dorms that students lived in. Some cells were multi-racial. Some were all Black and some were all white. Others were comprised of different ethnic and racial groups. Since we were fighting racial apartheid, the existence of all white or all Black cells sparked debate. We had to constantly think about infiltration. So, not trusting the university telephone, we transmitted information through the cell-based communication network.

It wasn't exactly Ten Days That Shook the World, but it was twenty-seven hours that shook Princeton and pushed the anti-apartheid movement forward in campuses across the United States. Years of divesture talk between Princeton student activists and the administration hadn't worked. On April 14, at 8:45 a.m. the takeover began. Student activists came in and lined the walls. We had many supporters outside Nassau Hall. There were plenty of students who were afraid that their scholarships and grants would be threatened, so we told them to stay outside and protest there.

We announced our demands for divestiture shortly after we took over the building. The protest was nonviolent, but we made it clear that business-as-usual would only be conducted over our live bodies. Princeton staffers did try to go about their business, but they were more nervous than we were.

Dean of Students J. Anderson Brown came to talk to us (there is a famous photo of him scrunching down to talk to me in a hallway), but we would not be moved. News quickly spread throughout the country. We had telegrams of support from many parts of the world including a national student association in Greece. There was a big cheer inside the building when that telegram was read by US, Rep Charles Diggs of Michigan, Chair of the United States House Foreign Affairs Subcommittee on Africa. That meant a lot to me: Diggs was also the co-chair of the 1972 National Black Political Convention in Gary.

The building was closed, and we refused to leave. Princeton was afraid to physically remove us. So, we held fort—literally—all night. That night, there were serious political discussions had and even some dancing in the corridors of Nassau Hall. In the morning, tired and hungry, we voted one-hundred and sixty-eight to forty-two to leave the building the next morning.

We came out and were swarmed by the hundreds of students that had stayed with us throughout the night. It was a victory rally. We saw the ABC News cameras and explained to the world what we had done, and why we had done it.

All 205 of us — including prominent student leaders George Castro, Allan Nairn, David Ayon, Sharon Kalemkarian, George Riley — were given official warnings in connection with our participation in the sit-in. Administrators ruled that the event constituted "a serious violation of University regulations." There was a hearing to determine the appropriate punishment. Princeton was not used to such direct action.

At that hearing, Riley spoke for many of us when he said: *"Many Americans have long condemned the racist South African government, but their words carry no weight against a 400 percent increase in U.S. investments in South Africa since 1960. Blacks in South Africa risk penalties from five years imprisonment to death to speak out against foreign investments. We bear the responsibility to carry their cause in this country with our own voices... If we did, as Dean Brown charged, create a tension in Nassau Hall or in the community at large, it is certainly a healthy thing. Secluded as Princeton is from the harsh reality of oppression and poverty which dominates so much of the world, we tend to lapse into academic lethargy. We are oblivious to the sufferings of our fellow sisters and brothers to whom we are joined by humanity and to whom we share a special responsibility by nature of our economic ties to their oppressors. Thus, if the tensions created by our movement challenged Princeton's insolent complacency, it is certainly salutary to the University's educational mission, and in no way an offense or a threat to the University... We recognize that any society is governed by rules and that rules need to be respected. Yet respect for the rules is conditioned in the long run by respect for human rights and human dignity.... Regardless of the punishment, we remain firm in our conviction that our decision to stay in the building was correct, and we unite with opponents of apartheid all over the world."*

No student was punished. However, some students and faculty suspected that one faculty member did not get tenure because of his support of and participation in the sit-in at Princeton.

Princeton did divest from a couple of companies, but I learned from my reading that capitalism was an intertwined system. We had made our point, though. There were campus anti-apartheid protests before ours, and there would be many, many after ours, well into the 1980s. But today, the survivors of the two hundred who took over Nassau Hall are proud of our status as one of the earliest ones.

It is hard to explain in this present day, but in trying to force a major Ivy League institution like Princeton to take a political and economic stance against a United States ally during the Cold War could be academic and political suicide for any college student protesters. Princeton could have expelled us.

The movement on Princeton defined me almost as much as my work in Newark did. I saw that under the right circumstances, activists could move a campus, the entire nation, and the world in the right direction.

I would step back from the leadership of the People's Front as I transitioned from being a Princeton undergraduate to a Princeton graduate student, but I would still be involved. We had new chairpeople or coordinators who were highly capable. Women provided excellent leadership to the People's Front. In my senior class, there were leaders like Marsha Bonner, who would one day become the Director of Programs, Community Grant Making and Special Initiatives of a major foundation. Natalie Byfield was in the class that followed. Byfield led the next People's Front sit-in in 1979. She reminds me of the strong young women from high school on, who more than demonstrated leadership capability. Later Byfield would go on to be an editor at the *Daily News* and the author of *Savage Portrayals: Race, Media and the Central Park Jogger Case*.

So those reins were passed on, but I really didn't stop. In 1979, as a Princeton graduate student, I helped organize the New Jersey coalition of Black Student Organizations. We had a march in Newark, on Broad Street. We stopped in front of the Prudential's international headquarters, and we discussed Prudential's investments in South Africa.

That was a wonderful period. It was the first time in my life where I really saw strong evidence that Black people and white people could work together on issues. In Newark, very few whites were interested in working with Black radicals on social justice issues. At Princeton, Black people were a significant minority; it was not unusual to put out a call for people and have more whites show up than Blacks.

All my activism at Princeton prevented me from finishing my senior thesis in time. I was allowed to participate in the graduating ceremony, with the expectation that I could complete my thesis over the summer before the beginning of that fall semester. I had to force the thesis — an intellectual exploration of my time at the Newark Board of Education — out of me. I didn't even work that summer. Charlene, Laini, and I were living on Tremont Avenue in My Mom's house. I spent July and August in mom's sweltering, hot, no air-conditioned, attic. I couldn't wear clothes. I wore a sheet I had put a hole in and put my head through. I had a fan that blew my papers around but no real relief in the form of cool air. Literally, all of July and August I was up there, typing, on a manual typewriter. My academic work occurred before the PC revolution. Upon submitting it, I received my Bachelors' degree, graduating *cum laude*. The thesis is still in the Mudd Library at Princeton University.

Charlene and I were having problems. She wanted me to leave Princeton after I completed my undergraduate work and move our family finances into a zone befitting someone who had a Princeton degree. She had already endured my living on campus without her for the first semester. The Princeton administration said having my wife with me during my freshman year would be too much of a distraction. By the time I got to my sophomore year, she didn't want to come because she had gotten a job at General Motors. She was making a decent wage back then. This was back in the day where, if you had a high school diploma and worked in the auto industry, you could easily make $100,000 a year, with overtime. The GM plant was arduous work — you had to come to the factory, turn your head off and go up to a line and repeat a motion one-hundred times an hour — but it allowed you entry into the middle class. And they couldn't get enough people.

She didn't move to Princeton when I became a sophomore. She and our daughter moved in with me when I was in graduate housing as I entered graduate school. By then Princeton had formally offered me a full fellowship for my doctorate. This was too much school for Charlene.

I remember that my friends helped move us into the graduate housing, down by the wildlife preserve. One of them was Bill Smith. After our divorce, he told me, "Man, we knew, we knew when we moved you down that that wasn't going to last too long, because that woman had made her disdain *verbally clear*."

She did not want to live in Princeton, even though we had a nice apartment. She probably didn't like the fact that I was a poor graduate student, and she was a full-time autoworker who had to be on the road at sunrise to get to the GM plant in Linden. It was easy for resentment to build during this period.

She had to work, and I had to read. I was satisfied with my life path, and she wasn't. I started graduate school in 1978 and a little more than a year later, 1979, she left me. Charlene left — and took everything, even the bed, in one day. It felt like something out of *Mission: Impossible*. In the morning on my way to class, I had a life and a fully furnished apartment. In the evening, I came home to an empty apartment, with not even any food left in the refrigerator.

Princeton Redux: Apartheid and The People's Front

My failure echoed throughout the empty pad. I had to go ask a professor and Resident Assistant Mike Mitchell for something to sleep on. Thankfully, he gave me some blankets and I slept on the floor. I was devastated. I couldn't focus on studying, in Princeton, by a wildlife reserve, without my wife and Laini. *I'm doing this for my family*, I thought then, *so without my family, what's the point?* I was broken and exhausted.

The break-up of my marriage was the first major mistake. And it was followed by the second - I didn't finish my graduate work. I blame myself for both mistakes. I think I should've been tougher because I was halfway there. I had my required eight courses. I still had to write papers for the last three courses, but I had just had it. I just felt so isolated at the time. Forty years ago, Princeton was not the most socially conducive environment for Black students. Perhaps I would have finished if I had gone to another school, closer to a Black community. Also, it seemed that graduate school encouraged isolation. That isolation was an anathema to my personality, which thrived in the Movement.

So why did I want to be a professor? Because I thought teaching and writing books would help me make a living and raise my family. I thought it would afford me some latitude to be an actual academic. However, the reality is that the work of teaching and the process of gaining tenure would have taken me away from activism for sure. In the brief time I was in graduate school, I had to attend class and do my own research work, give lectures, and grade papers. The experience soured me on the idea of academia facilitating some degree of activism.

Would I still have formed the People's Organization for Progress? Probably not. I had no patience as a young man. If I had toughened it out, I might have gotten my doctoral degree. With that, I might have ended up teaching at Princeton and living there. I would never have returned to Newark and formed the POP. I don't think I could have formed a group like POP at Princeton. My academic work would have interfered with the creation and maintenance of POP. Most academics, buried in teaching and administrative work, academic publishing, and their family lives, don't have time for nuts and bolts, on-the-ground social justice organizing.

When I finished my undergrad and my time in graduate education at Princeton, I was more committed to the struggle then than when I left the first time. Much of that had to do with what I learned, on my own, inside and outside the classrooms.

When I left Princeton 1971, I knew I would eventually return. Back then, I only wanted two things: my degree and a grassroots political movement. From 1971 to 1974, I fought hard for the second, through electoral politics and activism. In 1974, at age twenty, I thought I could have a more conventional life by finishing my degree. Then I would go on to advanced degrees and get a job teaching, because this was the closest I was going to get to working for myself while taking care of myself and my family. I thought that a doctoral degree would be a helpful tool in building the movement that I wanted to build. My doctoral work, like my undergraduate senior thesis, would be on political organizing. I wanted to make enough money to have a house and the same things most people want. I was kind of oriented towards doing that.

But for many reasons, that didn't work out. It was the personal disruption, the divorce from Charlene and other things that led me to put down the doctoral work. But I still wanted to do the political organizing. I ended up leaving the university for the second and, unfortunately, the last time. Princeton had been liberating but painful, and there was only so much pain I could take. When I graduated *cum laude* and started graduate school in 1978, I thought it would take four to five years for me to do my doctoral work, so I'd be finished around 1983. Giving up that timeline because of the end of my marriage and my refusal to accept the monastic loneliness of Princeton graduate school life has been my life's huge regret.

Lawrence Hamm track win

Arts High School Newark, NJ 1971

A Life in the Struggle

David Hammond
Arts High Mayor 1968

Lawrence Hamm
Arts High Mayor 1971

Harry Lewis, PhD.
Arts High Principal 1968

Lawrence Hamm
Arts High Mayor 1971

Captain Larry Hamm becomes
Arts High's first cross-country
Champion

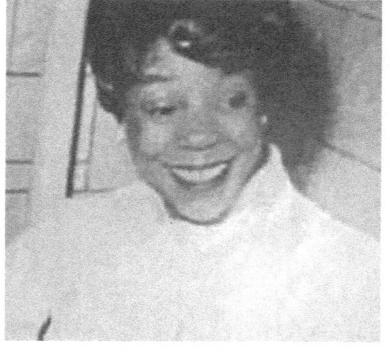

Theresa David Arts
High Principal 1971

Princeton Redux: Apartheid and The People's Front

Newly appointed to the Newark Board of Education 1971

Russell Bingham (Baba Mshuri) and Larry at the Essex County Political Convention. Leading up to the NJ Statewide Political Convention and Nation Political Convention Photo by Risasi Dais

New Ark Student Federation Button

Adhimu Changa noted in Black New Ark newspaper 1972

A Life in the Struggle

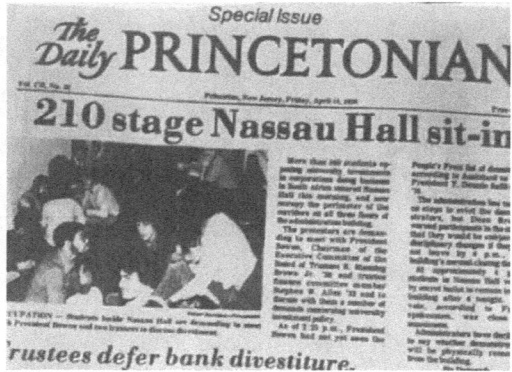

Muddy Library Archive

Sitting in Nassau Hall
April 14, 1978

Larry and his daughter Laini at Princeton
rally against Apartheid. photo by
Kim Pearson Mudd Library Archive

The following morning April 15, 1978
Leaving Nassau Hall. Muddy Library Archive

Princeton Redux: Apartheid and The People's Front

Laini Hamm with Muhammad Ali after Larry Hamm and Ali spoke at the UN on Apartheid in South Africa in 1978. Photo by Larry Hamm

Earl Williams, Earl Faison's father

A Life in the Struggle

rt to lft Lisa Davis and Zayid Muhammad protest at Justice Monday

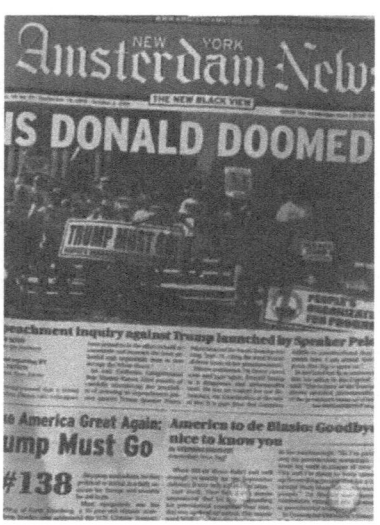

Coverage of POP

Trump Protest in Newark. Picture by Annette Alston

Princeton Redux: Apartheid and The People's Front

Lft to rt. Amina Baraka, Pam Africa, and Muneer Muhammad
at a POP Commemoration of Rosa Parks.
Picture by Annette Alston

Protester at Anti-Trump Rally
Picture by Annette Alston

Faison Protest in front of the police building

Princeton Redux: Apartheid and The People's Front

Lft. to rt. Dr. Cornel West, Imani Hamm, Lawrence Hamm, Nia Hamm, Dr. William Howard

Orange Transcript October 28, 1999

1980S:
CO-OP TO POP

My immediate post-Princeton life began with a run for Newark's West Ward district, and I did win. Other aspects of my life evolved from Princeton. While at Princeton, I met people that were part of Ralph Nader's organization. When people think of Nader now, they probably can't get further than his Green Party run in the 2000 Presidential election. Everyone lost but George W. Bush. But that's really not fair. Nader did his part to create consumer protections and enhance the environmental consciousnesses of this country. He created a baseline for consumer safety standards. GM hired people to stalk him and wiretap his phone. Nader sued GM and won, then used the money to fund his activism. One entity he founded was Public Interest Research Groups (PIRGs). They were on campuses across the nation in the 1970s. Some members of the PIRG at Princeton got involved with the anti-apartheid movement. I was very close to two of the students that established the Princeton PIRG, Alan Nairn, and George Riley. Nairn is an activist and freelance writer who was often on Pacifica's *Democracy Now!* Riley became an attorney for Steve Jobs and Apple. He died in June of 2016 of leukemia. It was through them that I learned about independent energy cooperatives. Nader was trying to get Jimmy Carter and other Democrats to establish a national cooperative bank that would provide capital to start cooperative projects, which is essentially an alternative economic model.

The cooperative I learned about was the fuel oil distribution company founded by Joe Kennedy Jr. He had set up his own company which obtained fuel oil directly from Venezuela at a discount. He then distributed this fuel oil to low-income communities in the Northeast because he was based in Massachusetts. I thought that establishing a co-op would be one way to provide service and it would be a way for me to essentially work for myself. With this, I could have the freedom to do the political work that I wanted to do. Theoretically, it was sound. Practically, it wasn't the sure fire shot I thought it would be, because the cooperative both structurally and practically had its own dynamic that had to be fulfilled. There was the dynamic of providing a service as an energy cooperative and then there was the community organizing component. The two parts were intended to overlap. To establish these cooperatives from the ground up required a lot of time and effort. As a young father, I quickly saw that just that became a job in itself. As any entrepreneur will tell you, there are huge tradeoffs required: on the one hand, the potential for economic growth and being your own boss, while the other was spending twice as much time to get the thing up and running. I had to figure this out.

The People's Energy Cooperative (PEC), had a grassroots name and grassroots ideal. I had assembled about 400 families I knew and put together a brochure. If people were interested, they would tear off the coupon and send it in to the PEC. One of the questions on the coupon asked how much oil a person or family used in a year. Once I totaled up the oil needed — two to three million gallons a year — I identified the few large companies in this area. I then told them that I had formed an association of fuel oil consumers and that we were soliciting bids per gallon price of home heating oil. I explained that the PEC was soliciting bids. The company would send us a quote. I would ask for the standard discounts. And I also asked what kind of discounts they would give on their fees for servicing furnaces. Often at the start of the winter months, many people need to have their furnaces cleaned and serviced. The company submitted a proposed discount for the PEC while adding the remittance they were willing to pay to the cooperative. It could be 1.5 cents per gallon on the total amount of fuel oil PEC members purchase from the company over the course of a winter period.

I operated the People's Energy Cooperative for three years. There were 400 families using more than 800,000 gallons of fuel oil. If I could have stayed with it long enough, if I could have kept it going, I might be representing four thousand families for eight million gallons of oil.

The Co-op presented several challenges. First, I had hoped that this would be a vehicle that would help build the kind of political movement I was looking for. However, by the time I finished doing everything I had to do for the Co-op, I didn't have a whole lot of time left to do the political work that I wanted and needed to do. Though I did run for Newark West Ward district assembly and win. More on that later. The second challenge, the dilemma between building the movement and making a living. I had hoped that the Co-op would resolve this problem, but it didn't. The Co-op barely generated enough money to pay its operating expenses and the extremely modest salaries for myself and the office administrator. I was struggling to pay my bills. Eventually I left the Co-op to take a job in corporate America. I left the PEC to my assistant, Joyce Riley, and I joined AT&T Informational Systems as a second-level manager. A friend with whom I had done some consulting, Don Saunders, a labor relations specialist, and negotiator with whom I had done some consulting while I was a student at Princeton hooked me up with AT&T, a really good job at the time.

My life had reached another milestone with my second wife Michelle Miller who I met through a PEC board member. Michelle and I were married in her parent's house. I was glad that it was a large house because throngs of people were there. We moved to an apartment on West End Avenue in Newark. Nia was born and the three of us would eventually move to Montclair— Michelle's hometown. After our apartment in Newark was broken into a couple of times, Michelle had had it. It was move to Montclair or have a very brief marriage. Imani was born three years after the move.

In 1984, my life was becoming more conventional and somewhat middle-class. The 1970s had ended for me and many other activists with the hard thud of Ronald Reagan's election. It was a critical point for me: do I stay radical, or do I join the system?

Nonetheless, I still strove to be an activist and continue political work, even while working for corporate America. This too was a challenge. I had to do my nine-to-five and then after work hours, carry out my family responsibilities and try to engage in political activities. This was very difficult, but it would be the nature of my life for more than three decades. It was like working three jobs, a constant tug of war between them. There are only twenty-four hours in a day. And as human beings we have only a limited amount of energy to deal with it. I was only able to navigate this contradiction because of the cooperation of my wife and children. Yet friction and tension were unavoidable. As most working people know, our jobs inevitably infringe on our personal and family lives. Add to this, involvement in political activity, my own flaws and shortcomings and you have twice the tension, friction, and sometimes emotionally explosive situations. Michelle was a publicist, later a teacher. She was a hard-working woman, a great mother and homemaker. So, she had multiple jobs too. Including picking up the slack for me when my political activities interfered with the activities I should have been at with my children. As my wife, Michelle would have appreciated more time just with her. Inevitably, the things left undone often became the source of great consternation for Michelle and perhaps for my daughters as well. It was difficult to explain this to my children, though sometimes I think they understood. And as they became older, they sometimes participated in the political struggle I was clearly tethered to. It's important that we as activists consider the impact our political activities will have on those closest to us. Those of us who choose to have families need to think very hard before doing so. Make sure you are ready and prepared for the challenge. Make sure you have those long discussions with your life partner before you are married. There was the constant pull of something larger than us: the people's struggle around the world. South African apartheid was still in the ring, slightly bruised with the attention and threats of divestitures but still standing with the stench stretching through President Reagan's Voodoo economy. This was not the time to act as though anyone had "arrived." The constant struggle against injustice exacts a price.

The People's Organization for Progress (POP) is, in many ways, an outgrowth of PEC. POP was founded because many of us involved in PEC saw that its potential as a political organization would be extremely limited. Ed Steed and his wife, Connie, key members of the PEC board, were founding members of POP. We met regularly once a month starting in 1981. After two years of monthly meetings, we realized we needed something else.

Prior to organizing POP, I decided to run for District Leader in the Twenty-eighth District of the West Ward of Newark with a desire and design for social change. From the beginning, I had no illusions. It was never about helping me personally. I always felt that running for office had to be part of a larger strategy and a larger fight for structural, social transformation. I know my degree will say I was studying politics at Princeton, but I knew I was really studying social change and people's revolutionary movements while exploring the evolution of large cities across the country like Detroit. The Detroit Alliance for a Rational Economy (DARE) was an organization that I looked at as a model for what I wanted to do in Newark.

While simultaneously establishing the PEC, I established the Twenty-eighth District Assembly. The Twenty-eighth District Assembly was an embryo of the POP, and it was established before POP. If you look at the POP Constitution under local political organization, it says, "POP units shall be established at local levels. These units are subsidiary organs and have been created to assist the realization of the goals of the organization to the establishment of district committees."

The idea of establishing district committees came from the Twenty-eighth District Assembly in the West Ward. We came up with a central organization that had local units. Newark has five wards. At the time, each ward could have up to forty-five districts. The idea was to set up a type of unit of POP in every district, or at least in most districts in the city. And that would be the basis of the political organization that we would essentially challenge for political power at the local level. That was the grand idea. We didn't know what it would be called. But the District Assembly was an experiment. We met once every month. We even had a newsletter. The idea was to evolve the role of the district leader. Each district is supposed to have a male and female district leader—a term that lasts for two years. These district leaders come together to elect the County Democratic Chair. That is really their purpose, and they don't see their purpose as more than that. Now in general political theory, the district leaders are supposed to be grassroots leaders of the Democratic Party. The job of the district leaders should be to muster Democratic votes for the party line during the elections. I have never known there to be an election where there wasn't somebody who challenged the regular Democratic Party choices. The regular Democratic Party choice was on line A and the others were on lines B, C, D, E or F. After the primary, they muster the votes again for the general election in November. But my idea was to take this district leader and make them into political activists because district leaders are the most grassroots of all the political leaders that are elected.

For me, this position would not be just about getting the vote out for primaries and general elections, and it would not just be about electing a Democratic Chair. But the district leader would be party functionaries that educated, organized, and mobilized the people around issues, in this case those that affect the district.

The district leader position was a move up politically because now I'm actually doing political work with people. But it limited me to the district. I couldn't be in other districts because the other district leaders would be upset.

This was disappointing because I held to the idea of POP being an amalgamation of district committees. I held on to that idea for a long time. Long enough to include it in our POP Constitution which took over a year to write.

In a nutshell, this idea was way overly, politically ambitious because the amount of time and effort it would take to establish just one ward worth of district committees would've been nearly impossible. I mean, I would have meetings with these other district leaders, but these other district leaders were so loyal to the existing political leadership. They had a political allegiance to the councilmen, particularly the West Ward councilman. And what I was talking about wasn't what they were talking about.

The Twenty-eighth District worked because I was there. But we couldn't really get the other districts to buy into the idea. It was time to build something that was larger than the district. The district idea had become too parochial. But it was that experience that led to the formation of the POP in 1983.

The previous year a few of us had started meeting. I had purposed to reconnect with some of the former student activists of the Newark Federation. Ed Steed worked for the postal service and his wife, Connie, was a nurse. They were some of the first to attend the meetings. There was Angie Johnson, a Newark public schoolteacher, and Greg Adams, who lived in Newark's South Ward. Connie Smith was on the board of the PEC because of her background as an attorney. She came to some of the first meetings and introduced Michelle, who would become my second wife. Michelle was at some of the first meetings as well. There was a core group of about nine people. There were never more than a dozen folks at a time. We met for nine months without really giving a name to what was forming. I was trying to convey to people my thinking hoping we could build unity from it. It was a long discussion process, and it wasn't a real formal thing.

The idea: if we could just get control of local governments through the election of Black mayors and Black council people the condition of Black people would change for the better. And we weren't seeing that. At that time, we felt that the traditional civil rights organizations in the city, county and state were not really putting up a sharp challenge to the status quo. We wanted something that was going to be more militant, more connected to the masses of people and more direct in calling for and implementing fundamental change. Electoral politics was no longer viewed as the panacea for progressive change. By 1980 Black mayors in large cities were no longer anomalies. No one had to study Marx to know that structural changes were needed. But structural change is rather broad. There's a whole lot under the tent of structural change. I think one of the motivating ideas that brought us together *was how do we explain this now?* Looking back, a lot of us explained it using the race analysis, saying we had elected Uncle Toms to represent us and that was the problem. We elected people who were selling us out, the analysis went. We had to elect the correct ones — the right ones, the militant ones.

But a Marxist analysis goes deeper. A Marxist analysis would say, and even if you will let Jesus Christ be the mayor, the outcome is not going to be much different because the socio-economic conditions of Black people result from a capitalist system. The situation with urban areas is a part of the real estate industry. And one of the cornerstones of capitalism is real estate. Marx spoke of three forms of profit. They are rent, interest from bankers and exploitation of labor. Those are the three sources of value — or the extraction of surplus value Karl Marx gave: rent/landlords, interest from bankers and labor surplus from the capitalists.

Most of the early POP members were really Pan-Africanists. They realized and articulated that we needed public officials who have a progressive, people-centered agenda. The goal was to have real choices——to be able to vote for people with integrity—no sell out. That was a centerpiece for many of our discussions. Some of them had participated in Gibson's elections in 1970, when I was still a high school kid reading the *adventures of Superman* in DC's *Action Comics*.

Our analysis back then was as simple as a comic dealing with heroes and villains. The problem didn't have gray areas for us: the Black people were being oppressed by the white. I didn't understand anything about social classes, economic systems, or social super structures. Apartheid seemed to be our central problem, getting rid of the white oppressors our collective goal. So, we replace them with Blacks and then have to struggle against them! By 1983, with sixteen years of Black Power in Newark, large tracks from the Newark Rebellion were still visible. Drug- and rat-infested brick high-rise public housing complexes like Hayes, Stella and Scudder Homes were unchanged. Toward the end of the

Gibson administration, there seemed to be a trickling of development. But the pace of change was too slow. Then there was still crime. When I got back home in the late Seventies and early Eighties, there was a rash of car thefts and home break-ins, particularly in the Vailsburg section of the West Ward. It was so bad, some in the community were calling for our 1967 adversaries, the National Guard, to come in and patrol because they felt Newark police were not doing their jobs.

It took a lot of brainstorming, but we finally came up with a name. Connie Steed was the one who thought it up. The People's Organization for Progress, or POP for short, clicked. Initially we met at people's houses. We'd meet at Ed and Connie's house, Angie Johnson's home and there may have been some meetings at My Mom's house on Tremont Avenue as well before my second marriage.

We worked on the constitution for more than a year. Here's the process: I would write something, bring it to the meeting, they would debate it and come to a unifying position. We put the constitution together with the thought of POP as a vehicle to establish something larger that would consist of district committees. But we could never get anyone to run for district leader. Though we never developed POP district committees, over time we did begin to develop POP branches throughout the state and New York.

We began slow. We had one of our first public programs on February 24, 1983, at the Messiah Baptist Church in East Orange. It was about the economic recession entitled, "These Hard Times, Which Way Out?"

Our next forum was held on Malcolm X's birthday at the Black Organization of Students (BOS) building on Rutgers campus May 19, 1983. The focus of this forum was educating the public on who Malcolm X was and to publicly announce the formation of the POP.

We started meeting at the BOS building regularly. That building had particular significance because it existed as part of a demand after Rutgers-Newark students took over Conklin Hall in 1969 to protest the lack of Black students on the Rutgers-Newark campus. By 1983, a number of community groups would meet there. One of them was People United for Better Schools Coalition (PUBS), headed by Junius Williams. He was the director of Gibson's 1970 mayoral campaign, and is an attorney, education activist, author, and musician. Williams performed with *Return to the Source*, his singing band, for decades. POP was a part of that coalition in the fight for a type two elected board over a type one appointed board. Even though I attempted to represent the community when I was an appointed Board member, it became clear to us in the Eighties that community decision-making was essential to community involvement. And that meant school board elections. We won that fight for an elected board but lost the meeting place when factions within PUBS had a physical confrontation. This turned into a fight that spilled into the hallway and tore the door off its hinges.

We may have had a few meetings after the door was fixed there, but eventually we had to find another location. Our next meetings were held at the Newark Coalition for Neighborhoods office. Richard Cammarieri, a true progressive we could always count on, was the executive director.

Co-op to POP

He let us meet there right above the Ward Coffee and Nut store on Broad Street. Sometimes we had POP events and forums in the senior citizens' building across the street because our meeting space wasn't physically accessible to everyone because of the stairs. Unfortunately, the space didn't lend itself to a large audience.

First, we were meeting monthly. By this time in 1983, we were meeting weekly. We were impressed with this idea via a poem written by Amiri Baraka, *Afrikan Revolution*. It was written in 1973 and read by Amiri at Amilcar Cabral's funeral in 1973 after his assassination by the Portuguese in Guinea.

Be conscious. Meet once a week.

Meet once a week. Talk about how to get more money, how to get educated, how to

Have scientists for children rather than junkies, how to kill the roaches, how to keep the toilet from stinking, How to get a better job. Once a week. START NOW. How to dress better. How to read. How to live longer. How to be respected. Meet once a week. Once a week.

All over the world. We need to meet once a week. All over the world Afrikans, Soul   Brothers and Good Sisters we need to meet.

How to live longer, live healthier, build houses,

Run cities, understand life be happier.

Need to meet once a week,

OK All over the world,

Once a week...

Black History was something everyone in the group could rally behind. Many believed that if we could just get all our kids to know their history, we'd be straight. We'd get seventy-five to one-hundred people coming out for the programs. We would try to turn those crowds into members.

It's interesting to me that none of the people originally active with POP when it formed are active now in 2024. It's interesting, though certainly not encouraging. I think what it was is that the initial people that came together to form POP had in mind a more conventional political organization. They weren't really animated by the same ideal or vision that animated me. It's not that they didn't believe in the same things. They just weren't willing to commit the same amount of time. I was young and had graduated from Princeton and studied revolutions. I thought people might be ready to start one. I was living and breathing this stuff and they were sympathetic and perhaps saw things the same way, but they were living life. I had studied a little Marxism, but none of the early members were Marxists. When I was young, I wanted a revolution. Now that I'm an old man I'm happy just to have a political movement that is going in the correct direction.

POP was formed to be a non-ideological organization — that's why we're not called The Black People's Organization for Progress or the Socialist Organization for Progress. That means we organize around the common ground in which we agree — and believe me, it takes a lot of debate to find it. We confront the system. We raise the consciousness of the people, so they want to join us to confront the system.

The Eighties were both exhilarating and terrifying. If people couldn't see a need for change with the Voodoo Economics President Ronald Reagan, in office, then this country was in a stupor we might never get out of. In our POP Constitution, we had a place for political endorsements. That section was a big part of our beginning with the upcoming 1984 national election brewing. But it was the local elections that almost ended us completely.

1980S: RACING WITH THE RAINBOW

It was the twentieth anniversary of the 1963 March on Washington and Jesse was the keynote speaker. This was the moment to take King's legacy to the next phase. The stars had aligned. The ebb and flow of struggle merged into 1983 with a level of consciousness amidst a vibrant anti-apartheid movement and three years of Reagan's oppressive regime. Perhaps to the chagrin of some of the Black leaders of the time, this keynote speech, made in such a historic place on such a historic anniversary, would be the shot of a Presidential run. The Rev. Jesse Jackson was going to enter the race for President and shame on anyone who got in the way.

No, Jesse was not the first African American to run for President of the United States. Frederick Douglass was actually the first to run in 1888 and then George Edwin Taylor in 1904 in the National Negro Liberty Party which interestingly had its roots in Little Rock, Arkansas. Guess what they were fighting for in 1904? Self-government of the District of Columbia. The first Black woman elected to the U.S. Congress, Shirley Chisolm was the first candidate of a major party and the first Black woman to run for President. Ms. Chisolm's run in 1972 was a litmus test for America. Jackson's run would serve as the next.

Much had changed in the twenty years since the first March on Washington. In 1963, you could watch television and almost never see a Black face on television shows or in commercial advertisements. The year 1983 brought us *The Cosby Show*, Vanessa L. Williams as the first Black Miss America and Michael Jackson's *Thriller* album. More importantly for me, Chicago had just elected its first Black mayor, Harold Washington. For those of us who fought for Black political leadership in America's cities, it was a major advance.

I had watched Jesse for a long time and admired his young, vibrant leadership coming out of what by 1983 was Harold Washington's Chicago. Jesse was a natural bridge from the Sixties— SCLC-Operation Breadbasket, the Gary Convention, and PUSH (People United to Serve Humanity). Some in the Movement viewed this as the opportunity to take the platform we had set at the Gary Convention in 1972 and make it the platform for the Democratic Party. If that didn't work, some of us thought, maybe we could start our own party. The latter turned out not to be what Jackson had in mind.

When Jesse ran in '84, he was really depending on Black elected officials and Black ministers — people already in place on the ground level in cities throughout the nation. It is an effective strategy. It seems Al Sharpton, who was the youth director of SCLC's Operation Breadbasket in New York around the same time I was nominated to the board, used the same strategy when he ran for President twenty years later in 2004.

In line with this strategy of cities providing the lifeblood of the 1984 Jesse campaign, Newark stepped up when he made it official. Mayor Gibson — the elected official and outgrowth of the Newark's Black Power Movement, the man Jesse had to speak at his Operation Breadbasket rally in 1970 — would head his campaign in New Jersey. It was clear to us that the national Jackson campaign had not really kept up with the local climate of Newark. Eighty-four was a long way from 1970 when he was first elected as mayor. The revolutionary spirit had faded into a kind of political malaise, and even the threat that Reagan posed couldn't revive it. By 1984, a lot of people were feeling alienated from the Gibson administration. Many of us privately winced when he once said, "I'm a manager of resources, not of hope." Gibson was an engineer, not a charismatic leader.

In 2022, it's very interesting to see the role that Mayor Ras Baraka has played in terms of upholding the contributions of Ken Gibson. We must remember that Ken Gibson did make a significant contribution. He essentially was the battering ram to break down the apartheid political system that was in Newark. And regardless of what happened after that, you must recognize the benchmark role that that event was. Mayor Baraka has rescued that Gibson legacy. But in 1984, Ras' father, Amiri, and Gibson had become political adversaries. Brothers United no more. The discord or friction had reached its peak ten years earlier because by 1974 the mainstream political Black elite had pretty much undermined the Kawaida Tower project in which Baraka was engaged. This mainstream cadre included Gibson and Donald Payne Sr. It's interesting now to see that the sons of Baraka and Payne — the latter now a congressman representing Newark, like his father — are working closely together when their fathers were at odds.

By '84 there was a divergence. There was clear opposition to Gibson with the divide only swelling over time. I'm not sure Gibson was ever cognizant of that gulf. I think he felt secure politically to the point that it may have seemed that he didn't even care. Maybe he didn't think the gulf was going to affect him, but it did. And two years later, in 1986, it unseated him. However, back in 1984, the die was cast, and Gibson was Jesse's campaign chairman.

Yet Jackson's announcement created some grassroots energy that the newly-formed POP was proud to see. Those outside of the establishment would not be denied this moment to make tracks in history. People went about setting up their own Jackson campaign support committees. And POP did too. We named it Friends of Jesse Jackson. When possible, we did attempt to work with the existing campaign structure. But when it didn't seem possible, we went out and did things on our own. We had our own events. We didn't rely on the main campaign organization to give us anything.

In fact, in April of 1984 we had a rally that focused on the significance of the Jackson campaign's progressive platform, one that pushed many of the issues we always wanted to see discussed and debated in the political marketplace: reparations for Black Americans, declaring South Africa as a rogue state, ratifying the Equal Rights Amendment for women, supporting Palestine. We invited a person who had recently headed the delegation with Jesse Jackson to free Lt. Robert Goodman, a downed pilot captured by Syrians. Jesse's successful negotiation for the freedom of this imprisoned Black man impressed Black America. Reverend William Howard, Vice Chair for the Religious liaison of Jackson's campaign and Executive Director of the Black Council of the Reformed Church of America, was our keynote speaker. Amiri Baraka, Newark Councilman Ralph T. Grant, and New Jersey State Assemblyman Eugene Thompson also spoke. Rev. Elia Tema of Soweto, South Africa, really struck a chord with the implication of Jackson's candidacy on an international level, particularly for Third World nations. It was a great event. We educated, we motivated, and we mobilized. Reverend Howard, always the diplomat, urged all the Jersey Jackson campaigns to work together statewide. Many years later, Dr. Howard would return to Newark as Bethany Baptist's senior pastor and later head the transition team for the future Newark mayor and future Democratic Presidential candidate Cory Booker.

We were fine with working together, but we were not waiting for Gibson or anybody else to match our stride. We had another rally a few weeks later with Ben Chavis as the keynote speaker. Then we had our state-wide rally and parade scheduled a few days before New Jersey's Democratic primary. There was so much stuff going on within our organization that Gibson started publicly complaining. I was concerned about local schisms in that it might have an adverse effect on the overall campaign. But we really believed that if the campaign was going to be successful in New Jersey, then there had to be room for all in our diverse community to participate.

As history will tell, Walter Mondale won the primary. Jackson came in six points behind Hart in New Jersey. Overall, Jackson had about twenty-three percent to Hart's twenty-nine percent and Mondale's forty-five percent. Our dream was deferred; Reagan would have another four years to torment the working class and people of color. Despite the outcome — in fact, because of the outcome — we had an obligation to keep the Jesse fire lit. Jesse reminded us that this run was not a thirty-yard dash, but it was a decathlon.

POP learned the importance of networking early. We had a charity run with the Black United Fund in May at Weequahic Park in Newark. That was the culmination of a series of events that began with a forum in Plainfield titled *Racism at Home and Abroad*. Plainfield is approximately forty minutes south of Newark in what is Central New Jersey. a history that parallels that of Newark in terms of its racial history. Plainfield had their own rebellion from July 14 through the 17th 1967. The difference was that Black people raided the Plainfield Machine Company. Missing were at least forty-six M1 carbines. The other difference was that no residents were killed, while there was a police officer killed. Two people, a man, and a woman were convicted of the murder and sentenced to life.

With its working-class population. Plainfield was a good setting for this forum because of the centrality in the state. Newly-elected Plainfield mayor, Rev. Richard Taylor, spoke on the role of community-based organizations. Taylor was only the second Black mayor of Plainfield.

What assisted POP in keeping the energy going was the growing anti-apartheid movement. It had everything we needed: Africa for the Pan-Africanists, socialism for the socialists and trade union organizing for unions.

Maybe just as importantly there were open displays of white racism for liberals. In 1985, ABC went to South Africa and conducted some of the most in-depth reporting on South Africa we had seen up to that point. America got to see for the first time a sort of déja-vu of events from its own not so distant past—cops beating protestors with batons like whips and people grieving over children, men and woman who had died at the hands of South African police. All this helped bring a sense of urgency to bear, even after South Africa started banning reports on insurrections.

We began to hold forums on apartheid. Nomazizi Sokudela spoke on *The Destruction of the Black Family Under Apartheid* and I spoke on *Black America and South Africa: Same Struggle, Same Fight*. The title was taken from the Sales/Anderson pamphlet I used years before on Princeton's campus. A few months later, we were one of three groups to sponsor a series of anti-apartheid cultural events. We worked with the Works Gallery, which was founded a year before as a vehicle for showing contemporary African American Art, and Newark Mediaworks, an organization that was formed to assist community groups in using electronic and print media. Our goal of course was to broaden awareness on South Africa, apartheid, and the United States' economic and political role in it all. The United States politically supported South Africa because it was an anti-communist state, and many U.S.-based corporations were doing business with South Africa. The United States was, in effect, a full supporter of the apartheid regime that had killed and imprisoned many in its Black population, including Black leaders like Steve Biko. It helped that Bishop Desmond Tutu, noted South African cleric, had received the Nobel Peace Prize in 1984. It raised consciousness about apartheid throughout the world.

We believed that the naked violence of apartheid deserved a higher stakes protest. In December of 1984 eight of us were charged with failing to leave a federal building. We were among about 75 people protesting South Africa's policies and the U.S. trade policies with that country. Here's my memory-informed list of who was charged that day: Arthur S. Jones, President of the New Jersey Council of Churches and pastor of St. Mark's AME in East Orange; Rev. William Rutherford, then Irvington Branch NAACP President; Mignon Curry Arthur of Orange; James Love, a Rutgers University student; Marcia

Brown of Newark; Jerry Coleman, a Rahway City Councilman; Neal Garfinkle, an executive board member of Local 8406 of the Oil, Chemical and Atomic Workers Union in Bayonne and myself. We left before being arrested but the charges and fines still arrived at our doorsteps. The charges were dropped at a subsequent hearing though we had to pay court fees of about $75. However, this was one protest indicative of many throughout New Jersey that was conducted for the express purpose of putting pressure on the state to divest its $10 billion pension funds from companies doing business with South Africa.

Apartheid supplied clarity and purpose. Everything we did after the 1984 election was about divestiture from South Africa. The momentum worked. In August of 1985, Governor Thomas Kean — considered by some to be a liberal Republican governor, a former member of SCLC when it was a multiracial organization — said he would sign a divestiture bill that would remove $2 billion in New Jersey investments from companies that do business in South Africa. We had won a major battle, but the war showed no signs of ending. Mandela was still imprisoned. Black South Africans were not free and for that matter, neither were we.

It was in September of 1985 when the Ku Klux Klan got so brazen as to try to have a march going down Broad Street in Newark. That took a helluva lot of nerve to choose the Blackest city in the state and try to march down its main street. Of course, Gibson denied them the parade permit. But these unabashed racists decided they were going to take it to a court as a freedom of speech case. That's when the Newark City Council stepped in and had one of their most pronounced moments. They decided to allow the permit only if they walk down Broad Street unmasked. Needless to say, there was no

Klan march down Broad Street in Newark. But there was an anti-apartheid march in Newark a couple of months later with more than 12,000 people of all races, colors, and creeds.

I was everywhere but home during this period. Maybe that's why when Ben Chavis offered me a position at the United Church of Christ Commission for Racial Justice (CRJ) as the Director of the Commission's Community Organizing Program, I jumped on it. Although I had a decent job with AT&T at the time and the money was good, I knew that wasn't enough for me.

It was a few years now since I formed the PEC in 1981 and Joyce Riley was still running the PEC, so that was no longer a factor. POP was now having regular programs. However, the two trains, AT&T and POP, were running simultaneously and parallel. It all began to clash. I became discontented with my role at AT&T. I started at AT&T in 1983. I had only been there about a year before running into Ben Chavis. It had been almost a decade since I met him as a Princeton student organizer. Chavis and the rest of the Wilmington Ten had finally been released by 1980. It would be thirty-two more years before they were finally pardoned by Governor Beverly Perdue.

Transferring from AT&T to the struggle for social justice in the Reagan years resulted in a pay cut but Chavis was offering me an opportunity of a lifetime. Chavis promised there would be salary increases but that didn't matter at that moment. This is what I studied for. I didn't go to school to be conventional and become Mr. Corporate America. But by the same token, I had a family and children to feed. If I could do all of that and be part of the change the world so desperately needed, then the Commission would be the place for me.

My working for Ben Chavis during that period was key in terms of him giving me support and permission to work on projects related to building POP. Ben adopted POP as a project of the Commission perhaps in an unofficial way. He allowed me a significant amount of time to do work either around organizing POP or organizing POP-sponsored activities. He always saw POP as part of my work for CRJ. That was critical, especially in those early years that were crucial to the development of POP and the New Jersey Rainbow Coalition. There was so much work to do. We still weren't free, despite the successes of Cosby, Williams, Jackson, Washington, and Jesse Jackson.

It was disheartening to see in 1986, twenty-two years after the Voting Rights Act was signed into law, there were folks in the South being harassed and threatened when they tried to vote. The Justice Department trumped up charges against some Black people in Alabama in an effort to intimidate them and keep them from voting. The Commission for Racial Justice sponsored a "Freedom Riders of 1986" ride through the South, following the route of the Freedom Rides of 1961. Seventy-five people participated, many of them from Rutgers University. A Rutgers Black student leader, Lisa Williamson, who is now known as the popular novelist Sistah Souljah, was on the bus with us going down there. It was fitting that largely students went because that's who was primarily on those rides in 1961. Coretta Scott King would write years later of those early young activists eagerly trading the privileges of youth for a season of suffering.

I actually tried to get out of going because I was sick. I had an eye infection, so my eye was swollen, and I looked like Quasimodo. But Chavis said, "No man, you've got to go." So, I went, and I was glad I did in spite of being sick for about a week.

We had stopped in Virginia, and I ate some catfish for the first time. That food did not agree with me at all.

This trip was a real education for me. That might sound interesting, knowing my past. As you know, it wasn't that I hadn't had any historical contact with the Movement before I met Chavis. The education came from an opportunity to travel a historical road where Freedom Riders forged a new world through blood and fire. We weren't met with angry white mobs, beatings, bombings, or jail cells when we stopped in various Southern towns. Instead, we were greeted by Black elected officials. It was John Hulett, the Black elected High Sheriff of Lowndes County, who greeted and watched over us as we lay the wreath at the grave site of Viola Liuzzo. Liuzzo was a white Detroit housewife who decided to answer the call to be a part of the Movement. She was assisting with the coordination of the Selma-to-Montgomery March when she was murdered by the Ku Klux Klan in the presence of an FBI informant in 1965. Following that, we went to Dr King's Dexter Avenue Baptist Church in Montgomery.

The thing that I remember most about the trip was the extreme poverty that still existed in 1986. People automatically think Newark is so bad. Well, we went to a town where they had elected their first Black mayor and we had to sponsor a drive to raise money to purchase furniture for the City Hall. We went to towns such as Eutaw and Chickasaw that didn't have sidewalks.

These were the towns where voter intimidation was rampant. There are parallels between what we witnessed in 1986 and the voter suppression tactics that started after the Shelby vs. Holder Supreme Court case stripped away section five of the Voting Rights Act. The Reagan administration was using the federal government to repress the Black vote and cut Black voting strength in Alabama. The Justice Department concentrated its investigation on certain counties in Western Alabama which had the greatest number of elected Black officials. Charges were subsequently lodged against Black individuals for voter fraud. All charges targeted absentee ballots, which were crucial in the Black Belt area. It was clear to us the federal investigation and subsequent trials were designed to create a veil of fear among Black voters before the June primaries.

We met with longtime Movement activists Albert and Evelyn Turner. The couple's home was firebombed two weeks prior to our meeting. Movement stalwarts Spiver Gordon and Spencer Hogue had been indicted and falsely charged with voter-fraud. We also met with several elderly voters who had been questioned by the federal government. Some elderly voters were transported from Perry County to Mobile, nearly one hundred and sixty miles away, for finger-printing and additional questioning. One ninety-year-old woman told us they couldn't get her to change her answer. She told us she wasn't so old that she didn't know what she was doing.

We stayed at the home of Senator Henry "Hook" Sanders and his wife Rose Sanders. Both were community activists involved in a wide range of issues. They helped guide us as we walked through recent Movement history that had at the time only begun to be documented by history books. We were confronted with the pain and anguish of living that violent, terroristic history. We visited the grave site of Jimmy Lee Jackson, a Black veteran who was participating in a peaceful voting rights demonstration when he was brutally beaten by troopers and then shot by one. I went to the Sixteenth Street Baptist Church, and I met the father of Denise McNair. Denise

McNair was one of the four girls killed when the church was bombed. Her father took us on a tour of the church, and I cried. It was just like being there, hearing his voice and visualizing the eternal internal torture. That day, I cried for some children that I had never even met. They had a bronze plaque on the wall with engraved pictures of the girls. We were also guided to where the old part of the church was left standing. It was literally like a giant saw had sawed the church in half, split it down the middle; you could see where the old church was and where the bomb blew out an opening to the new church. We could stand in the sanctuary and look straight down and see this new edifice on one side and the old edifice on the other side. They showed us the stained-glass window that the people from Scotland sent to the Black people in Birmingham when they heard about this church being bombed killing the four girls. Seeing that had a major impact on me that day. As Mr. McNair spoke, tears came to my eyes, and they would not stop.

The following year, in 1987, the Commission sponsored another Freedom Ride. This time, we started in Selma and rode up to Chicago to make sure that people came out to vote in the city's Democratic primary. Harold Washington was up for re-election, and every vote had to be counted. This year was also the sounding bell for Jesse's next run. Everyone had to be in place for Jesse to have a chance in 1988.

By 1987, some began to view POP only as a political vehicle. Those seeing our organization in this way weren't looking at it as a vehicle for social change as much as they were looking at it as a tool to help people get elected. They looked at POP and saw campaign workers and fundraisers. It's funny because we wanted to establish a political organization, but when we say "political," we say it in the broadest sense. Those approaching us for endorsements weren't thinking about a political movement or transforming society to make social change. Instead, the focus and message were, "I want to run for school board. I want to run for city council. I want to run for mayor. And if you're a political organization, you can help me get that done."

Theoretically we could, but there was but one problem—fissures inevitably creating splits. This wasn't like the apartheid-like situation where Gibson was elected. It wasn't even like the 1984 Jackson campaign where we had a real opportunity to possibly see sweeping change on so many levels. These elections were a little more complex in that we were talking about Blacks running against other Blacks. And POP would always break down into camps. We'd have two people both wanting to run for the City Council's West Ward council seat. There were times when there would only be three seats up at the time on the school board and you've got five people in POP that want to run for the school board. And why did I have to choose that year to try to run for State Assembly? I was a third-party candidate. Had I run in the primary as Democrat I might have won. In fact, a political powerbroker was trying to work out a deal with the local Democratic leaders. They were going to support me as a Democrat for the Democratic County Freeholder position, if I did not challenge James Zangari for his seat on the State Assembly. But there was this whole third-party tendency that was very strong in POP at that time. I would bring back the deal that was proposed before the POP general assembly and they would be like, "Hell No. We're not making a deal with the Democratic machine."

So, I ended up running as a third-party candidate with the famous civil rights attorney and law professor Arthur Kinoy.

Our campaign slogan in 1987 was "People's Needs First." Now, whenever people try to challenge me, I say, "Look, I'm the only one in this room that ever ran as a third-party candidate. It's hard to beat the established line. It can be done, but it's hard to beat the line." You have to have an enormous amount of money to beat them.

While POP was supporting me in my run for assembly, they had also voted to support Wayne Garner for the Board of Education. Wayne was a good guy. We all liked him, but people felt that I didn't work hard enough for Wayne. There was a falling out behind that when he didn't win. That meeting was so contentious that the following week when I showed up at the BOS building for our regular meeting, it was just me sitting there.

Then Brother Roosevelt Hobbs walked in. Hobbs had been around a long time. He said he had been part of Paul Robeson's security detail when Robeson performed at Niagara Falls. He told me he knew W.E.B. Du Bois as well. Removed from that time, he walked in wearing his usual cap, goatee, and the outfit of his former days as a long shoreman and truck driver. He sits down in one of our chairs, placed in circle formation back then. The seating arrangement was deemed more egalitarian. He sat quietly with the air of wisdom his years commanded, for a moment looking at me in the circle of two. And then said, "Brother Hamm, I think we need to stay away from the electoral arena for a while."

At that moment, with an assembly of two, we suspended the constitution where it says we can endorse candidates. Following that incident, I had to recruit a whole new group of POP members.

When delving into the Jackson Presidential campaign of 1988, it's important to remember how we got there. The 1984 campaign had served as a catalyst for an awakening, a realization of the power that we knew was within our grasp. The momentum created by the anti-apartheid movement and the Jackson campaign continued into the mid-80s. In May of 1985, two hundred of us were together at St. Michael's Chapel in Piscataway with the goal of building a permanent national Rainbow Coalition. It was probably in Piscataway first because we had strong Central Jersey representation. We also attempted to rotate meetings throughout the state. It was time for this campaign to become a movement. It was first called the Progressive Rainbow Coalition of New Jersey. This meeting represented a marriage of northern, southern and central New Jersey. a coalescing of anti-racism and anti-nuclear activists. It was a network where we began to identify key pieces of state legislation that we wanted to support. We also began looking at people running for office that supported our platform. It was a pivotal convention with speakers like local Black public affairs television producer and host Gil Noble, Neo Mnumzana, a representative of the African National Congress, and Rev. Henry Atkins of the New Jersey Sanctuary Movement.

By 1988, you could feel the energy in the raps of KRS-One, Public Enemy, and others. You could also feel it among Blacks in the New York City area, who had become radicalized because of several beating incidents and deaths of Blacks by groups of white thugs in and out of uniform.

In Newark, we had "new" political leadership to deal with in terms of the Jackson campaign. Mayor Gibson had been soundly beaten by Sharpe James in 1986. The New Jersey Rainbow Coalition, as it was renamed when we became the first officially certified chapter of the National Rainbow Coalition that year, was not involved in the Gibson/James fight as an organization. Of course, some individuals were involved in the election contest. Two-thirds of the members didn't get involved at all because they didn't live in Newark. Of the third that did live in Newark, only half of them were involved. Most of them supported James who was one of the original candidates on the Community Choice ticket.

James, who was a more activist mayor, decided to play this campaign smart. He said, "I'm going to have one campaign and I'm going to bring Larry in and make him campaign co-chair and we're going to work together." And that's what happened. That's what made 1988 different. As chairman of the New Jersey Rainbow Coalition, I now had one thousand members, county chapters, and institutional support from the Black establishment of the city and the state. We had state conventions, which had the full participation of Black elected officials such as Donald Tucker and the national Rainbow's Executive Director Ron Daniels.

The New Jersey Rainbow Coalition continued after the Jackson campaign was over. In 1989, we now had if not a machine, an umbrella of Black and white activists, union organizers and radicals. We organized over racial incidents in Atlantic City, Trenton, and Vineland. We pushed the state to establish a racial violence study commission and a multicultural state curriculum commission, but our efforts were unsuccessful.

Our biggest effort focused on voter registration. We organized voter registration campaigns across the state and called out New Jersey on its institutional attempts to quash voting registration. Both in 1985 and 1989, I advocated for same-day voter registration. I contended that registering to vote should be as easy as playing the lottery or paying your water bill. I argued that a person should be able to register to vote when he or she pays the water bill. I still believe that today. At the time, New Jersey had a state-of-the-art computerized system for the lottery, but not for voter registration. Alan Karcher, a Jesse Jackson supporter, Middlesex County assemblyman and Speaker of the House, tried to create an avenue for legislation by going to court on behalf of the Rainbow Coalition to fight for same day registration in the state of NJ. We didn't win that battle, but we did get the number of days that a person has to be registered to vote prior to an election reduced from thirty days to twenty-one days. And it's still twenty-one days today. Though that was progress, I think it's ridiculous that we even have the twenty-one days — especially today with all of the technological advantages that we have. I still support same-day registration and in a number of states it does exist.

In some respects, POP took the Rainbow Coalition on as its project. But POP had its own identity. Many joined POP believing us to be more radical or progressive. And our role was to be in the establishment to push the most progressive position possible with them. The Rainbow Coalition on the national and state level was very broad. The people who wanted a third party were only one color of the Rainbow, but a strong part of POP. However, the people who wanted Jesse Jackson for President spanned the liberal spectrum in every way. We tolerated the differences, knowing that we had to have a united front. We were trying to reach a goal and we knew we had to have a broad kind of united front for Jesse to win the election and to build the kind of movement we wanted to build.

We stayed together a few years after the final votes were cast in 1988. We liked the idea of the Rainbow Coalition, which, by the way, wasn't an original idea. Fred Hampton of the Black Panther Party talked about a Rainbow Coalition in 1968. While people understood the need for all-Black organizations, they also understood the need to work with other like-minded groups with similar goals and ideologies. It's like having different tools in the toolbox. You need an all-Black organization to accomplish certain things in the Black community and to address certain types of issues in that community. But for other issues, you would need a broader constituency to develop political consensus around those issues. You'd need a Rainbow Coalition, which is simply a different tool in the political toolbox. You have to be open to using different instruments to get the job accomplished. There were many people who moved from the Rainbow Coalition to POP during those years. Among them were Gladys (Ayo) McMillan and Charlotte Munnerlyn, who I attribute much of our organizational growth in that period.

The Rainbow locally lost steam by the time William Jefferson Clinton was elected president in 1992. So, we transitioned into the 1990s — a decade where we realized that under Bill Clinton, the struggles were going back to being more local, as POP had become an established community- oriented, educational organization. We would always be a part of coalitions, but now we had to build ourselves internally. Inside baseball was now in vogue in the Black community. This was the decade of the Million Man March, the Million Woman March, and more attempts at Black institution building. In Newark, the State of New Jersey took over our school district as soon as we got money from an important school parity ruling. We won the court case but lost the district. We had to deal with police brutality while partnering with organizations trying to stop the rising tide of drug- and gang-oriented violence.

1990S: PERPETUAL PROTEST, PERMANENT POWER

Another one of my life's regrets is not continuing my running. I once believed I had the raw material to become an Olympic athlete. I was state champion. Had I slid seamlessly from high school to college, maybe I would have taken athletics to another level. But the four-year interruption of the Board, study, my job as a security aide, activism and my new family, something had to give. I determined to leave running alone. At least for a while. I don't know what had gotten into me, close to turning thirty-six and deciding to run my first marathon. It was October of 1990 and I had entered the Atlantic City Marathon.

I really can't explain the need, but I know my body and psyche demanded it. At thirty-five, I had settled in, and my body was settling down to the point where I was beginning to feel uncomfortable. My cholesterol was going up dangerously. It was at that point that I decided to cut meat from my diet. Running the marathon was a personal goal that I would use to get myself back into shape. I didn't know what was beyond that new decade starting line, but I needed to be ready for it in every way.

Our nation and world needed clarity and vision, Maybe we were on the brink of some. And yet, there were ingrained factors that ran so deep it seemed out of our control-no matter what we did.

The year 1990 would see Nelson Mandela released and free from South Africa's prison system and on the cusp of becoming president of the country. David Dinkins, the first Black mayor of New York City, would greet him on his first tour of the US, But within four years, Dinkins would be replaced with Rudy Giuliani, someone whose fascist politics moved our people backwards.

When preparing for a marathon, you set training goals. The goals always push you forward a little closer to the end. You fall backwards when you are injured, or your body runs out of fuel. I learned that lesson in 1990 as I was drawing to the end of my 30K run in Atlantic City. It felt as though my insides were on fire. It turned out that I had used all my reserve and my body had begun to feed on itself. Seemed like such a contradiction. While trying to build myself up, my inner turmoil was eating me alive.

The same thing was happening to our communities across the country. Bill Clinton, the first Democratic President we had since Jimmy Carter, was in the White House. A moderate advance by a moderate politician.

At the same time Newark was averaging about one-hundred murders a year and crime was at an all-time high nationally. Carjackings, thefts and drug activity were at such a high that Black people were ready to put their own children behind bars. As quiet as it was kept, more people were for Bill Clinton's crime bill than against it at first. This was a bill that put a disproportionate number of people of color in prison for minor crimes.

It was such an epidemic that rappers had gotten together that year and produced the song and video *Self-Destruction*. Everyone on the street could recite Kool Mo Dee's famous line, "I never ever had to run from the Ku Klux Klan/ And I shouldn't have to run from a Black man."

There was hope in getting an opportunity to finally see my friend, Ben Chavis, come into his own as the head of the National NAACP. I as well as other hopefuls saw shades of Fred Hampton's unfinished and radical Rainbow Coalition in play as Chavis reached out to gang members, The Nation of Islam, Sistah Souljah and other progressive radical groups for a solution to what Dr. Cornel West dubbed in an essay as "Nihilism in Black America." Hope and then the contradictions that came with Chavis' brief rise and fall — ousted from the NAACP after only seventeen months — forced us to continue to look at our internal contradictions as a Black radical movement. Black nationalism began to openly fail while the masses looked to neo-conservative solutions.

But we didn't give up. We couldn't give up. To give up would be committing suicide. We refused suicide but we still had to deal with homicide. A sixteen-year-old Black boy, Phillip Pannell, was shot in the back by a Teaneck, NJ police officer, Gary Spath in 1990. Despite the protests and demonstrations that many of our POP members attended, the officer was acquitted two years later in February of 1992. His acquittal was followed by unrest, the overturning of some police cars and continued demonstrations. People were beginning to take notice of a trend. A few months later the officers that had violently beaten Rodney King in Los Angeles would also be acquitted in May of 1992. This set off displays of outrage throughout Los Angeles for days.

While people around the country were watching the cases of Phillip Pannell and Rodney King, people in Newark were focused on still another case. Eleven months earlier, there was sixteen-year-old Tasha Mayse, Black, pregnant, and gunned down in Hillside, a township bordering the southward of Newark, while in a stolen van with other teens. Newark police were responsible for the fatal wound to Tasha. Salaam Ismial, President of the United Youth Council of Elizabeth, led the charge in support of Tasha's family. POP supported them. Most argued that shooting thirty to forty bullets into a van that's not shooting back at you was beyond the pale. This case would not receive the national attention of King or Pannell. It did serve as an indicator of how many other cases of police brutality across the country most people will never hear of.

One thing every marathon tests is your endurance. The Nineties would turn out to be one long marathon with various events-shootings, court cases, the Million Man March and aftermath- marking its trail. The finish line, like the light at the end of a tunnel of a bad dream, tends to move further away.

More contradictions unfolded as the Nineties rolled on. On one end there seemed to be a burgeoning, post-Reagan/Bush optimism. But on the other, there was still the hideous head of racism that kept trying to swallow up any sense of hope.

In 1990, the Commission moved from New York City back to Cleveland. I didn't go with them. Heading the Jackson state campaign had afforded me some political connections. With the support of Willie Brown, a Newark assemblyman, I secured a job as a research associate in the Assembly Majority Office.

Perpetual Protest, Permanent Power

A significant development during this period was the favorable ruling by the NJ Superior Court in the *Abbott vs Burke* case brought by the Education Law Center that challenged the funding formula for public schools. It was found that funding for schools in poor and non-white districts was not on par with the funding provided to wealthier suburban school districts. The needs of poor and non-white students in largely poor and minority districts educational needs were not being met. The NJ Supreme Court finally found the state funding formula to be unconstitutional nine years after the initial filing.

My new position as a research associate gave me an opportunity to work in part on the state legislature's response to the landmark decision. That response took the form of the Quality in Education Act. QEA was the first step toward implementation of parity funding for urban districts. Was there a glimmer of something on the horizon for our youth? Not if the Republicans had anything to say about it. QEA and Governor James Florio's assault weapon ban were enough leverage for control of the assembly to be flipped. I would soon be looking for a new job. But I didn't know that in December of 1989 as I was looking down a decade of marathons of all sorts. I didn't know we would have to wait another eight years before we saw any semblance of full implementation of *Abbott* funding. Under *Abbott*, funding would be earmarked for poorer districts termed *Abbott* districts, with the purpose of closing the achievement gap between wealthier districts and poorer districts. Free early childhood programs, afterschool, enrichment programs and capital facility improvements would eventually result from the prolonged effort.

Marilyn Morheuser was the director and lead attorney of the Education Law Center. And she was an absolute powerhouse when she came to Trenton and spoke before the assembly and senate. On one occasion, I had an opportunity to meet her and invited her to a POP meeting. Eventually, she came periodically and updated us on the process of getting the funding to our districts.

I worked for a few months in 1992 for the Small Business Office of the Port Authority of New York and New Jersey and then landed a position with NJ Transit. I had the usual juggling act of balancing a new job, my family and my old passion, POP. There was a segment of the Rainbow Coalition in Teaneck that was still active, particularly with the Phillip Pannell case. POP sent people to Teaneck regularly to participate in the demonstrations. Brother Ismael worked consistently with the family of Tasha Mayse.

And I was still entering marathons. I ran in the New York Marathon in 1991, 1992 and 1993. I achieved a personal record in 1991: finishing time was 3 hours and 42 seconds. I damaged my knees in 1993 and I haven't run that kind of marathon since. POP would turn out to be its own sort of marathon.

In 1993, we co-sponsored a rally with the Metropolitan Ecumenical Ministry (MEM) on drugs, crime and violence in the Black community. Steven Jones was the executive director of MEM at the time. We held the rally at the Deliverance Jesus is Coming Church on Springfield Avenue in Irvington. This was such a principal issue for POP that we had a special membership form drawn up to give it the focus needed. Out of this event, POP formed a committee on drugs, violence, and crime. Darryl Graham became the head of what was renamed the anti-violence committee until he died several years ago. We were advocating for thoroughly funding our schools, more job training and jobs, and increased living wages. We wanted increased police services in our communities. About the same time, Lisa Williamson—a.k.a. Sistah Souljah— attended some POP meetings. She helped with a major fundraiser at George Washington Carver Elementary, where Public Enemy performed.

However, by 1994 President Clinton had stamped his Three Strikes law and the Black Caucus at the time, cosigned it. The only ones critical of this law were the radicals. And in Newark, we were marginalized on this issue. People just wanted this shit to end. Clinton's plan was not the answer. In fact, his plan was devastating.

This is probably the point where many of us began to realize that we must play a critical role in the positive development of our families and communities. When Brother Khadir Muhammad approached me and asked if I would help organize NJ for the Million Man March, I said "yes." I have a great deal of respect for the Nation of Islam. Some white people have a tough time with this because they focus on what they believe to be anti-Semitic statements from the Nation. Though I have a respect for the positive work of the Nation in our communities, that doesn't in any way cloud my thinking about the ultimately deadly encounter between it and Malcolm X.

In this case, the situation was more important than the contradictions. I felt that the Million Man March would be a major contribution toward mobilizing hundreds of thousands of people in opposition to the status quo. So, after Brother Khadir came to me, I called a meeting at Ruben Johnson's restaurant at the Nevada Mall on Court Street. Ruben used to let us have fundraising parties there. And we'd have jamming parties there. People would be lined up outside to come into our parties. It was about the time that 98.7 WRKS-FM (Kiss-FM) changed its format to classic R&B and that was really a kind of backlash to some of the Gangsta Rap that had started to dominate the Black music industry.

August of 1994, we had our first Million Man March meeting. I called POP members, Rainbow Coalition members, people from other organizations and Sister Fredrica Bey, a well-known Newark activist. At the time Bey was a member of POP. In fact, we would have some meetings over at her house.

There was a perception that only men could go to the Million Man March even though the official line is that was never the policy. But there was a perception, even an enunciated perception, that only men could go. Now POP has always had women in leadership roles. So, when I brought this to the POP meeting and asked them if this was something they wanted to do, and everyone said yes. Fredrica Bey asked what women can do to help the Million Man March. That's when I said, "Let's form a Women in Support of the Million Man March Committee." Fredrica and the other women working with her like Charlotte Munnerlyn and Ayo McMillan, took that committee and created a real vehicle for women to be a part of the March. It was the beginning of turning this committee into an institution and corporation—a legacy. Despite the perception, women by and large not only supported the idea of a Million Man March but played a prominent role in the event.

The media also played a role. At first the media tried to ignore the Million Man March. That was their first strategy.

Then when it became clear that they couldn't ignore it because Farrakhan was going to different cities and holding humongous rallies of forty thousand to sixty thousand people. He was filling up stadiums that sports teams couldn't fill up in Atlanta and Houston. That whole year, he was going from city to city having these huge rallies. They couldn't ignore it anymore, so they rolled out people that would criticize it.

But make no mistake about it, the masses of people were with the Million Man March and with Farrakhan. This march touched something deep within Black people. That's what drove people, including Black ministers that would have ignored it because it was the idea and creation of the Nation of Islam. They couldn't ignore it because their own congregations were saying our church needs to send a bus to the Million Man March. Keep in mind: the majority of people that went to the Million Man March were not Islamic. In the end, close to two million Black people converged on Washington, DC with two hundred and fifty-five buses from our New Jersey coalition roster. Many other buses were from groups that were not part of our coalition. Thousands of men left New Jersey for Washington on trains and the roadways. Altogether, I think as many as sixty thousand to seventy thousand people from New Jersey may have attended the Million Man March.

So, what were the factors behind this mass movement of Black men? Yes, there was police brutality, white racist violence, attacks on affirmative action, Rodney King, but this went beyond that. Yes, there was that O.J. Simpson verdict, but beyond that. Beyond the violence in our communities and the mass media's negative portrayal of the Movement. It transcended all those things. It went right into the heart of Black people's longing. Just the idea that a million Black people could gather together. Sometimes you have to take something that seems so simple. And yes, some people may have been disappointed in what seemed like a million Black people coming together to pray. But you can't take away from the fact that it happened like that and no other organization in the Black community could do it.

Farrakhan told people to go home and adopt Black babies and then adoption rates went up. Farrakhan told people to go back and register to vote and voter registration went up. In fact, Farrakhan may have helped Clinton get re-elected! In New Jersey, we were able to keep things going connected to the Million Man March for the next couple of years. However, it's important to note that the Million Man March was fundamentally complete when the buses came home. There was a basic sense of accomplishment and great success. There is an element of this that transcends material reality. There's a spiritual component. The Million Man March was a spiritual act that had to happen. Black people needed an affirmation of themselves. And once that happened, the main part of it was over. The rest of it was like the Big Bang and the creation of the universe. The Big Bang is it and the rest of the universe is just the particles from the explosion. The Million Man March was like that. The explosion was on that date, October 16, 1995, and everything else was the particles flying out from that.

I couldn't have said this in 1996. I would have said that we tried to make it into a movement, talked about all the activities we tried to have and would have attempted to justify everything we were doing after that. But now, only with the benefit of hindsight, can I look back and say, October 16, 1995, it was done. The main thing to accomplish was bringing a miraculous number of Black people together to be amongst themselves, with themselves, without violence. It was an unmaterialistic moment of brotherhood, sisterhood, and personhood. A deep psychological yearning for Black people to be together. It was a symbolic demonstration that yes, Black humanity can be together.

The particles of that cosmic experience were seen across the country in various ways. In New Jersey, a year later, we tried to harness some of the energy generated from the Million Man March in a March on Trenton with Rev. Reginald Jackson, pastor of St. Matthew AME Church in Orange, as co-chair. We were hoping to get about ten-thousand people to gather and go home eager to mentor, tutor, coach youth sports teams, build low-income housing, raise funds for scholarships and of course, elect politicians that would work for us. We had the largest gathering in Trenton up to that point with seven thousand people. A new Republican governor, Christine Todd Whitman, wanted to come out to address everyone and I told her staffers, no. Whitman was part of the problem. At this point, it had been six years since the *Abbott* case was won and QEA was passed, and all hell broke loose. Six years later, our children are still being cheated out of a thorough and efficient education. The phrase "thorough and efficient" was and still is a part of New Jersey's state constitution in reference to providing an education for all students.

It was so intense that they were talking about amending the constitution to change that phrase. "Thorough and efficient" was really the legal basis for *Abbott*. It was under the Whitman administration that funds that were mandated by the court were cut back for *Abbott* districts. Those districts were supposed to be getting additional funding. I knew we were going to need to do something to get needed attention and focus on this issue. One of the last things we did as a NJ Million Man March Committee was call Black fathers together statewide to take their children to school. Then we called everyone together and announced a fast to draw attention to what we believed was an injustice to our children.

Fifty to one hundred men and women joined me in, taking in only liquids. I fasted for forty days. I would have fasted longer, but on Day 41, my arm went numb and so I went to the doctor. That's when I knew it was time to come off. Though the action did get the attention needed, and money did start to come in, there would be state takeover of Black and Brown districts, placing the state in complete control of funds. In addition, a continual back and forth with ongoing amendments and implementation delays to the school funding formula for many years to come.

The New Jersey Million Man March served its purpose. The contradictions kept it in its space in time. One of the contradictions was the religious contradictions. I think that a lot of people felt that the Muslims were in charge of it, and they couldn't fully participate in something that Muslims directed. And I think too, there was a certain degree, nobody ever said this, but I know if I had been a Black Christian minister and I had to sit and watch the biggest March in the history of the United States called by a Black Muslim, I would feel some kind of way. It was good we were able to work within our common ideology, even if for a moment and remain respectful to the point where when we have to come together again, we know we can.

There was still another contradiction. And that is, the Nation is really more about self-help—building up Black communities from the inside by encouraging Blacks to own property and start businesses. They're about doing things like Fredrica and Women in Support of the Million Man March (WISOMMM, Inc), did. The Nation focuses on accomplishments that are largely tangible. The women of WISOMMM took over a mansion, created office space, turned it into a school, created a hall. They had a vision and they saw it through.

Activist groups like POP have fewer tangibles as we engage in confrontations and protests. Yet these were the kind of protests that were defining the 1990s. I have to say that brothers and sisters from the local mosques have given us support on numerous occasions. The trend that started the decade with the shooting of sixteen-year-old Phillip Pannell and the beating of Rodney King, continued in the form of racial-profiling, the sexual-police assault of Abner Louima and the 41 bullets shot into Amadou Diallo. There would be no relief from issues of police brutality, but I didn't fully realize that yet.

After the Million Man March, I actually thought I might be able to put my life on pause. I wasn't going to quit the Movement but maybe I would reorient myself and not be a primary player. I still had a growing family that was not getting the quality time the rest of the world was getting in abundance. I was studying for an MBA and beginning to focus heavily on the corporate side, trying to be a good worker at a major transit agency.

And then Abner Louima happened.

A lot of people came out to our special meeting at the main branch of the Newark Library on the Abner Louima case.

That's when Steve Hatcher first joined POP. Today Hatcher heads the Plainfield POP branch and he is our membership chair and Field Marshall. He leads membership recruitment as well as the voter registration drives called Empowerment Saturdays. Several other POP members——like Alfreda Daniels, Nat Williams, Tyrone Lockett, Daniel Abdullah, Sharon Hand, Marcella Simadiris, Jimmy White, Brad Ringold, Douglass Tucker, James Simms and Aminifu Williams——diligently set up space on the corner of Broad and Market through much of the year on Saturdays getting voter registrations and recruiting POP members.

In 1997, the thought of what New York police did to Abner Louima, was horrendous. It just ripped your soul to know that something like this could happen in America. Not that these things hadn't happened before. But I think sometimes we can become so unconnected to the past or some of us are just so unaware that when we hear these things, they strike us like it's the first time that such heinous acts have been committed against Black people. But it's not and it's not the worst thing that ever happened. I mean, it was commonplace for white people to castrate a Black man either before, during or after a lynching. It wasn't uncommon to hear that they would cut off a man's genitals and put them in his mouth.

Louima survived with physical and emotional scars he'll carry the rest of his life. He did continue to breathe while other victims of police lynching breathed their last. Amadou Diallo couldn't survive 41 shots.

Nothing pulled me back into the struggle. I turned around and walked back into the thick of it. Because it wouldn't be long before we would see the same kind of senseless police brutality on our own front door reminding us that police brutality is not limited to New York City. It's a national trend, a national emergency but only to those who are the most oppressed.

Earl Faison, still in his twenties with two young children, a fiancée, and a promising music career, would never see his children grow up or realize any of his musical dreams and aspirations. New Jersey's Orange police ended his life and maybe five of them would face a modicum of justice. The Nineties would clearly end the way they began. The last thing you want to do when you are looking toward the millennium is feel as though you are running backwards.

But retrospection can intrude on any forward movement. My mother died in 1998. Just prior to her death, I experienced another period of severe introspection. This was a moment that made me question everything I thought I knew about myself and my very roots. I was turning forty-four and discovering my name at my birth was Anthony Leroy Burton.

INTERLUDE: SUDDENLY, ANTHONY

My life changed dramatically without changing at all on my forty-fourth birthday in 1997. That day, six months before she died, I went to visit my mother at the White House Nursing Home in Orange.

As I was leaving, my mother said: "When you come back, I have something to tell you."

"Well," I said, "don't keep me in suspense! Tell me now."

That's when she shocked me. With the news, in this order:

I was adopted. My birth name was Anthony Leroy Burton. My birth mother, Theresa Burton, had recently visited her in the nursing home, with her brother. I believe that had that visit not happened, this family secret would never have been revealed.

According to my adopted mother, when Theresa Burton was pregnant with me, she was put out by her parents. Lawrence Hamm Sr.'s brother, my Uncle Albert, and his wife, took Theresa in off the street. When Lawrence Sr. and Uncle Albert's father died, Lawrence Sr. and Grayce traveled to Virginia for the funeral. Before heading back to NJ, they stopped off at Albert's house.

"Do you want a baby?" Albert asked Larry and Grayce. They say yes. So just like that — *with Theresa not even there!* — Grayce and Larry take me back to New Jersey on a train. My mother later told me that every time the train stopped, they shook in fear, because they thought the police were going to get on the train and arrest them for kidnapping.

After talking to Theresa, I discovered that Theresa met Grayce and Larry when they arrived. Albert and his wife talked to her about giving me up for adoption. Theresa still was not totally convinced or sure that was what she wanted to do. They then suggested that she take some time to go out and enjoy herself and they would watch the baby. When she returned a few hours later, I was gone. Personal and financial challenges prevented her from going after Grayce and Larry. She liked the couple and thought maybe I would have a better life with them than she could have offered at that time. The pain was immense, but she felt she had to let me go.

Four years later, she would begin searching for me again, even going with her brother to the last known address she had for me, Ridgewood Street in Newark. But by then, I was no longer there.

Somehow, Grayce and Larry obtained a birth certificate for me with my name as Lawrence Hamm, born in Washington DC. This was back in the day when people were born at home, so this is not as unusual as it sounds. I got a Social Security card with the name I know on it.

Interlude: Suddenly, Anthony

So many things were answered by this story. For example, I always wondered why I didn't have brothers. I used to always ask my parents for a brother or sister. I now know it was because my mother couldn't have children. When I needed a duplicate birth certificate after the 1977 fire that burned my family's house to the ground, Columbia Hospital in Washington, DC couldn't find one. On those times when I couldn't get that needed documentation, the 1960 U.S. Census was used to verify my birthplace, age, etc.

I have talked to my birth mother several times over the years. My assumption was that no one in our family told her where Grayce and Larry took me. I have found out many things about her. One of the most important is that she was a prominent local activist in Washington, DC. The pictures she has in that Washington, DC senior citizens complex apartment, photo-ops with government officials, plaques — Man, talk about genetics!

We began to meet, and I began to listen. As I write this, she is still alive — in her early 80s. She told me that at certain points in her life, she wanted to find me. She said she even contacted the Make-a-Wish Foundation once. It's very clear that she loves me. These conversations can sometimes be difficult, because try as she might, we can't pick up where we left off because we never started. Often, she cries over the lost time, the lost love. There's little I can do at these moments: I respect her, and I am her son biologically, but forty-four years is a long time. By the time we met, I was married to Michelle and Laini, my oldest child, was an adult. My second child, Nia was a teen and my third child, Imani was in elementary school. I'm happy to say that my daughters are happy to see and treat her as their grandmother. One of our sticking points is that she has not told me who my birth father is. All she has told me is that she suspected he was involved in some illegal activities and might have been shot and killed. That's it.

After recovering from the shock, I asked my mother, Grayce, the obvious question: Why didn't you tell me this before now?

"Because I thought you would stop loving me," she said.

I said, "Ma, I will never stop loving you."

She died the following August.

So, at forty-four, firmly into middle age, I now found myself with a trilogy of names: Lawrence Hamm Jr., given to me by my adoptive parents; Anthony Leroy Burton, given to me by my birth mother, and Adhimu Changa, my chosen name, given to me by Amiri Baraka. It seems like it took a village to name me. But I know who I am, and the Ancestors know, too.

1990S-2000S: POLICE FORCED: THE CASE OF EARL FAISON

By the late 1990s, everything had settled into a groove. I was an administrator in the public service industry. Michelle and I were married more than sixteen years, and our two daughters were growing up too fast. We had moved out of Newark and were homeowners in Montclair. The POP had become established in Newark and in the parts of Essex County surrounding it.

The year was 1999. All around the world, people were contemplating the future. Were the United States and the West now at, as historians had begun to write in those pre-911, pre-ISIS days, the end of history? The end of history was a concept in which society would reach a place where human life continues indefinitely into the future without any further major changes in society, system of governance or economics.

The collapse of the Soviet Union had forced many in the Movement to chart new directions for social justice without the Cold War. It looked like a great time to divert funds that were going to a defunct armament program toward peace initiatives like better health care, ending poverty, education. Yet, the worldwide revolt against capitalism and the Third World bloc against Western imperialism didn't turn out the way that any of us thought.

Many of the Baby Boomer activists, those who thought and knew worldwide revolution was near two decades ago, were now well into middle age. The Black Power Movement was a chapter in some history books. Apartheid South Africa was another chapter. I was forty-four. My *nom de guerre*, Adhimu Changa, meaning "Important Youth," represented a time when I had my youth. However, my youth was gone. I was recuperating from a torn ligament in my leg, so I was no longer running marathons or running at all. I had been a vegetarian for nine years, so I was still trying to be health conscious. Time had begun to stretch out, become slower.

But there was always something to do, particularly when it came to POP. The group's cohesion, hard-won after sixteen years of organizing, had dividends. The members began to understand each other and operate as much as a family as a close-knit group of activists. Our community teach-ins and commemorations of Malcolm X and Martin Luther King — just to name three annual activities — became established, anticipated community events. Mass incarcerations, education parity and police reform were issues we kept in the forefront. Getting our press releases and pictures in the newspapers was no longer a struggle. We had significant access to Rutgers-Newark, churches, and other city institutions. In short, everything had begun to work like clockwork, the impending year 2000 and its threatening zeroes be damned. We had serenity of purpose.

Then, in April of 1999, a Black policewoman, Joyce Carnegie, was shot in the head and stomach by an armed robbery suspect in Orange, one of the many townships that surround Newark. In response, police departments in the county went on a blue rampage, looking specifically for bald Black men. The rumor on the street was that the police wanted the head of Carnegie's killer on a platter. Authorities picked up three Black men for the crime — Terrance Everett, James "Malik" Coker and Earl Faison.

Everett and Earl Faison were beaten by police. Faison, a twenty-seven-year-old father of four who had ambitions to be a hip hop music producer, died in a hospital after only forty-five minutes in police custody on April 11, 1999, three days after Carnegie's death. He had fled from the taxi he was a passenger in when police asked for identification. Faison, who was not bald but had a record, was innocent of the Carnegie murder. Another man, Condell Woodson, would eventually confess. Police said Faison also had a nine mm handgun. Although he was a severe asthmatic — the police took his inhaler from him. He was handcuffed, beaten, robbed and then pepper-sprayed in the nose and mouth at point-blank range, triggering a seizure caused by his suffocation. They never found a gun. The Orange Police Department, no different from any other police department confronted with the issue of police brutality, denied any wrongdoing, and tried to keep it business-as-usual. One of the at least nine officers involved in Faison's arrest was up for promotion.

POP was about to change in permanent and powerful ways because of the Faison tragedy. History, as it turned out, showed no sign of disappearing. It's not like POP had never been part of police-brutality demonstrations. We had constantly crossed the river over the New York police-brutality cases of Amadou Diallo, Abner Louima, and others. We and other activist organizations in New Jersey had been having demonstrations as far back as 1990, when 15-year-old Phillip Pannell, was shot by the Teaneck police. Then in 1997, Danette "Strawberry" Daniels, a thirty-one-year-old young Black woman, was shot in the head and killed by the Newark police. An activist group known as the Black Nia Force, led by a young Newark activist-schoolteacher named Ras Baraka, was in the forefront there. In Northern New Jersey, we are bombarded with New York City's news. So much so, that what happens in New York City feels like a local event. In fact, we publicly mourned the acquittal of the official involved in Diallo's death while struggling for Faison.

DeLacey Davis was head of a group called Black Cops Against Police Brutality. Davis told me he had been inspired to be an activist when he heard me speak at Arts High in the early 1970s. Davis had risen to the rank of sergeant in East Orange and formed his activist group to be a community check against police aggression and to give officers a voice to talk to the community. He introduced us to Faison's family.

And I want to say this about Davis. As difficult as it is to talk about police brutality in today, it was much harder in the 1980s and 1990s. I have a great deal of respect for him, because his outspokenness affected his police career. After many years on the force, he lost his rank due to his activism, even after the community appealed to the East Orange mayor who had been the subject of Davis' remarks and incurred the mayor's ire. There were also appeals made to the city council to no avail.

Davis gave me the phone number for Faison's father, Earl Williams. He and the family met with POP and talked about how Earl had been beaten and how an excessive amount of tear gas had been used on his asthmatic son. In that first conversation, he shared the image of viewing the body and seeing a footprint on his son's head. This was the beginning of an association between the Faison family and POP that spanned several years.

Police Forced: The Case of Earl Faison

Faison was killed on April 11. Three days later, POP organized its first Faison demonstration with about two hundred people outside of Orange Police Headquarters. We were careful about this because we didn't want to be accused of ambulance chasing. I remember an incident that occurred before Faison. A Black woman in Newton, New Jersey, was assaulted by a white racist. Because we hadn't contacted the family, we didn't go. I had regrets about that, but we as an organization, decided that we would be involved only if invited by the grieving family.

Even with the family's permission, we had some debate over whether to have the protest that day, because it was the same day as the wake for police officer Carnegie. She was a person who had roots in Essex County. When she was killed, many were outraged—and it wasn't just police. Carnegie was well respected in the community. There was a lot of sympathy for Carnegie and her family, but when somebody in that POP meeting said that "a life not in a police uniform is worth just as much as a life in a blue uniform," that ended the debate. Those who wanted the demonstration on April 14th won by a very slim margin. And the way it worked out was that the wake was early enough for me to personally go. I went to the Carnegie wake before the demonstration, personally balancing the community's various feelings.

We were demonstrating at the police station, and the police director, Richard Conte, called me upstairs to speak to him. He talked to me in a very causal way. He said, "Mr. Hamm, this kid was not a victim of police brutality."

Earl Faison was twenty-seven years old and had two children at the time. He was far from a kid. This was the mentality in which we were dealing. I asked, *If he was not a victim of police brutality, then, what was he a victim of?* Crickets could be heard.

I went downstairs and the demonstration continued. R.D. Strong, then POP's Vice-chair was on the front stairs, holding the POP banner saying, "Stop Police Brutality." He was joined by many others including Joe Fortunato, an activist-attorney. Earl Williams was speaking on the bullhorn. Williams told us then that there was going to be an independent investigation and autopsy into his son's death: "The truth will come out and hopefully, justice will be served." By November of that year, Conte resigned reportedly over a dispute between then— Mayor Mims Hackett and him over officer promotions.

That demonstration was important. But it was the next one— on May 1st—that was most profound. Because, for the first time in POP history, we demonstrated in police crosshairs, openly under the barrels of guns. There we were, in all of our predominantly Black power with some very conscious white friends of the struggle: POP, The New Jersey Coalition Against Police Brutality, Black Cops Against Police Brutality, The Newark Coalition for Neighborhoods, The Black Ministers Council of New Jersey, Women in Support of the Million Man March and the Nation of Islam's Muhammad's Mosque number 25.

We marched from the police headquarters to the Board of Education building on Main Street in Orange. I can never forget how when we turned onto Main Street, the police had sharp shooters on all the roofs of the buildings, especially and including the U.S. Post Office. I was just thinking, *how they got their guns pointed on innocent people trying to get justice for an innocent person killed by them. Shouldn't they be arresting and training their guns on the people that killed Carnegie and Faison?*

Police Forced: The Case of Earl Faison

In those early demonstrations, we had support from 99.5 WBAI-FM, the Pacifica station in New York City. WBAI would announce our actions. This time, it was New Yorkers who crossed the river to join us. Even Reverend Al Sharpton came to speak at one of our demonstrations.

I remember two things about those rallies. First, there were a lot of young people at those early demonstrations because Faison's family, and its circle of friends, was quite large. Second, POP had begun to make the large police brutality victim banners it's now known for; the Faison banner R.D. held is one of our oldest.

It is now commonplace everywhere for people to demonstrate against police brutality. But in those days, even though we had those notorious cases like Louima and like Diallo, keep in mind that a lot of that was in New York City. (Of course, the Rodney King case in Los Angeles was a huge and historic exception.) In New Jersey, there were only a handful of organizations that were conducting ongoing anti-police brutality work. POP was one of them.

There were as many tensions as opinions. The 1997 shooting of Dannette "Strawberry" Daniels by a Newark police officer had hundreds of South Ward residents, led by Black Nia Force, march out of the ward to downtown. Salaam Ishmial had his group, the National United Youth Council, based in Elizabeth. Wilbur Kornegay was a stalwart activist with his own group from the South Ward, and he seemed to be at every demonstration we had or joined.

POP members used their long-term mobilization skills well during this period. Marion Pitts, Brother Nello Ramsey, Brother

Roosevelt Hobbs, Debbie Brown, Gladys "Ayo" McMillan, and Jan Cheema would call one hundred and twenty-five people in one night if asked to do so.

Part of the reason that there had been such a debate about how to respond to the Carnegie murder within POP was because of the anti-violence sentiment in the community at the time. POP had our first rally against drugs, crime, and violence in 1993. This was the *other* violence in the community: the civilian-on-civilian violence. We had our first rally on those topics at Deliverance Church on Springfield Avenue in Irvington in 1993. This anti-violence sentiment was strong. And probably in places like Newark, it was probably stronger than the anti-police brutality sentiment, because the notorious police-brutality cases were happening in New York. These incidents of civilian-on-civilian violence were happening in New Jersey, but they were not blasted across the New York tri-state area by television and radio. New Jersey 12, the state's twenty-four-hour cable news station, was still in its infant stages during much of the 1990s.

But I have to be honest here. Another conflict was the fact that, in the early stages of the Faison case, very few ministers and elected officials wanted to publicly criticize the police. There were not a lot of elected officials on our side. Sixty letters would go out asking for their involvement, and three would come back. Sharpe James, the mayor who had ousted Gibson in 1986, even once tried to stop POP from having a march for Rodney King. When Mayor James couldn't stop it, he joined it. As he went along, James even came close to creating a civil police review board after the Strawberry Daniels shooting. So, as the 1990s was nearing its close, there was much room for growth.

Police Forced: The Case of Earl Faison

Murder is defined by state statute. Essex County did not bring any indictments against the officers that killed Faison. The county prosecutor, a representative of the state attorney general, was not going to pursue the case. We continued to press. We never let the state go. We wrote letters. We made phone calls. We even had meetings in Trenton with the assistant state attorney general. The state never brought any charges against the officers who killed Earl Faison, and it said it wasn't going to bring any charges.

We communicated with the family. We joined the family and demanded that the federal government come in and investigate this case. The feds responded affirmatively on the investigation. We were pleased, but we knew that federal involvement would not result in a murder charge; With the state refusing to file murder charges, the feds were left investigating for civil rights violations. The feds carried out an investigation that lasted more than a year. Robert J. Cleary, U.S. Attorney for the state of New Jersey, announced the resulting indictment of five officers on June 22, 2000 — the same week that would have been Earl Faison's twenty-ninth birthday.

It was the regional medical examiner for the federal government that announced the results of his autopsy. Three autopsies done, and the third got it right. That examiner said that Earl Faison died in a "stairwell of torture." (Later, Dr. Mark Flomenbaum, an assistant medical examiner in New York City, would testify, "Mr. Faison would still be alive today if it had not been for the catastrophic event and I say this within a reasonable degree of medical certainty.") The state didn't even convene a grand jury.

The news and its public aftermath carried serious consequences. People were fired (like Patricia Hurt, the first Black woman to be Essex County Prosecutor), and resigning, like Conte, but justice was slow in coming. Only five people were indicted. A Black reporter for *The Star-Ledger*, Kevin Dilworth, was the first to ask me why only five when so many more were involved. *Why only five when there were so many other hands doing things? Like the night that Faison was killed, they came in and cleaned up the car, removing the seat from the car he was beat in, and wiped up the blood. That's called tampering with evidence. What about the arresting officers that covered up for the officers that brutally beat and kicked Faison before and after he was in the car handcuffed?* Later, Officer Jackson, who is Black, would testify that his supervising officer was beating Faison so bad that he had to pull him off Faison by the belt, and the force of that pull, threw both on the ground. It was clear that the new acting police director, Don Wactor, was pretty sure that most of his department would be indicted in some way when he approached the Orange City Council requesting additional appropriations to hire more officers because of "imminent manpower shortages." Wactor anticipated federal indictments of up to twelve officers in his department. But we were not letting this get swept under the rug. What happened in Jersey would not stay in Jersey. The state's Attorney's Office got involved. The criminal case was argued by US Attorneys Patty Schwartz and Rafael Valentin.

The Faison family had two attorneys, while the police officers — Lt. Thomas Smith, his brother, Brian Smith, Andrew Garth, Tyrone Payton and Paul Carpinteri Jr. — had five attorneys. Each of the five charged had an attorney — a total of five white attorneys. It looked like a damn football team sitting over there. And guess who the lead attorney was for the five? Michael

Chertoff, who becomes the first U.S. Director of Homeland Security after 9-11.

We believed the fix was in already. The all-white jury was sworn in on Halloween, so we sighed, knowing it was all tricks and no treats. Then one of the jurors became sick and was replaced by a Black alternate. We prayed, but we didn't hold our breath.

I attended the trial almost every day. Not all day long, but I came in on my lunch breaks during work as well as after work. I took several vacation days to be in that courtroom, particularly on days witnesses were called. Fred Wright, who updated POP about the trial, was retired, so he attended the trial every day.

I was there for most of the key testimonies. Every time I entered the courtroom I was struck by the stark racial segregation. All Black on one side, mostly white on the other, with the judge seated in the middle of history.

Calm ruled. No protests in the courtroom during the entire trial. Or outside because we thought it was too important for us not to witness. The bottom line: family had confidence in the U.S. attorney, and we had confidence in the family. I think the family's respect for the attorneys and for the process shaped how the community who came out in support of them responded. The family set the standard for everyone else. For instance, family members walked out of the courtroom when they were overcome with emotion.

Carmen Espichan may have been the difference between guilt and innocence. She was Latina and a resident on the street where the police stopped and beat Faison. The police did not know she was watching them at the scene. Espichan turned out to be a late-Nineties version of smartphone video. She had been contacted twice by the FBI. The first time she was contacted by the Bureau, she said she wouldn't testify, didn't want anything to do with it. But the second time, they convinced her to testify. She came in the courtroom nine months pregnant. She was so large, there had to be concerns that she would give birth right there in the courtroom. Her painful detail of how Earl was beat down, thrown on the ground, validated all our work. Her next words caused a big gasp in the courtroom. Espichan said one of the officers backed up to the fence — he was about maybe twenty or feet from it — and he ran and kicked his head like he was kicking a soccer ball. *My God.* She said he kicked him in the head so hard that his whole body came up off the ground. That's before they took him to the police station before they put him in the car. That was the first of three collective courtroom gasps I will never forget. The second gasp was when the judge asked her why she didn't testify after the FBI had asked her several times. She said, "I didn't want to get involved in it. I had a daughter. I didn't want what happened to him to happen to us."

The jury tended not to show emotion. I certainly didn't hear any sounds from its racial majority. That's why we thought — we *knew* — the verdict would be not guilty. Instead, the verdict was *guilty* on all counts. Third gasp. The officers' lawyers were so stunned they asked for each jurors' individual verdict, and it was unanimous. A victory in a nation that couldn't convict the police who murdered Diallo. This was something out of *"Perry Mason" or "Law and Order"* — in fact, it was wilder than both.

The newspapers, including and especially *The Star-Ledger*, had to take what we had been saying all along seriously. I remember us being in front of the courthouse, answering reporters' questions. My only regret is that we didn't have POP's "Justice for Earl Faison" banner.

We felt vindicated, but we still didn't feel like it was complete justice because they were convicted on civil rights violations and conspiracy, not murder. They were convicted in December. So, I'm driving down Route 280 in May of 2001. I got a call from a reporter asking me, "What do you think of what U.S District Judge Lifland did?"

"What did he do?" I asked. "He overturned the verdict." Lifland decided to throw out the conspiracy charges against the five. I didn't even know at that time that a judge could do that. I thought that the jury's decision was the final determination of the case. And the first word we got was that the U.S. Attorney's Office was not going to appeal.

The officers didn't come to the sentencing. The verdicts were overturned before they could get to the sentencing. The judge used some technicality to overcome the jury verdict. *Bullshit*. Not only were they not going to get jail time, but a couple of them thought they might get their jobs back.

The appeal was happening, but the case was moved to the Third Circuit Court in Philadelphia. Philadelphia! More than two hours away from Newark. It was time to march. We were not thwarted. We rented buses and marched in Philadelphia, banners held tight, in front. Almost another year passed. We took two busloads of people to fill up the courtroom every day. The judges knew what was going on, because I know it's not every trial where they look out in the courtroom and view a sea of Black faces. Even though we weren't at the moment of justice, that was one of our proudest moments.

One of the people there with me was Nello. He was a member of POP and one of my closest friends. I think he carried the red- black-and-green flag when we marched over the Ben Franklin bridge into Philly because we didn't go straight to Philly. We went to Camden and told the buses to meet us at the courthouse. Then we marched over the Ben Franklin Bridge.

Our ability to put people in that courtroom really made us feel effective. The fact that they tried to move this outside of our sphere of influence to somewhere outside of our grassroots did not work; we would not be denied. We filled that courtroom on workdays. It wasn't just us, but it made me know we had a strong organization.

The 3rd U.S. Circuit Court of Appeals reinstated the guilty verdicts in June of 2002 citing that Lifland had erred when he threw out the convictions. We certainly were jubilant, even though there wasn't a lot of fanfare about it. We had won at the district court level, and we won the appeals level. It had taken more than three years to get to this point. It would take two more years for the actual sentencing and an additional year before any of the officers would be behind bars. Now that the ball was kicked back to Lifland's court for sentencing, he wasn't hearing it: no more shenanigans.

One of the things I remember most about that day was what Lifland said specifically about Orange Detective Keith Jackson, the Black officer who broke ranks to give his version of what happened the night Faison died. Jackson was the first of several officers to come forward after initially lying to the federal investigators. His reward was constant death threats. Lifland felt the need to publicly warn everyone that if anything happened to any of the witnesses, the perpetrators would be found and persecuted to the full extent of the law. Of course, Jackson was subsequently fired from the police department along with Detective Anthony Tortorella, the second to speak out. I used to see Jackson in downtown Newark, near where I worked. He had to be surrounded by FBI officers who were providing round-the-clock protection. Jackson had quoted a conversation with a defendant, in which Jackson was told, "I'm so hooked on this lie, I don't know what the truth is."

True over Blue.

The short life and tragic killing of Earl Faison changed POP permanently. Two months after Faison was killed, the family of Stanton Crew came to a POP meeting. Crew was shot twenty-seven times on the New Jersey Turnpike by state troopers. By January of 2000 we were marching for Max Antoine, a victim of police brutality in Irvington. POP was becoming a go-to-space to deal with New Jersey police brutality cases. After 9-11 and our anti-Iraq invasion protests, we continued and expanded our coalition forces with groups like the Frontline Artists, The New Black Panther Party, Million Man Montclair, Communications Workers of America (CWA) and Service Employees International Union.

The coalitions resulted in larger demonstrations. The Trayvon Martin demonstration was larger than any of our Faison demonstrations, yet there was something about the Faison tragedy. The impact was deeper. It's like the difference between a topical application on your arm and an intramuscular injection. Faison was like an intramuscular injection: it didn't cover as much area topically, but the impact was greater. We went with less trepidation into other police brutality cases because of our

Faison experience. In the last twenty years, there have been at least twenty-five cases in which POP has been involved post-Faison. Every Monday for more than four years, a vigil/protest is held in front of the Newark Federal Building to remember Jerame Reid, Jahqui Graham, Kashad Ashford and Abdul Wakil M. Kamal - all New Jersey victims of police brutality and lack of justice. Shelia Reid and her companion Muneer Muhammad are there with banners and posters in hand consistently and through all kinds of weather, remembering her son Jerame. We've worked with other groups in New Jersey like the National Awareness Alliance. The founder and chair, Walter Hudson has supported the Reid family while fighting for the family of Darryl DeRose Laqua Fuqua, who was gunned down while by Bridgeton police officers.

Earl Faison taught us. We learned how difficult it is to get justice within the criminal justice system. It is very difficult to convict police. There are all kinds of ways to subvert the system. Money. Having the state on their side — police are officers of the state — means they can, and do, routinely escape the same punishments that regular citizens would get. Every once in a blue moon, somebody in blue is convicted. This is why, credited or not, struggle is imperative.

We were overwhelmed by the evidence of criminal guilt, and so we were upset that this substitute-for-a-criminal trial stopped short of saying that Earl Faison was murdered by state-sponsored thugs in a dim stairwell of a police station. Those officers did not go to jail for murder. They went to jail for civil rights violations and conspiracy. The difference was apparent. Four of them, Tyrone Payton, Andrew Garth, newly retired Lt. Thomas Smith, and Paul Carpinteri, *each got only thirty-three months*. Brian Smith, the younger brother of Thomas Smith who sprayed the pepper spray into Faison's face, jump-starting his seizure and subsequent death from it, was sentenced to nine years. Lifland reduced his sentence to seven years. I remember telling the news media that the now-former officers "were afforded considerations that the average citizen never would have received." As a result, we consider the Faison matter to be a cold case. We believe that like the murder of Emmett Till, no one paid the price for either of their deaths.

During the four years the Faison case dragged on, the Faison family was a POP fixture. We were in constant contact with Earl Williams. He and Sagirah Williams were our main contacts with the family. Our time with Carolyn Faison was short in that she died a year after her son died. She was sick at the time of his death, but I don't think she would have died so soon had he not been killed. It was just too much for her.

We didn't make any moves without checking with the family first. From the beginning, we saw this as their struggle, not ours. We were behind them, not in front. We were a known quantity, and we used my familiarity with the news media to their advantage.

These protests always follow a pattern. After a death, there is an upsurge in participation. But most people come into struggle jaded, so when things don't happen rapidly, disappointment and disillusionment set in. And then they fall back.

In our work here in New Jersey, some families just went by the wayside because they just didn't have the energy or the wherewithal to keep it up. There are situations where families can't get to the finish line because they disintegrate in the process. Sometimes our people experienced grief at a level where they just can't go forward anymore. We've had families that didn't want a protest because their lawyers tell family members to not say anything because public statements might hurt the case.

The Faison family was not like this. They are a Sunni Muslim family who understood the Civil Rights and Black Power movements. They understood the power of steadfast faith and militant works. That family was prepared for struggle. It was not a good thing that their son died, but I don't think there could've been a better family to carry that ball across the goal line of justice. They were determined they would fight to the end. Earl Williams attended the protests after his leg was amputated. We would just call him, and he'd come and speak. He showed up with one leg. I loved that brother. We struggled side by side.

The Williams family, like so many in Black America, we're working class. This translates to being one or two paychecks away from homelessness, one paycheck away from destitution. I don't know what the financial situation was for the Williams family when burying Faison. But I do know that many families are strained with the cost of burial when their child is suddenly taken from them. And then attending the funeral viewing the body of that person, that person's face, you recognize—how devastating that must be. That one whole circle of life completed while others permanently broken. Faison's life and sudden death has long-lasting, personal impact that is off camera. Because Earl was killed, his kids grew up without a father. In December 2017, Earl Williams passed away while months earlier, Mikki Wilkins, the mother of Faison's children, had already died of cancer. The ripple effect that these events have, the dysfunctions amplified- are all off-screen.

Police Forced: The Case of Earl Faison

The strength of the Faison-Williams family — its determination to get justice, its ability to go the whole way without falling apart, and its willingness to let others in, to share their grief and to fight alongside them for justice — were critical in winning those cases.

I don't want to over-emphasize the role of activism. It was particularly important that the Williams family had strong, competent legal representation. Our role was to help create an atmosphere where it was possible to obtain a conviction of the officers involved in the murder of Earl Faison. I believe the following to this day: if there hadn't been a whole lot of protests around Earl's death, the state would have swept it under the rug because they didn't even bring charges. Without the protests, I doubt that the U.S. attorney would have taken the case further. There was too much anger in the community to ignore it. It couldn't be covered up. That anger made those in power say: *We've got to take a look at this.* Because it stank from the beginning.

More than twenty years have now passed, and POP is still calling for the Faison case to be reopened as a homicide. When I think about the case, I think of Sagirah Williams, who was always quiet but right on point when she did speak. "We will not rest until authorities reconsider the evidence surrounding the death of our son while he was in police custody on April 11, 1999, and then pursue murder indictments." The State Attorney General's office in Trenton, has not announced any plans to pursue a murder indictment against the five officers.

A LUTA CONTINUA: 381 DAYS-PLUS OF UNWRITTEN HISTORY

Mr. Hamm, this is your life. That's what I felt like when I was sitting at the National Education Association Human Rights Award Dinner in July of 2016. I was being awarded the Martin Luther King Memorial Award. My biological mother, Theresa Burton, was sitting next to me in a ballroom with hundreds of people watching my life on these jumbo screens. The event was in DC, where she lived, and I felt it right for her to be there. She had been somewhat of an activist herself in her day. I knew she'd want to be there.

Images of POP — in their bold gold (our name for our T-shirts) and coalition groups, standing on the corner of Springfield Avenue and Market Street holding up the six-foot black and white banners we had become known for — flashed across the huge screens. Three hundred and eighty-one days. That's how long we were determined to stand on that corner mobilizing with a number of other organizations in coalition.

The "new" POP — now being referred to in the news media as a "human rights watchdog group," now getting calls from media about our activities, instead of us always doing the calling — started having multi-day protests. Forty-one days straight, one demonstration went in 2000, to highlight the forty-one bullets shot into Amadou Diallo. We extended that demonstration to forty-five days for the forty-five minutes Faison was in the police station before being killed. More than ten years later, we would take it to another level.

I watched the myriad of scenes with the knowledge that this award was not for me. It was for everyone who knew the battle was still in its throes and the war was far from won. It was for those who thought it not robbery to take days and hours from their lives to remember those whose lives were unjustly taken or forever changed. It was for everyone who understood and accepted the importance of history's unwritten words, sharp symbolism and often-painful mandate.

How did we come up with the idea? We dedicate a portion of the POP meeting each month to "This Month In History." We can't push forward unless we understand where we come from. So, on December 1, 2010, we remembered Rosa Parks. It wasn't the first time we poured over the significance of Rosa Parks within the framework of the Modern Civil Rights Movement. We gave context to the struggle by inviting Claudette Colvin, the high school student who was arrested nine months before Rosa Parks for refusing to give up her seat in Montgomery, Alabama. Colvin was actually one of five plaintiffs that filed the first federal court case by civil rights attorney Fred Gray, challenging segregation on the buses. We examined the intensity of a 381-day boycott and its place in the protracted struggle for integration and human rights. The death of Emmett Till was the spark, but the steady burn came with decisive clarity that Jim Crow was on its deathbed, and it was time to speed things along.

A Luta Continua: 381 Days-Plus of Unwritten History

We study history so that we can learn from it, and we question our own fortitude. We constantly ask critical questions of ourselves, debate each other sometimes. So, the question before the body now was: do we have what it takes to create a movement in the Obama era? Do we really understand that sustained change takes place only over the course of a protracted struggle?

Could we start a movement surrounding the issues that needed to be addressed in a time when people were so relaxed? In some quarters of Black America, there was a low murmur of sustained satisfaction. To many, President Barack Obama represented our dream come true, a landmark that gaged the distance we had come as a people and a country. Many of us were suddenly blind to the fact that there were still real issues that had to be addressed. Not to mention that ever present knee on the neck of Black people clearly did not exclude our Black President. Obama ran and won on the promise of change. What could have been a transformative movement appeared stymied on every front. We were on the verge of losing the US, Senate and didn't know it because we were blinded by the Black shadow of the White House. People who saw the Presidential election as the most important would soon be proven indelibly wrong.

It had become clear that we would have to demand the transformation we needed. The minimum wage was, and still is, not a living wage. The Affordable Care Act had just been signed into law in March and though it didn't go far enough, it was still lambasted by the right for going too far. Instead of troops coming home, there was now a build-up in Afghanistan. And racism, police brutality—none of it vanished with the presence of a Black family on Pennsylvania Avenue. If anything, it became more pronounced. It was Dr. King who said, "With each modest advance, the white population promptly raises the argument that the Negro has come far enough. Each step forward accents an ever-present tendency to backlash."

This was as good a time as ever to create a movement. Obama would need help, a groundswell to push forth a more progressive agenda. It was becoming clear that the transformational leader we thought we had put in office was more status quo than we had bargained for.

So, all of that brought us to that moment of December 2010, at our regular meeting place at Abyssinian Baptist Church. We determined to turn an abstract history lesson into a concrete transformative tool, daily, from 4 p.m. to 6 p.m., for 381 days straight—a homage to the length of the Montgomery protest.

This was quite an undertaking; one we knew that we could not do alone. We formed committees, created a coalition of local grassroots organizations, religious groups, and unions. We met initially at the Rutgers Paul Robeson Center and then regularly at Bethany Baptist Church, where Dr. Howard was still pastor.

Our "381 Days for Jobs, Peace, Equality and Justice" was launched in February 2011. This was the symbolic protest in which we were now invested. It would not only memorialize the days that the Montgomery Bus Boycott lasted but it would bring more than one hundred and seventy-three organizations together with one collective voice. We could not be ignored.

Ingrid Hill oversaw the registration list composed of each organization that signed up for specific days and weeks to join us. Organizations that came out regularly were the NAACP's

Newark, Irvington and Oranges and Maplewood branches, Nation of Islam Muhammad Mosque no. 25, American Civil Liberties Union of New Jersey, Black is Back Coalition, Newark Education Workers Caucus, Newark Anti Violence Coalition, The New Black Panther Party, NOW-New Jersey Branch, New Jersey Jericho Movement, New Jersey State Industrial Union Council/Solidarity Singers and the Veterans for Peace UFCW Local 108. These were Ingrid's A teams. Her B and C teams came out less frequently, but they committed to times. Those groups included The Newark Teachers' Association, the NTU and a number of other local unions, churches and grassroots organizations. Each group was given an opportunity to present their platform, which was always in line with jobs, peace, equality, and justice.

POP's Brad Carlton, Keith Martin, Aminifu Williams, Ingrid Hill and I were there most every day. As POP Chairperson, I had to be there every day unless something pressing came up. I know that people are motivated by example. And then there was the added incentive of media coverage. The last thing you'd want is for the media to show up at an event and the head of the organization is missing in action. The media didn't come all the time, but they would pop up here and there. There may have been a couple of occasions when I had to speak out of the state and could not be there, but with those exceptions. Most every day after work you would find me at the corner of Springfield Ave and Market Street.

But the average protester didn't show up holding up banners, signs and fists expecting to get their pictures, names, or quotes in the newspaper. There was no paycheck nor fame, no chance for egotism, no visible incentive or gain. Yet, in the spirit of our historic homage, they were still there. That was amazing for me to see. We were making a people's history that, decades later, maybe only we would acknowledge and remember.

Other members that would be out there before I was to make sure that people had whatever they were supposed to have. I would bring the banners and sound system. Ingrid was out there with literature, posters, sign-up sheets, and voter registration forms.

The regulars did important tasks. Doug Tucker, an old friend track runner from my high school days, diligently posted flyers everywhere. He was also the one who brought current event news clippings to the meetings. When POP got coverage, Doug had the clipping at the meeting.

Brandon Rippey, a Science Park High history teacher, union activist and head of the Newark Education Workers Caucus, would be there every Friday and often with his students.

Ninety-year-olds Henry and Mary Shoiket showed up most Fridays. Some might say Henry's penchant for running with more radical groups spans back to his days at the City University of New York participating in several months of meetings with the Young Communist League along with Julius Rosenberg. Henry and Mary would often get rides from a couple of other members to get to the POP meetings. However, often they would take a bus from Bergen County to Newark to participate in the marches and demonstrations even if they couldn't stay the entire time. Their small frames would stand holding the signs there and years later at the Justice Monday marches and the wind at times would almost look like it would blow them over. But they stood strong. And when they were ready, they would get back on the bus and head back to Bergen.

Charlie Hall from the Retailer Workers brought his people out. The Verizon workers were striking, and they came out to support us. We in turn, marched down the street to protest in front of the Verizon building.

Bethany Baptist Church used part of the celebration of their one-hundred-and-fortieth anniversary by marching the congregation to the protest, holding up signs and banners. That was one of our largest turnouts.

We held the signs and banners while others distributed literature. Being in the intersection of Springfield Avenue and Market Street, traffic was heavy, and people got to know us. With our megaphones and sound equipment, we educated and made noise. And we expected everyone who saw us to practice making noise as well, even if it was just honking their horns. And so that happened across the spectrum—regular folks, public service workers, bus drivers, it didn't matter. People pulled out their smart phones to take pictures and threw up their fist – "Power to the People."

Through rain, sleet, snow, cold and holidays. We would not miss a day –even if we did not stay the full two hours, we were there.

Oh my God, I remember one day it rained like hell and the wind was so strong that you couldn't bring an umbrella. I tried but the wind turned my umbrella inside out. People still came out and stood out in the rain.

I was never out there alone. There were times when we had meetings and events that we had to get to so we might

A Life in the Struggle

have shortened it so that we could get to the Black History event, support Verizon workers in their strike, meetings related to the struggle or other POP program. But we didn't miss a day.

We ended that protest officially in July on the day of the celebration of the Newark Rebellion. We marched from Springfield Avenue and Market Street up to the Rebellion Memorial on fifteenth Avenue and Springfield Avenue. However, there was a contingent of POP members that wanted to go beyond the almost 400 days we had protested at that point. Brother Aminifu was on that side. He understood better than most any of us what protracted struggle looked like because he lived through the history. He was in the audience the day Malcolm X made the statement about the "chickens coming home to roost," after Kennedy's assassination. He was part of the first Kwanzaa celebration in California with Maulana Karenga. He's been to Africa numerous times and proudly wears his African garb, beads and red, black and green scarf. At the time, he had to be in his seventies, and he was determined he was going to be out there holding out the signs if he was the only one there. He was not. Some of the POP members voted that any member that wanted to continue could. It was election time, so some thought it a good idea to stay there through the coming election. And we did. So, we went well over the 381 days we had intended.

Back at the NEA event, I looked over at My Mom and realized that she probably had not seen any of the images flashing on the screen. So much of my history had been robbed by circumstance from her, so it was good for her to see my public highlights.

She had followed much of what I did as best as she could from Washington DC. However, New Jersey news is not often national news. The New York media shadow again. They're showing pictures from the Million People March for Peace and Justice in 2015. We didn't expect to get a million people but with the coalition-building we built on, we had over one-hundred groups represented including the various unions, church groups, the Masons and Eastern Stars, fraternities and sororities. Thousands of people came out making it the largest demonstration we had ever held.

It was Dr. King who said that a movement that moves only people is merely a revolt. A movement that changes both people and institutions is a revolution. The justice system was and still is in need of major surgery.

The U.S. Department of Justice was called upon by the ACLU and Newark Communities for Accountable Policing to come into Newark and investigate their police department. They opened the investigation in 2011. On July 22, 2014, the DOJ published their findings. The agency revealed a pattern or practice of constitutional violations in the Newark Police Department's (NPD) stop and arrest practices, its response to individuals' exercise of their rights under the First Amendment, the department's use of force and theft by officers.

A Consent Decree was issued which mandated reforms. The establishment of a system for civilian oversight of the NPD was one of the mandated reforms. One of the first, if not the first executive order the newly elected Mayor Ras Baraka issued created the Civilian Complaint Review Board. This is something that Baraka's father, Amiri, had called for fifty years earlier. Finally, his son had a chance to make manifest a demand the community had almost given up on. Baraka made sure the Board was comprised of community representatives and that it had investigatory powers.

The Newark City Council passed the ordinance that was necessary for the formation of the commission. In response, the Fraternal Order of Police promptly went to court and obtained an injunction that prohibited the CCRB from going into effect for many years. It was clear that the CCRB could set a precedent for the rest of the state. Newark was not the only place that needed oversight.

Throughout New Jersey there were cases that forced us to challenge the U.S. Attorney General for NJ.

The 381 day protest laid the groundwork for February 1, 2016, when we had our first "Justice Monday" protest in front of the Federal Building. We felt that if we could do more than 381 days straight, then we could have a demonstration one day a week in front of the Federal Building where U.S. Attorney General Paul Fishman's office was located.

We demanded federal civil rights investigations into the police shooting deaths of Abdul Kamal, Jerame Reid, Kashad Ashford and the shooting of Radazz Hearns by police. Thirty-year-old Kamal, unarmed, was doused with pepper spray and then shot several times by Irvington police amidst a domestic dispute on November 11, 2013. Twenty-three-year-old Ashford was involved in a police chase in Lyndhurst. He was shot when police said he tried to ram his car into theirs. It would take three years to get the video released. Kashad was killed in September of 2014. Thirty-six-year-old Reid, unarmed, was stopped in his car by Bridgeton police on December 31, 2014, and two minutes later he was shot dead. Fourteen-year-old Radazz Hearns, unarmed, survived being shot seven times by Trenton police as he ran away from them. We struggle to make sure these people are not erased from contemporary history because they were not from Harlem or Brooklyn or Chicago or Detroit or Houston or Los Angeles.

The mother and stepfather of Jerame Reid were in front of the Federal Building regularly with the rest of us holding up signs and speaking out on the sound system. Shelia Reid and Muneer Muhammad recruited other parents to join them on occasion.

We didn't have to tell people to honk their horns anymore. It's as if we had picked up where we had left off from the three hundred-and eighty-one-day protest. Cars, trucks, buses knew what to do. They saw the "bold gold" — us with the black-and-white signs and large banners and they honked their horns. We made sure we had a banner for each of the victims and we continued to say their names; we continued to bring them forth into the present.

Jacqui Greadington, president of the East Orange Education Association and president of the NEA Black Caucus, finished her introduction of me and I walked on the stage. I was really honored to stand there before some of the most powerful people in the world — teachers. Here was an opportunity for institutional change within the mindset of people educating our children. I was receiving an award named after Dr. Martin Luther King, but how many had read any of his six books? How many had charged their students to read any of them?

The images on the screen showed the fight for institutional change within the justice system. But I was there that night to remind everyone that structural change did not end there. I was happy that I was being honored in the context — in the historical continuum — of protracted struggle, the same one King was in from Montgomery to Memphis.

THEY STOLE US, THEY SOLD US, THEY OWE US

People chuckle when I call myself an old man because they still see the shadow of my youth, not my actual 68-year-old gray-headed self, trying to keep in stride; trying to keep up. But with God's grace, it almost looks like I am progressing. I was 65 when I made this speech at Good Neighbor Baptist Church in Newark for its Black History Month program in February of 2019, far away from the days of CFUN and New Ark. This "sermon" is here as a chapter because I had been through more in the previous five years — physically, spiritually, developmentally — than I had during the previous almost sixty years. In addition to the Good Neighbor congregation, present was the Newark Public Schools Superintendent, Roger León and a few Newark public school classrooms of second grade students from Mt. Vernon Elementary. This speech will describe and condense the period of serious challenges that I experienced since 2010.

I walked through my *public* life in Newark and in struggle. But there are things I didn't bear witness to that day, parts of me that I have kept somewhat private. I didn't mention the fact that I divorced for the second time while going through my other trials. My two wives went through much with me. I will always deeply respect them and the sacrifices they made for our children.

A Life in the Struggle

This presentation is proto-typical of my melding of the personal and political. As a written document included in this telling of my life, it presents an opportunity to connect my political grounding to our larger historical experience and truth. I attempted to create out of one, many: our collective historical testimony of how we got over.

Praise the Lord. Giving honor to God, Pastor Blackwell and the first and leading lady, Mrs. Blackwell of his church, Reverend Rountree, the young Rev. Malik Stewart. And let us give a round of applause for all the young people that are here today and honoring us with song. I'm so glad to be here with you this morning. I'm so glad to see the Superintendent of the Newark Public Schools here this morning. And if I don't recognize everyone, please don't hold it against me. I only have a few minutes to be here, so I recognize everyone for whatever contribution that you made to this church, to the uplift of this community and the uplift of our people. I want to start by saying, first, like the publican, "Lord, I am a sinner." And I ask for God's forgiveness and ask God to help me wrestle with the sin of pride and vanity and vainglory because we know the pride goeth before the fall, but also want to thank God. I've heard testimonies here today about the wonderful work of God in our lives and I ask that God pour out His blessings here in Good Neighbor Baptist Church. Pour out his blessings on this congregation. Its members and all people of this church and this community and for the good work that Good Neighbor does in this city. I ask that God pour out his blessings on our Elders.

This morning. I had to go to New York City and do a radio show [Open Line on WBLS-FM] early in the morning and I had to take some people with me. People who were going to be on this particular show and one of them was so infirmed that he couldn't make it from the car across the street to the sidewalk or the door of the building without asking for help. He had to lean on me. I had to think of that song Lean on Me.

You ever had someone, had anybody have to lean on you? They need to hold on to your arm. and hold on to your shoulder and help them up the stairs or across the street. I felt that this morning and so I ask God to pour out his blessing on our Elders who are sick and infirmed and who are struggling with disease. And who have given so much to us, we should cherish and love our elders and respect our elders in our communities. I ask that God pour out his blessings on all the adults, all the parents who must shoulder the responsibilities of familyhood. I've raised three children. I know what it is to struggle to be a parent. I came from a single-parent household. My father died when I was four years old. My mother had to raise me. I want to say something for all Black women that have raised so many children successfully by themselves in our community and I want to praise the fathers who have shouldered their responsibility to be fathers and I want to praise the men who may not have had biological children but have treated children in their families as if they were their biological children. I want to praise our children. Yes, and I heard that song this morning, O-oo-h Child *and some of y'all might be old enough to remember who wrote it. The Five Stairsteps. You remember? And I think of Marvin Gaye. In 1970 he composed an album called* What's Going On. *You Remember? And on that album, one of the cuts is what?* Save the Children. *Save the Children. God says, if you harm one hair on one of these little ones, that you might as well take a millstone. Y'all know what a millstone is? That's that big stone you use to grind grain. Take a millstone, tie it around your neck and throw it in the river. Our children are our future, and we must do everything we can to ensure that they grow up with a happy and healthy lives. We love our children.*

A Life in the Struggle

I want to thank God for this blessing that he's given to me. I'm so glad to say that in this past December I saw my sixty-fifth birthday. I don't know but at sixty things started to happen. I was doing push-ups one morning and suddenly my left arm fell under. And I wasn't paralyzed, but the doctors diagnosed a compressed nerve, and it was a nerve compressing on the motor nerve to my arm and although I wasn't paralyzed, I couldn't lift a pencil. But God guided the physicians to heal my arm and I could move my arm today. A few years after that, I was doing a workout and suddenly blood started coming out of my nose. They had to take me to three hospitals. They couldn't even do work in Jersey. They had to send me to Mount Sinai in New York. I was literally bleeding out my life, but the Lord staunched the bleeding, and I am here today. I was driving my car across Eighteenth Street at the intersection of Eighteenth Street and fifteenth Avenue, and I was hit by a stolen car in my car. The car, they said, T-boned me. It hit me on the driver's side. They hit me so hard witnesses to the accident say their car flipped over. I had broken vertebrae from my neck down to the lumbar. Seventeen of my twenty-four ribs were broken. My hand was broken. One lung was filled with blood and one lung was collapsed. My spleen was punctured, My liver was lacerated I had all kinds of wounds I had tubes in my body in every orifice and hole in my body. Two tubes were placed down my neck, pumping the fluids out of my body because they told me everything was not working in my body. They told me I left here twice. But God brought me here this morning to be with you. (SUSTAINED APPLAUSE.)

Last year [in 2018], *I was diagnosed with prostate cancer. And I want to talk to the men in here this morning. Don't be squeamish about your health. Yeah, I know some of us have some hang-ups about the digital examination. But I tell you an ounce of prevention is worth a pound of cure. I had prostate cancer. They said, "Mr. Hamm, we're going to have to take your prostate out." And I had*

had friends who died from prostate cancer. I've had friends that had their prostates removed and all the terrible side-effects and I prayed on it. They said, "Mr. Hamm, we're not going to take out your prostate," but then they said, "We're going to have to give you 55 radiation treatments." Fifty-five radiation treatments! *You know, sometimes the cure is worse than the disease. And I prayed on it and the number went down from fifty-five to five radiation treatments. Then they did the follow-up examination and I'm cancer free today.* (SUSTAINED APPLAUSE)

I'm so glad to be here. So glad. I've seen so much. I have to conclude that I am only here by the will of God. If you knew my life. If you knew me. You'd say, "Lord have mercy." Let me tell you, I've spoken before presidents and prime ministers, I've spoken before academics of the highest rank, but let me tell you, there's no greater honor than to be given the podium in the house of God. No greater honor.

And no greater honor than being given that opportunity in the house of God where you grew up. Where people know your going in and your going out. I'm so glad. I love you so much. And I thank you for the great work that you've done, and you've asked me to talk about Black History Month. And this is so important. I'm so glad to see that this church is celebrating Black History Month I see the children with their kente cloth on. I saw people here with African clothes on. If I had known it was allowed, I would have had my dashiki on. I still have my dashiki. I've lived long enough to remember, you know, [Newark School] *Superintendent Roger León, to remember the last white Superintendent of Newark Board of Ed, Franklin Titus. Jesse Jackson was in town yesterday. He is Black History. And we thank Reverend Jackson for all his contributions to our people. They honored Rev. Jackson and talked about how he played a role in the Black struggle here in Newark for self-de-*

termination and political power. That when other would not come, he came to Newark and campaigned for the first Black mayor of Newark, Ken Gibson. I'm old enough to remember that campaign. I'm old enough to remember how Newark was before Gibson was elected. I'm old enough to remember when this was a very segregated city. I'm old enough to remember when I couldn't cross Clinton Avenue, much less Lyons Avenue. I grew up on Ridgewood and Avon. How many remember Esther's Restaurant? *How many remember the Ridgewood Bar on the corner of Ridgewood and Avon? I've seen Black History.*

This year (2018) marks the 400th anniversary of the enslavement of African people. This year is an important anniversary. The founding of the United States is marked at 1607 with a colony in in Jamestown, Virginia, but by 1619, twelve years, only twelve Africans were in what today we call the United States, but then it was the American Colonies. Africans had been here much longer than that in the Western Hemisphere.

Africans have been here as long as 1492. That's the year that Columbus came, and you know our children every year sing Columbus sailed the ocean blue/ fourteen hundred ninety-two/ Many weeks he was at sea/ Sailing ships that number three. The Nina, the Pinta and Santa Maria. *Little Black and Brown children cut out the little ships and put them into windows of the school. How ironic because Columbus was a slave master. Columbus was engaged in the slave trades before he arrived here in the Western Hemisphere. Columbus learned the art of navigation in what was called then the Guinea Strait, when Portugal first ventured out along the West Coast of Africa. That's where he learned how to sail ships. That's where he learned how to sail ships. And when he got here in the Western Hemisphere in the Caribbean, he encountered the indigenous people; The Arawak, Carib Taino and others. Columbus took enslaved people on his first voyage. When those ships returned, they had enslaved people and before we were enslaved, there was one-hundred years of enslavement of indigenous peoples.*

But that didn't work out. And they came up with all kinds of rationales. You can't enslave and treat people as beast of burden knowing that they are human beings. So, they had to come up with a rationale. They had to come with a pseudo-science. They had to come up with a narrative that would justify removing nearly one hundred million Africans, Du Bois tells us in the book, The Suppression of the African Slave Trade. *They came up with something called racism. An idea that some people are inherently superior and some people inherently inferior. And I'm here to tell you that racism is a lie. Because God does not make any superior or inferior human beings. There was enslavement for nearly two hundred years in the Caribbean. You think of enslavement only in North America when enslavement was throughout the Western Hemisphere. Africans were brought all the way down from North America all the way down and even down to Chile. All of these countries have descendants of African people. And we have to get over these divisions that we throw up and others between us. We all came here on slave ships. It's just that your master spoke Spanish, their master spoke French, other masters, our masters spoke English. But we're all one people. We are an African people. Let me tell you another secret. All of humanity is African because you can't tell a story of humanity without telling Black people's history. Because mankind begins in Africa — in Eastern Africa. Ask Dr. Leakey. Ask an archeologist. Ask the anthropologist. It's no dispute now that the origins of mankind go back to Africa. And when you tell Black history, you cannot begin with enslavement because we have 6,000 years of history that precedes enslavement of Black people. We have 6,000 years of great civilizations on the African Continent throughout Asia and the rest of the world. I know we have a lot of problems around us today and*

A Life in the Struggle

I know our communities are plagued with a lot of ills but I'm here to tell you that I'm proud to be a Black man — a descendent of African people in the twenty-first century. Say it loud. I'm Black and I'm proud. Say it loud, I'm Black and I'm proud.

I'm not saying this to exercise any kind of chauvinism on anybody else. Our struggles have liberated other people. There is not one thing we have struggled for that other people have not benefitted from. And the world we want to build is not a world with racism in reverse. A world with superior or inferior. We want to build a beloved community of God where all people can prosper together. Where all men, women, every human being can realize their full potential.

But in America, we start in Jamestown, Virginia. In 1619 Africans come here in to Point Comfort in Jamestown. That was the colony, Jamestown, but the ship actually landed at Point Comfort. And then we can talk about New Jersey. New Jersey was a Dutch colony. It was New Netherlands and New York City originally was New Amsterdam. There was a split in the congregationalist church in the New Haven colony and that split caused one half of the church to come down to this Dutch colony called New Netherlands and in 1620 they founded New Jersey. It's called New Jersey because Europeans were fighting a war — a hundred years of war, uninterrupted. and the Dutch were fighting the English. The English overcame the Dutch. So New Netherlands became New Jersey because Jersey was and still is a place in England.

And then the colonists that came down you can still see today. If you go down to the Robert Treat hotel, you'll see a big mural on a wall there. You'll see that the leader of the new colony, Robert Treat, purchasing New East Jersey as it was called from the Hackensack Indians. See, we must never forget, brothers and sisters. Columbus didn't really discover anything. Columbus was lost. And

They Stole Us, They Sold Us, They Owe Us

somehow when Black people make mistakes, it's got to be corrected right away. They have been calling the indigenous people Indians for 500 years because Columbus thought he was in India. He took that idea to his grave. He was wrong. He was in the Western Hemisphere and all this land that we walk around today was the land of the Native Americans. The school right up the road here, Weequahic High School, has as its mascot, the Indian. Why? Because this area was covered with the Lenape Indians. All of the Western Hemisphere was filled with Native Americans. Where did they go? They were murdered. They were exterminated. They died from diseases that were not indigenous to the Western Hemisphere that the Europeans brought with them. In fact, if you want to know the truth... I know that the truth can be painful some time. But this country was founded on oceans of blood. This country was founded on the theft of land from the indigenous people and 400 years of stolen labor from Black people in this country. I know that's a hard thing. I'm just saying we too can understand that this is the most rich and powerful country in the world today, because our ancestors made it rich and powerful and that's the truth. If you don't believe it, test anything I say today. It's easier for you to test it today than it was twenty-five years ago. All you have to do now is Google it.

In 1620 New Netherlands was founded. In 1624 Black people were here. Don't let anybody tell you "Go Back To Where You Came From." We been here longer than anyone else but the indigenous people. It's as much our country... We been here since 1624, building the roads, clearing the forests, building the buildings. giving them free labor. If you couldn't get rich off free labor, God help you.

When I was a little boy, Rev. Rountree, I lived on Ridgewood and Avon. You know, we didn't go downtown in Newark.

A Life in the Struggle

Anyone who lived long enough, you remember Black people didn't go downtown. We did our shopping on Prince Street. We did our shopping in the neighborhood. Y'all talk about Jim Crow and Dr. King. Jim Crow was right here in Newark, New Jersey. All the movie theaters downtown were segregated. Black people could not sit in the mezzanine. No, they couldn't. They had to sit in the balcony. You couldn't eat at the restaurant in Bamberger's. *You talk about* Woolworth's *in North Carolina, but you couldn't eat at the* Woolworths *on Broad and Market here.*

This was in my lifetime. This isn't something I read. In 1960, it was my mother, her sister, my grandmother's sister, and me. I was one of those bad kids they had to send down South every summer. ("Lord, if you don't send him...") They had to send me to my cousin Johnny and Martha's farm in Gainesville, Georgia. That's where my people from.

We got on a train. A train that still runs, Mr. León. It's called the Silver Meteor. *Yes, if you go to Newark's Penn Station today, you look up on that big board and you'll see the* Silver Meteor. *It's an Amtrak train. But in 1960 there was no Amtrak at Penn Station in Newark and when we got to the nation's capital, the citadel of democracy where the Lincoln Monument and the Jefferson Washington Monument still stand today, Black folks on the train heard, "All y'all got to move to the rear of the car." Why was that? Because Washington DC sat on the Mason-Dixon line. and once you went into Washington, the segregated laws for interstate travel took effect. The conductor came over and asked us quietly and nicely, "Please move to the rear of the train" and my mother, God bless her, she's such a passive woman. Everybody loved my mother 'cause she never gave anybody a hard time. But her sister Gladys- Lord have mercy! Gladys raised so much sand, the only reason we moved to the rear was because we couldn't afford another train ticket.*

I went to the National Theater. Remember the National that was on Belmont Avenue? That was the Black people's theater. At one time, most of the Black people in Newark lived in what today we call the Central Ward. But then it was called the Third Ward. And because of redlining and discrimination, most of us went there and we didn't go downtown.

We went to the National Theater, and I saw that Cecil B. DeMille movie The Ten Commandments. *And I tell you, I was a little boy, like four years old. I tell you that movie put the fear of God in me. I saw the Red Sea parted, I saw the pillar of smoke by day and the fire by night and the seven plagues and I was like, "Oh my God." I felt so sorry for the people who were enslaved by the mean Pharaoh, but I want to tell you something, you know what the record said? The real record says that those pyramids were not built by slaves. I know that comes as a shock to a lot of people and I know that won't make me popular, but I didn't come here to sing y'all a nice song. You told me to talk about history.*

Here's the history but here's the odd part about it. I felt sorry about these slaves and when they taught us about The Civil War, they taught it in such a way I didn't understand that they were talking about me and our people. I didn't understand that, but did you know that in Newark in 1838 there was an antislavery society? Here in Newark. It was here in New Jersey. There were places in Newark that were stops on the Underground Railroad because slaves that had sense and kept going. They didn't stop in New Jersey or New York. They went to Canada. What ended slavery? What did it take to end slavery? Of course, it took prayer. We're a great people. But we didn't get here on our own. We got here because of our courage. Because of our faith. Because of our strength.

Every day you turn on that television and they tell you that you are less than this and your less than that. That you're not courageous, that you're not brave, that you're not industrious. I'm telling you that that is a lie. Because if we had not been a courageous, strong, industrious, unified people, we would not be free today. We wouldn't be free today. We're a great people. I hear some of y'all talking today. "Negroes can't do this and Negroes can't do that. Colored people got to do this, and colored people got to do that." We're a great people. We overcame enslavement. We overcame Jim Crow. Other people would have been wiped out. We still here. And the hands that picked cotton picked a President eight years ago. And I'm telling you, we're going to do more than that. We're going to do more than that.

And it took three amendments. The Thirteenth Amendment. It took the Fourteenth Amendment and The Fifteenth Amendment. Slavery didn't end with the Emancipation Proclamation. How many people in here have read the Emancipation Proclamation? Superintendent, I want you to make sure that our young people read the Emancipation Proclamation. I charge you today. It didn't free all slaves. It offered freedom to those who could escape to the Union and join the Union Army and we answered the call, Two-hundred and twenty thousand Black people joined all branches of the Union Army, 186,000. Lincoln wasn't winning the war. They weren't winning. They didn't even want to fight. And then came the radical Republicans Harriet Tubman, Frederick Douglass, Thaddeus Stevens and Charles Sumner. They came to Lincoln, and they said to put arms in the hands of the ones that have an interest in winning this war. And Lincoln said, "Give guns to the people we got chained up?" Because you know they had people chained up in the North too. A lot of those states in the North, part of the so-called Union, were still slave states.

But Lincoln had to do it because he wasn't winning. Confederate General Robert E. Lee, a leader with less men and less resources, was defeating the Union Army. One-hundred and eighty-six thousand Black men joined the Union, fought in battles like Gettysburg, where twenty-five thousand fell and Antietam, where thirty thousand fell. Sixty thousand Black soldiers killed in battle. One hundred thousand wounded. We are free people today because of their sacrifice. Their sacrifice and their contribution must never be forgotten. When Memorial Day comes and when Veteran's Day comes, we need to take our children out to the graves of Civil War soldiers and lay flowers there because had it not been for them, we may have stayed enslaved until the twentieth century.

The thirteenth Amendment abolished slavery, the Fourteenth Amendment gave us citizenship, the fifteenth Amendment gave us the right to vote. The anniversary of the Fifteenth Amendment falls on February 3rd, during Black History Month. Yes, but you know what? There were thirty-six states. It took twenty-seven of the thirty-six to amend the Constitution. New Jersey was not in the 27-state majority to ratify the thirteenth amendment. It's not even clear that they ratified the Fourteenth and Fifteenth Amendments. I believe that State Senator Nia Gill offered a bill just ten years ago to get Jersey finally on record to ratifying the fifteenth Amendment. This is our history.

Our children need to know our history. They don't even know the history of Black History Month. Nobody gave us Black History Month. It didn't come from a legislature. It didn't come from a city council. It didn't come from Congress. It came from a Black man named Carter G. Woodson, who wrote The Miseducation of the Negro. He was the second Black man to graduate from Harvard University in 1912. He started writing columns about our history. Most Black people in the twentieth century couldn't read. So, Carter Woodson was writing these columns in Black newspapers. What happened? Black people took Carter G. Woodson's columns to church. And when service was over. People would stay back and the one who could read would stand up and read Carter G. Woodson's Black history column to everybody else. I'm telling you congregation, there would be no Black liberation if it wasn't for the Black church. The Black church has always played a prominent role in our struggle.

They say, "Well Larry, they gave us February, the shortest month of the year." Nobody gave us anything. Carter G. Woodson fixed Negro History Week on the second week of February, the week of February 12th, Abraham Lincoln's birthday, and the February 14th birthday of Frederick Douglass. Why those two? Because they were the giants of the Civil War.

See, you've got to understand just how cataclysmic the Civil War was. More Americans died in the Civil War than in World Wars I, II, Korea and Vietnam combined. That was the conflict that broke the back of the slave aristocracy because everybody was making money. Human commodities. They were making money in 1860, the largest investment of capital in the United States, greater than banking capital and industrial capital combined, was the investment in slavery. And you and that industry made this country rich, and they knew it.

That's why Thaddeus Stevens in 1865 issued HR Twenty-Nine. Well, let me go back for a minute. General Sherman issues in 1864 General Field Order Number Fifteen. What did he do? He confiscated 400,000 acres of slave masters' land and said, "This is the price of the sedition. We're going to take the land from the slave masters and distribute it to the slave." Thaddeus Stevens said, "That is a good idea and I'm going to put a bill in Congress." HR Twenty-nine would give every free person or their surviving member, if their family member, fought in the Civil War, forty acres and fifty dollars. See, where did the mule come from? How many y'all raised on the farm? If you ain't got a beast of burden or a tractor, you can't farm. You got to bust that land up. So, what happened? Sherman used to take the mules that pulled the canons and give them to the formerly enslaved people so that they would have a beast to pull the plow. So, it was 40 acres and fifty dollars. It passed both houses of Congress. See, they knew they owed us.

You walk around saying white people don't owe us nothing. The government don't owe us nothing. The government has given reparations to enslaved Jewish American brothers and sisters that were enslaved in concentration camps in Europe. It gave reparations to the Japanese who were incarcerated here in this country. If this government can give out reparations for our Jewish brothers and Japanese brothers, it needs to give reparations to the descendants of enslaved Africans in this country.

And that's what it was. It passed both houses of Congress. But what happened? On April 9th, 1865, John Wilkes Booth, an actor, assassinates Lincoln and who becomes president? Andrew Johnson. and where was Johnson from? Tennessee, a slave state. And what did he do? He gave back all the land that Sherman had confiscated. He vetoed HR 29. Can you imagine what the state of Black people would have been if all of us had gotten our 40 acres? They stole us, they sold us, and they owe us to this day. They owe us reparations for the stolen labor of our ancestors. But you can't understand the present unless you understand the past.

We have a Martin Luther King National holiday. They didn't give it to us. We had a campaign. We made it happen. We got a Martin Luther King national monument. We got a street that used to be High Street. Now it's named after Martin Luther King. You know when the idea first came up. I'm old enough to remember these things. When the idea first came up that High Street should be Martin Luther King Boulevard, all the colleges on High Street resisted. They didn't want to be on a street named after a Black man. But we persisted. It's Martin Luther King Boulevard today and all their literature, all their letterhead has Martin Luther King on it. But this is what hurts my heart. We have a holiday. We have a monument. We have streets and schools. Back in the 1970s, I was the board member that put forward the motion to change the name of South Eighth Street School to Martin Luther King. South Tenth Street School became Harriet Tubman. Robert Treat was changed to Marcus Garvey and South Side to Malcolm X Shabazz.

We have all this for Dr. King, but I want to know this: what school in the city of Newark, what school in the state of New Jersey, what district in the United States of America requires its students to read one of the six books he wrote? Those books are Measure of a Man, Stride Toward Freedom, Why We Can't Wait, Strength to Love, Where Do We Go From Here-Chaos or Community, *and* Trumpet of Conscience. *If you going to close the schools for the day, the students should at least know the ideas for which Martin Luther King fought and died.*

Lastly after this, twelve years ago, they passed The Amistad Act in New Jersey, put forward by State Assemblymen Bill Payne and Craig Stanley. The Amistad Act passed by the entire state legislature and was signed into law by the Governor of New Jersey. That bill requires not just Black History courses; it requires every course offered to teach Black Studies relevant to that particular subject area, because as we said, our children need our history. They need our history. There are 600 school districts. Every school district is required to put together an Amistad curriculum. Do you know of the 600 districts in this state, only a handful of them have actually implemented Amistad? I challenge this congregation, Good Neighbor Church. I challenge the clergy and the elected officials who were brought into office by Black people to make sure that Amistad is implemented in every school in the state. Our children should know our history.

But you ain't got to wait for legislation from New Jersey or an act of Congress or a proclamation from the President. You can teach Black History from your own home. You can go to Black bookstores and buy Black history books. You can sit around your dinner table and tell your story of how you had to deal with racism and segregation. Tell your stories of your Ancestors. Because all our history is the distilled essence of our collective experience. We've got to tell the story and pass our history on to our people.

e are great people and we're going to be a greater people. We're going to help bring into existence a world in which all people can live as brothers and sisters and prosper together. I don't understand how people can work 40 hours a week and not make enough money to support their family. You can't do nothing on a minimum wage. It should at least be $15. It should at least be a living wage.

When I went to Princeton University. How did I get to Princeton? Did I get into Princeton because I was smart or nice looking or whatever? No, I got to Princeton — and most have you in here who went to college got in —because Black people kicked down the doors of those universities open during the Civil Rights Movement. No. None of us in here would have those degrees.

You know what else? There was no financial aid before 1966. There was only the G.I. Bill and we talked about the Civil Rights Act and the Voting Rights Act. But we should talk about the Higher Education Act because that's what made it possible for our children and millions of other poor children to go to college.

The color bar is gone but there's a new bar. It's an economic bar. When our young people are going to school and graduating with thirty, forty, fifty, a hundred thousand dollars in debt, it defeats the whole purpose of going to school. The whole purpose. This country is rich enough to provide a free college education to every young person who wants to go to school and wants to go to college.

Lastly, where does the idea of public school come from? Public schools come out of the struggle of Black people. After we got the Fourteenth and Fifteenth amendments, what did we do with the Fifteenth Amendment? We elected the Reconstruction government., The Black state legislators in the former slave states. Some of those state legislative bodies in the former Confederacy were majority Black. Some of those state legislatures were a mixture of progressive whites and Blacks. And what was the first thing they did? They created free public schools — the same ones we know today. Tax supported, government supported. It came out of Black people's struggle for Freedom. If our children knew this, wouldn't they have a greater appreciation for the education they are getting? But there are forces who are trying to destroy free public education. In a minute, we're not going to have any free public schools. We must support the Movement to keep public education public and free for our young people.

There are negative forces that are trying to turn back the clock on civil rights and every struggle that Black people have participated in or led during the last one-hundred years. They're trying to turn it back on workers' rights. on environmental rights, on consumer's rights, on women's rights, on everybody's rights.

I don't know about you, but as for me: our people died too much, bled too much, sacrificed too much to go backward. I don't know about you; I AM NOT GOING BACK WITHOUT A FIGHT!

2019 TO 2022: PRESENT TENSE: CAMPAIGN, PANDEMIC, UPRISINGS

I don't like to talk about religion. I believe as Malcolm did: that you keep that in the closet. But I must be honest: On Saturday, May 30, 2020, I have no problem telling you that I prayed silently to myself from noon until 3 p.m.

Like the rest of the world, POP responded to the lynching of George Floyd in Minneapolis by having an emergency march. We did our extended call. We found out that there were other groups that were going to protest the same day. We also knew that our mayor, Ras Baraka, wanted to be involved. So, POP began quilting the groups together, unity-without-uniformity style.

POP has led many protests in Newark. Some had less than one hundred participants. Some, like that anti-apartheid march in 1985, had had more than ten thousand. And in 2008, there were thousands at the anti-war march we had in Newark and the Million People March for Peace and Justice in 2015. We were always prepared for an organized protest, no matter what the side. But even we were not prepared for what we saw when we gathered on Springfield Avenue. Thousands. More than we had ever seen before in decades. Mayor Baraka — who, at an earlier press conference on the steps of City Hall, had called Floyd's lynching "barbaric" — spoke at the rally and marched with us. I prayed the mike we had would hold out. Trying to get a back-up last minute amidst COVID-19 was a major challenge.

We had to watch the crowd as we left Springfield Avenue to head downtown, an apparent anarchist pulled out a bat, wanting to imitate the "political violence" that had swept Minneapolis and other cities the early days of the Floyd protest. It just took a few Newark marchers to quickly quell that proposed action. I had told the crowd at the start that violence was not going to be tolerated, and we had to show the out-of-towners that they were welcome, but that we meant business. We in Newark had pioneered violent rebellion more than fifty years ago, so we knew too well the consequences. There was a small group that pulled the American flag down from the bank at Broad and Market and set it on fire, but that was the extent of any property damage. Our restraint was impressive enough to make *The New York Times*.

But the times were also creating a movement. Suddenly, the possibly-COVID air was tension-filled and spontaneous based on the real-life, real-time Sci-Fi movie Pandemics 2020. The world was introduced to an invisible enemy called COVID-19. Stuck at home by municipal government decree, America and the world were then confronted with an almost ancient pandemic known to the darker brother and sister: the cases of Ahmaud Marquez Arbery, an unarmed 25-year-old man who was fatally stalked and shot by a lynch mob while jogging in Georgia, Breonna Taylor, a 26-year-old who was fatally shot by Louisville Metro Police Department officers and finally Floyd, 46, who died in Minneapolis literally with a police knee on his neck. All the victims were Black and unarmed (Taylor's boyfriend used his registered gun because he thought the police, who forcefully invaded the home on a no-knock warrant, were burglars). Two of the murders were recorded on cell phone video and endlessly rerun on the cable news channels, and all of this happened within weeks. And if that was not bad enough, about the same time Floyd was killed, a Black man birdwatching in Central Park simply asked a white woman to not ignore the postings in the park and put her dog on a leash. She in turn weaponized her whiteness and called the police on him. People could clearly see that the old evil was still afoot because they had no choice but to see while cloistered in their homes. COVID-19 had sufficiently shut the world down and forced everyone to see what Blacks had been saying the whole time. There was simply no denying it. Racism is alive, well and entrenched within police departments across the nation.

How would an activist group used to meeting and protesting side-by-side survive? We agreed with Mayor Baraka and his shutdown. Our city was filled with Black and Latino "essential workers," so we knew we were at greater risk. Almost instantly, people across the world were having every kind of club, work, organization, and church meeting using software such as Zoom, Go to Meeting and Google Meet. Unable to meet at Abyssinian Baptist Church, our adopted home for the last twenty years, we began meeting by conference telephone call.

Then we switched to Zoom. Zoom added a closeness that the conference calls lacked. For Ingrid and our Vice Chair, Larry Adams, it was easier to conduct roll calls and maintain order. We started using a stack system to ensure that everyone that wanted to be heard had the opportunity. Adams is a fellow

Princeton grad and labor leader forged in the people's struggle. He is adept at keeping order at the marches and the meetings. Adams and Ingrid make sure our in-depth discussions don't take us off course. Instead of the guard at Abyssinian signaling the time with the flickering of the lights, Ingrid or Adams will say, "Chair, it's 9:15... Chair, it's 9:30."

We were adapting to this forced physical isolation. Then Arbery happened.

When Ahmaud Arbery was lynched, there was a testing of the waters. Mid-May, the only protesters that had been out were the ones standing at state capitals with no masks or gloves but with Confederate flags, guns and MAGA caps, demanding that states open up.

POP didn't broach the idea of marching amidst COVID-19 lightly on our POP conference call. Sharon Baldwin was rightfully concerned about the example we would be setting by resuming our marches. Lisa Davis reminded us that, yet another Black man was lynched, taking us back to Trayvon. But this time, we watched the killing from our living rooms. White men see a Black man and feel empowered to accost the Black man and the Black man is not supposed to fight back. When he does, he's killed. Other members suggested ways that we could be socially responsible while making our point. We could socially distance, wear face masks and gloves.

Ahmaud was silenced but we could not be. The vote was taken. The march was scheduled for May 13th. We couldn't sit quietly in the comfort of our home knowing that people all over the country are the victims of racists and police brutality. I want to make it clear that Black people have a right to defend themselves, their families and their homes by any means necessary.

We didn't know it at the time, but historically, that was the same day as the thirty-fifth anniversary of the 1985 MOVE bombing in Philadelphia, another example of extreme police militarism and murder.

We had signs for Ahmaud Arbery and signs for Breonna Taylor. Her name had not even come up in the discussion at the POP meeting because most of us didn't find out about her case until the next day. Darlene Troutman and Alfreda Daniels took most of the pictures for POP that would be seen on Facebook or used in newspapers. Darlene was doing double duty, finding time to take pictures, and passing out face masks and gloves to those who didn't have them.

There are patterns in all these killings. I had to remind the more than three hundred people that came out that Breonna's death in Louisville, Kentucky was just like little Aiyana Jones' death in Detroit, Michigan in May of 2010 as police stormed this six-year-old's home and fatally shot her while she slept. It was another instance of a police raid of the wrong home. Breonna was a college graduate, a mother, a hardworking woman, and front-line worker. She was shot eight times. It seems that for the police, it's never enough to shoot someone once.

We can never forget. That's why we have to do a roll call of Black victims who have been shot multiple times: sixteen-year-old Tasha Mayse of Newark in 1991, New York's Amadou Diallo, shot forty-one times in 1999 and Sean Bell fifty times in 2006, one hundred and twenty-seven shots fired into the van she was in and the 2012 Cleveland police shooting one hundred and thirty-six shots into the car of unarmed Timothy Russell and Malissa Williams.

The pattern of police brutality must shine so brightly that it pierces through the shades too many people insist on wearing. We didn't know at the time, but we were at a tipping point and in less than two weeks after the march the world would not be able to shut its eyes quick enough or long enough. Eight minutes and forty-six seconds is a long time to watch someone die.

Suddenly, America and the rest of the world opened up as quickly as it shut down. Set free in a late May filled with sunshine, millions unable to physically go to work or school for two months grabbed their facemasks, the new necessity, and took to the streets in protest, many for the first time. Protests took place around the world. Floyd, Taylor and Arbery became worldwide subjects.

Somehow, I wound up spending fifteen hours a day running for the United States Senate against a popular and borderline progressive incumbent, Cory Booker. A year ago, this was nowhere near what I had planned for myself. But maybe I should start at the beginning — which, for me, was the summer of 2019.

When most people retire, they become more involved in their churches and civic organizations. When I was planning for my retirement throughout 2019, the front of my mind knew what my goals were: to spend more time with my family and POP and to work on this book. One of the rewards of forty years of ceaseless work is quiet and reflection. I was looking forward to a largely quiet 2020, with maybe doing some statewide Get-Out-The-Vote registration efforts before working with POP through Election Day to make sure Trump was voted out of office.

However, there was something in the back of my mind. Really, the thought of running for office first reared its head two years before when Menendez ran amidst questions of corruption. He was eventually found not guilty. But at the time, people were really concerned. Lisa McCormick, who would later run for Congress, ran against Menendez and did pretty well with about 169,000 votes. I was surprised because she was a total unknown to me. People approached me about running but it was May and not enough time to even get on the ballot. So, in the general election, I told people they needed to support Menendez. Democrats could not afford to lose a senate seat. But the possibility of my running for something; that seed was planted.

By September of 2019, I officially joined the Bernie Sanders campaign as its New Jersey state chairperson. Sanders was rising in the pre-primary polls, and grassroots Left groups saw a great opportunity to organize around Sanders and help him win the New Jersey primary. One of the issues we had as we organized for Bernie is that we wanted him to be at a high position on the New Jersey ballot. To get that position, Bernie needed to have a slate of state-sanctioned candidates. Slates of candidates can be as high as Row B. So, to make sure that Bernie wasn't buried on the ballot, I had begun to think about running for the U.S. Senate.

My mind went back to the last time Sanders ran in New Jersey. NJ Assemblyman John Wisniewski was the state chair for the Sanders campaign. I thought that when Wisniewski ran for governor the following year, that he would have gotten the endorsement of Sanders. Many suspected, but the Sanders campaign had confirmed that there existed a progressive wing of the Democratic Party in New Jersey. Sanders got 360,000 in the Democratic primary. That's a lot of people that aren't scared by the word, socialism. A Sanders endorsement for Wisniewski in 2017 would have consolidated that base. You've got to continue to stimulate that base so that they come out and vote, not just for Bernie Sanders, but for all progressive candidates running for office. Sanders didn't do that and that was a great disappointment.

So, conversations were had in the summer of 2018, and I told people when I was asked to be state chair, that we had to do something to consolidate the progressive base. It can't be everyone comes and votes for Bernie and then it's over. It was these discussions where that little seed that had been planted a year before began to sprout tiny roots in my consciousness. But I still wasn't there.

It wasn't until the spring of 2019 when the state legislature passed a bill that would allow Cory Booker to hold his Senate seat and run for President, that the idea of running for Senate blossomed in my mind. Several people had already approached me about being the State chair for the Sanders Campaign. Among them were Analila Mejia, the Bernie Sanders National Political Director and Hettie Rosenstein, the NJ Director of CWA.

I began asking if I could be the chairperson for the campaign and run for the Senate seat. I saw this as a way of really bolstering his campaign. Everyone knew Bernie needed help with the Black community. And to be truthful, I wasn't all that concerned at that point with winning as I was about expanding his base.

We had discussions from late summer through the fall. Then in December, I issued an announcement that we were going to have a meeting to discuss my run. I didn't say a meeting to announce. The press rolled with it as an announcement. And so, the discussion became a de-facto announcement.

I told my youngest daughter and latest graduate from college, Imani. She seemed a little surprised. I don't think my daughters thought I would run for anything at this point. And I didn't expect my other daughters, Nia, or Laini, to be into what I was doing at this time. Nia was newly married, and Laini was never into politics like that.

That announcement as it was, caught the attention of my bosses at NJ Transit and I was called to a meeting. It didn't matter that I was retiring in a couple of months. Transit depends a lot on federal funds and US senators have a lot of influence on the funding process.

I decided to have a general-interest meeting at REFAL Inc., also referred to as REFAL Center/Temple of Anu. The name comes from the Arabic word meaning healing and it's also an acronym for Reconstructing Economics For African Love. The center is an important Black cultural and educational meeting place on Ninth street in Newark for more than thirty years. I expected twenty people ready to have a sober, intellectual discussion. Instead, I walked into a room of more than two hundred campaign workers of all races and ages ready to go. I met the first two people who became a part of my campaign through POP member Dr. Matthew Johnson. Justin Dillard and Gerald Jackson were part of the "Black People for Bernie" group that Dr. Johnson had started.

It's a misnomer that Black people were not coming out for Sanders. The oddity was that when all the information came in, Black people were spending more proportionately on the Bernie Sanders campaign than any other candidate. Sanders had more support from Black people than anyone but perhaps Joe Biden.

I got to know Justin and Gerald through this group. They were a big help to me in organizing the rally when we brought in Dr. Cornel West to speak at Rutgers-Newark. One night, shortly after that rally, at a sushi restaurant on Central Avenue in Newark, I told them that I was going to run for US Senate. And they were really the first ones that said they wanted to help me with my campaign.

There's considerable overlap between the Sanders campaign and my campaign. Another person I met while campaigning for Sanders was Nikki Kurzynowski, I met her at a Sanders fundraiser that was hosted by Barry Brendel at an Asbury Park Sports Bar. Barry was one of the two chairs of the Sanders campaign. She said that meeting was the first one where she spoke out publicly. And there she was in Newark months later, ready to become a major part of my communications team.

I met Assatta Mann shortly before the Rutgers event in November. Assatta was the president of the Rutgers-Newark College Democrats. Justin introduced her to me hoping to bring her on board for a collaboration between Blacks for Bernie, POP, and her group. He succeeded. Working with the communications and social media committee, Assatta turned out to be a valuable asset in the campaign later when COVID-19 would hit.

Saleemah Hadi, a four-year member of POP with video and graphic designing skills, also worked with the communications and social media.

Allen Simmons was the chair of field operations. He had precious experience with other campaigns.

Leslie Scott was on the social media committee. She posted most of the professional grade social media posts for Facebook and Instagram as a volunteer.

I wound up addressing the enthusiastic REFAL crowd that would be my team and asking their opinion. Their response was a resounding *Yes, run!*

I was absorbed into the campaign. I crisscrossed every county of New Jersey, delivering thousands of signed petitions. When I retired from New Jersey Transit in late winter and early spring of 2020, it freed up a significant amount of time to do everything but rest. I was on the road all February. I was a regular on 107.5 WBLS-FM's *Open Line* Facebook second hour. As March approached, the biggest challenge I thought I had was fundraising and perhaps trying to get a televised debate with my opponent, US Sen. Cory Booker. Steve Bernhardt, a long-time POP member, agreed to be my treasurer. The time I would have been doing my heaviest campaigning was when COVID-19 spread in the air and covered the land. In two weeks, America and much of the world completely shut down most in-person operations. Even our "Justice Monday" protests had to abruptly stop. By then, those protests in front of the

Peter W. Rodino Federal Building had lasted every Monday for two hundred weeks. As I write this, POP did decide to resume "Justice Mondays," at the Rodino building starting on June 6, 2021. Those protests continue in so-called "post-pandemic" 2024 because of the need. Our demand for justice for the state's Black victims of fatal shootings has lasted for more than a decade.

However, in March of 2020, the pandemic had forced the campaign and its fundraisers to become more creative. All our campaign strategy meetings were now Zoom. Our Town Halls were Zoom webinars. Nikki Kurzynowski Josie Gonsalves, Lisa Davis, Assatta Mann and Annette Alston were instrumental in creating and implementing the Town Hall formats.

In the end, we were able to raise $97,590.21 to Senator Booker's $2,900 million ... We ended up with twelve percent of the vote with three percent of the money Booker had raised.

Struggles ebb and flow. Facebook and Twitter have become sources of minute-by-minute coverage of white supremacy and resistance to it. This public oppression has moved people into radical expression — moved people past their fears.

I am forced to admit that POP today really is not the organization that was envisioned when we first wrote the POP Constitution. The idea that you are not going to live forever carries special resonance when you realize you have seen more of the past than what you may have left of a future. And even if I live well into the next two decades, I will not go into the grave with the Chairman's gavel in my hand. Ultimately, I must be prepared whenever the time comes to work myself out of that leadership role. When you are running out of time, these questions of pragmatic impact vs. vision are important.

We face the challenge of how to create a financial foundation while retaining our autonomy. For decades I have been often asked why, as a nonprofit, all-volunteer organization, POP has not taken major grants from organizations, foundations, political parties, and local, state, and federal agencies? The answer is both simple and painful: We like to decide our own direction, and you cannot do that if you accept money from these power brokers, because money means influence. You can't be self-determining on someone else's dime.

But even volunteer organizations need, and often have, paid staff. We get by on the little bit of money we raised, but we never have more than a couple of thousand dollars in the account at any given time. It's been enough to help us continue, but it's not enough to help us expand. We must develop a system and a method of membership recruitment and retention because the power of POP is really based on the activity of its membership. The more active members we have, the more we're able to do and ergo, the more influence we have. This is harder than it seems because Newark is a big city, but relative to New York City, it's a town, a village smaller than any of the five boroughs.

We need a membership coordinator who can recruit and maintain a paying membership base of five thousand, a roughly four-fold increase over what we had prior to the Floyd/Taylor/Arbery uprisings. Believe it or not, POP on paper had about three thousand members pre-Floyd, but these were not all dues paying members. They may be on our social media, but most are not on the committees or regularly in the streets with us.

Just three or so years ago, we could stand on Broad and Market and in one day recruit fifty or sixty members to sign those membership forms. People will do that. They'll sign membership forms, but there's a total disconnect between that form and getting them to be active, getting them to the meeting. So many future problems with POP could be dealt with or prevented if we had a weekly meeting of one hundred active members — a dues-paying core of a community think-tank. We hope that the post-Floyd membership application upsurge and the energy we have created around the Senate campaign will assist here.

POP has become known for its work throughout the state. We learned that in 2018, when many of the New Jersey gubernatorial candidates, and most of the front-running Democrats in local and state races, came to our meetings. That had never happened before. I'm not sure that any gubernatorial candidate had ever come and addressed us.

We have done a good job of promoting participatory democracy at the grassroots level. We have discussions instead of issuing directives. We put items on the table, and we have some very lively debates about them. Sometimes we go for long periods with a general consensus, but every two or three months we hit an item where people have intense and different opinions. Some issues we have to leave alone. There should be a consensus on decisions made and when possible, a majority in agreement. It's probably the closest thing to a regular participatory democratic activity that you will see in our community.

Cities are characterized by two types of political activity: electoral and extra-electoral. POP exists primarily within the extra-electoral arena and is at its best when it links issues together. When we protest the closures of hospitals, we link it to universal health care. When we assist Newark to get a Civilian Complaint Review Board, we link it to police brutality. The purpose of our Floyd march was not to just protest his death, not to just revive all the names of all the Blacks in New Jersey who were killed by the police, but to call for pressure to be put on the New Jersey State Supreme Court to allow Newark to have a civilian complaint review board with subpoena power.

One of the things I have learned in trying to create that dimension is that it can't be done via social media. I wasn't on Facebook until 2015. I got on Facebook because I thought it would be a tool to help us organize and mobilize people. I went from having no Facebook friends to seven-thousand friends and followers. That has resulted in no appreciable increase in the number of people participating in the meetings or our activities. But what it has done is that it raised POP's profile. For example, one day after I had dropped my daughter off at school and I was going through the parkway toll booth, the toll operator, a white guy, looked at me and asked, "Are you Larry Hamm?" I was a little wary, but I identified myself. He said, "Man, you are all over social media!" So, I learned that if you can't get people to participate, you can at least win people over to support whatever it is you're doing. That's a good thing. But the acme of organizational acumen is the ability to move people to action. Again, we view the mobilization we've done about Floyd, Taylor, and Arbery as a positive step in that regard.

Trump revealed the underbelly of this republic and the need for POP and other grass roots organizations to be ever vigilant in their pursuit of a fervent and true democracy.

For thirty-seven years, POP has been consistent: It's a great accomplishment, but it's not how I judge political success. We're not as far as we should be for a community institution, a radical institution without walls. It's causing me to question some of my fundamental premises. What we envisioned in the POP Constitution is not what we have established, we have small, active branches throughout the state, admittedly only a fraction of the original vision. The question: Is it possible to build an independent grassroots organization in an urban community that is not dependent on outside resources and institutions? Is that possible? Is it possible to build such an organization on a voluntary basis? We have the self-reliance and independence we originally craved, but not the stabilizing structures of say, unions — organizations that have, for example, headquarters and many active members.

Although POP has been strong there are challenges. We can't get enough of our members involved. We can raise money, but will everybody remain on the same programmatic page, and fight to go forward? This is a question that bothers me in my quiet moments.

I am still Adhimu Changa in name, spirit and heart. But age catches up to all of us, including those who have run their whole lives. At the final finish line are the inevitable beings that you don't necessarily want to embrace right now, no matter how much you love your Ancestors.

Present Tense: Campaign, Pandemic, Uprisings

Until the advent of COVID, POP—— that unique mixture of Marxists, Pan-Africanists, Black nationalists, and others—— met at 7 p.m. every Thursday at Abyssinian Baptist Church on West Kinney Street, in my old ward. By the time you read this, we hope to have resumed that weekly meeting in our adopted home.

Our core group has met so long we know and act like the family we have become. We know each other's quirks and strengths. Because we are family, we sometimes fuss at each other. For example, my eyes are not what they used to be, so I might not recognize who is asking to speak from the back of the room. That might get some ribbing.

Our members have more health problems than they used to have. Aminifu had a stroke right in one of our meetings; he recovered for a time. However, between the Spring and Fall of 2021, we lost three long time POP members including Aminifu.

The Baby Boomer radical generation is now struggling to keep their health as well as their politics. That includes me as well; I'm a prostate cancer survivor.

But we are still out here, protesting, registering people to vote, having public forums, holding our collective memory together as oppressed people. Our bold gold shirts/sweaters are known throughout the state and in some activist corners of the United States. Our consistent struggle is our greatest collective accomplishment. I am still, in more ways than one, a product of Newark's Grayce.

The year 2020 was almost as extraordinary as the times that politically birthed me. I was approximately the same age as the four girls martyred in the Birmingham church bombing. My conscious struggle began after Medgar Evers, Jimmie Lee Jackson, Malcolm X, Martin Luther King. After 26 people lost their lives in the 1967 Newark Rebellion: Rose Abraham, Eloise Spellman, Eddie Moss, Michael Moran, Isaac Harrison, Frederick Toto, Robert Lee Martin, Albert Mersier, Jr., Rufus Council, William Furr, Tedock Bell, Michael Pugh, Jessie Mae Jones, James Rutledge, Leroy Boyd, Rebecca Brown, Hattie Gainer, Raymond Gilmer, Raymond Hawk, Mary Helen Campbell, Cornelius Murray, Oscar Hill, James Sanders, Richard Taliaferro, Victor Louis Smith, Elizabeth Artis.

My fifty years of struggle began after them. And during my active years, we have been constantly confronted with dead Black bodies or the threat of dead Black bodies, executed almost exclusively by police, other public servants, or those claiming to act on their behalf. The most recent of the second wave: Trayvon Martin. Eric Garner. Sandra Bland. Earl Faison. Abdul Kamal. Tamir Rice. Michael Brown. Aiyana Jones. Kenneth Chamberlain. And now: Rayshard Brooks. George Floyd. Breonna Taylor. Elijah McClain. Ahmaud Marquez Arbery.

Our only answer is what this brother from South Seventeenth Street learned at Arts High, the Newark Board of Education and Princeton University decades ago; a tried-and-true organizing and agitating trio of principles that were passed down to us from Dr. King, Fannie Lou Hamer, Amiri Baraka, and Ella Baker: take it to the streets, and the voting booths, and the courts. I may be now rewriting a popular cliché, but it is true: only when we fight, and do it from every angle, do we win. The only way to fail at struggle is to not act, to engage in what King called the silence of betrayal.

Present Tense: Campaign, Pandemic, Uprisings

The year of reckoning was 2020, the year we had to vote "45" out. We knew we would not have a better target, or a better set of conditions that would help people to see that there was no better time to organize and fight back than we had at that moment. The opportunity to create a new reality begins with the ballot, but it doesn't rest there. The challenge before us is not to fall silent, not to be discouraged if those who raised their voices in a racist rebel yell so successfully, do so again.

It has been, is and will be my honor and privilege to spend the reminder of my life assisting you, the reader, in all those efforts. Your autobiography in struggle awaits its creation.

CODA: CHAIRMAN
BY ANNETTE M. ALSTON

Larry always said: "If I get to the point where I'm in a wheelchair and there's a march going on, just wheel me on in."

His energy could match and surpass that of any of the Seton Hall University students staring up at him from Dr. Kelly Harris' Fall 2019 class. Students had just finished watching the documentary *Profiled* by Kathleen Foster about police brutality.

Said my chairman: "To understand police brutality today, you must understand the use of force and the evolution of force against African Americans. During the modern Civil Rights Movement, there were just as many violent encounters with the police as there were with the Klan. In fact, many of the police officers were part of the Klan."

Larry glides effortlessly from slavery through the Civil Rights Movement and into Black resistance and rebellions throughout the country, most of which were sparked by police brutality. One student asks the inevitable *What-do-we-do* question, "because it doesn't seem protesting works."

The question from the young woman had a slight air of a dis, though it really was not meant that way. Sometimes youth and those who are not-so-young jump to conclusions because they just don't know. They don't know about the protests that have happened on that campus for decades, stretching back to before I attended their campus as a Seventies teen. The SHU Upward Bound leaders, including Erwin Ponder and Leroy Wilson III, were among the late-Sixties/early-Seventies SHU undergrads protesting racism, staging teach-ins, and assisting Newark striking teachers in 1971. They're the reason SHU has a Martin Luther King Scholars program and that professors like Dr. Forrest Pritchett, the program's director, still exist. The student is clearly frustrated about the continuation of police brutality, but perhaps misses the irony that Harris was just hired the previous year, after student protest and demonstrations demanding the formation of an African American Studies Department.

So, I looked at Larry as he listened thoughtfully to this young girl's question, knowing his thoughtfulness bore more patience than I would be able to sustain. He was younger than most of the students in the room when he organized his first protest. Now his hair is silver, close cropped and neatly wavy. He came straight from work, so he is wearing his business shirt, tie and slacks which still appear neatly pressed at the end of the day. I know that the patience he displayed is just an innate part of his being and it comes with an understanding that he must convince this next generation to pick up the mantle he's carried so long. He answered in the only way that he would ever answer it: "There has to be more protesting and more demonstrations. The problem is that there are not enough." *Agitate, agitate, agitate, whispered Frederick Douglass from the Realm of the Ancestors.* The paradox of being patient while agitating is lost on many youths and many adults, too. Hamm has somehow mastered this in his activist life.

A couple of weeks later, Rutgers-Newark students and the POP co-sponsored an event with Dr. Cornel West. It was a great color visual — Rutgers students of all shades organizing side-by-side with POP members, all in bold gold shirts and sweatshirts. Adhimu Changa — in decades past, the "Important Youth" — now has the essence of an elder statesman, one who can humbly ask the powerful to bear witness. Both New Jersey Governor Murphy and Dr. West said they were there at the chairman's behest.

Looking around the Rutgers Dome, it was a clear victory for an organization that has experienced ebbs and flows. POP and the students seeing a result, and now wanting more. Possibilities. But for POP, that moment represented thirty-six years of struggle within and without to get to this point in time. It's been one trial after another. Larry is used to the ebb and flow — how conditions make situations. He has learned flexibility: sometimes he's leading the pack and sometimes it seems he's running against it. But his direction has never changed.

The first time I saw Larry I was about eleven-years-old. My parents were active participants in the struggles of the times, particularly with the Board of Education. I don't know why he came to my parents' door. I think it was to drop off some flyers or something like that. He didn't stay long. He was at the door and then he wasn't.

Ten years later, I was standing at the bus stop waiting for the Cheap Charlie bus to take me to downtown Newark.

"Southorangejavenue" (that's how we pronounce "South Orange Avenue") had two competing bus companies running down the same line. One was NJ Transit, charging their usual forty cents and the other was the company we dubbed "Cheap Charlie." The fare on that bus was only twenty-five cents. Those buses were usually the more crowded. If you wanted to ensure a seat, you paid the extra fifteen cents to take the NJ Transit. (Now, only the Cheap Charlie remains, the legendary No. 31 bus.) I was in my last year in college, so I was not averse to saving a few cents and standing a little while. As I stood on the corner of West End and South Orange Avenue, I would often notice a young curly-headed man running past Sunrise Avenue. Found out later he started from Tremont Avenue where he lived at the time. He would continue past West End, Vermont, Columbia toward the park. I admired how committed he was to what seemed to be a regular, if not daily regimen. One day as I was getting ready to step on Cheap Charlie, I smiled at Curly Head in acknowledgement, and he smiled back. The bus started down the street, passed Vailsburg Park, went under the Garden State Parkway Bridge and was passing the Pabst Brewery and Cooper's Deli when someone exclaimed, "He's keeping up with the bus."

I looked out of the window and sure enough, Curly Head was in stride. By now, everyone on this crowded bus was looking. And someone pointed out, "He's looking at you." Now the distance from West End Avenue to downtown is more than 3 miles. I was impressed when I got off the bus on the corner of Broad and Market and he was right there. I am not going to flatter myself and say he ran all the way downtown because of my smile. I found out later that this wasn't the first time he had run all the way downtown, not losing pace with the bus. But it had clearly been a while because he was absolutely sweaty and spent. And he clearly had not planned this out: he didn't have twenty-five cents to get the bus back up South Orange Avenue. We exchanged numbers and I gave him the quarter he needed. Just another of those strange things that happen when you're on a Newark bus.

Over time you learn that Larry's very nature is to spend everything he's got in him for the struggle. You see it when he is in front of an audience. As you listen to Larry run off information about names, dates, and events in history, you remember him saying he doesn't have a television or a computer. I'm sure he had a television when he was raising his kids with his wife because Larry and I would talk about various *Star Trek* episodes. But currently, outside of his smartphone, this brother gets his information the old-fashioned way. He reads and absorbs everything. When he's on the podium, you can't really call him a speaker because he's just too fiery for that. He's way too passionate to be a professor giving a lecture. And he might not be religious enough to be considered a preacher. But something much more akin to preaching is what he does. Maybe it's like the fiery abolitionists of old rallying the troops to fight. He pours himself out sometimes three or four times on a weekend moving from one speaking engagement to the next. It is slightly scary to watch when you know what he's been through physically.

I had the privilege of driving him to some of the events around Black History Month. He had ten activities back-to-back, literally in one weekend. Larry had already crashed up one car for falling asleep behind the wheel. Some of the POP members take turns now getting him around when we know, or he lets us know he has a crunched schedule. He can't really eat before speaking so he often goes the whole day without eating. He'll drink water sometimes or that blasted *Red Bull*. I just look at him and wonder, *how do you do this? I'd be done after the first speech.* But I realized he really gets a high from speaking. The adrenalin is pumping in marathon mode. He's just got to make it to the finish. But he never really does. Like Superman, there is always a villain to catch or expose. The villains include racism, sexism, and poverty. The struggle came in the form of educating, agitating, mobilizing and constant organizing while the day job was in continual peril of being lost. The sacrifice comes in the knowledge of what every superman comes to understand. There is little or no normalcy. The Spider-Man mantra "With great power must also come great responsibility" greatly frustrates a marriage situation. You expect sacrifice but constant sacrifices can manifest physically and stretch one emotionally.

No one has ever known Larry to actually take a real vacation. Some years ago, Larry went to speak in Bermuda at a Bermuda Industrial Union conference, He then turned around and came back the same day without seeing the sights or absorbing the sun on a beautiful white sandy beach. *Who does that?* Larry is someone who always sees a larger picture and the broader implications of not doing enough. He is very critical of himself and sometimes loses sight of all the people's lives he's given meaning to, particularly people like the Williams/Faison family and the Hearns family.

I was speaking to fellow POP member Ingrid Hill about this. Hill said he's driven; it seems as if he has been touched by the spirits of Dr. King, Malcolm X, Medgar Evers, Fannie Lou Hamer, and other ancestors. What people see is a genuine, unadulterated pure drive to realize a better world. (As a Christian, I often wonder about that Holy Spirit experience he had as a child with his aunt as he read the Beatitudes found in Matthew 5:1-12 for the first time — that moment he was touched by God's Word.) Those of us in the struggle often must question if we are half-stepping as we try to balance our lives while struggling to keep up with Larry. Balance is an exquisite luxury to activists. The pervasive sense of urgency that presses on the chest often precludes the comfort and normalcy that would permit balance.

POP is a family pulled together with common threads of pain and compassion, committed to meeting for a spiritual dinner once a week for the purpose of creating the change they want to see around them. It is a feast replete with remembering and honoring our past while pouring into the future. Sankofa. It is a way to heal our collective wounds through collective strength. Two hours go by fast and it's not uncommon to have agenda items moved to the following week because we wouldn't let the guest speaker go. "Susan on stack." "Lela on stack." "Daniel on stack." "Tyrone on stack," "Nat on stack,"

Questions for the speaker could go on until Adams or Hill say, "Okay Chair, it's 8:30 and we still have items on the agenda." And Hamm heeds the signal and lets everyone know, we'll take one or two more. He'll add, "And please make sure they are questions and not long commentaries."

Discourse creates pathways for understanding and leads to action. "We should write a letter to…," ""Let's invite ….," "We need to memorialize…," "We should join that group's efforts to…," "It's time to demonstrate."

The shooting of Phillip Pannell was the thread that pulled me in. I have two brothers and one of them was not much older than Pannell at the time of the fatal shooting. I wanted to see both of my brothers continue to grow and thrive without the threat of being cut down by an officer's bullet. Many years later, the thread is a cord that tugs at the conscience with the knowledge that without this organization, there's less movement, less heightened awareness of our collective possibilities.

Though Pannell and then, Faison pulled me in, my level of commitment pales in comparison to others in the organization. To keep an organization together nearly forty years regularly meeting every Thursday except Thanksgiving and when Christmas falls on a Thursday is a major feat. To find people, even for five, ten, twenty years, that recognize the imperative of the organization and are willing to commit to being more imbalanced than balanced is worthy of praise. They are the unsung heroes. Vicki White, who I remembered as impeccably organized, running the anti-war forums and workshops. Roosevelt Hobbs, the one left in the room when everyone else had gone. Doug, who Larry used to run with in his track days and who stuck with him throughout, keeping us all informed with the news clippings he brought to the meeting. Dr. Ed Lewinson, a former Seton Hall history professor, who was arrested five times in Civil Rights demonstrations. In 1949, he was arrested during a "sit-in" to desegregate the Greyhound Bus Terminal in Washington, DC. Lewinson managed to be at nearly every meeting and march with his seeing eye dog. Wilbur Kornegay, who founded the Clinton Hill Improvement Association in 1982 opened the door for our meetings at Abyssinian Baptist Church — the site where we have been meeting for the past twenty years. Curtis Knight, wrongfully imprisoned for fifteen-years, became a very active POP member upon his release. Curtis had his own baking service and would bake a cake for POP with the POP emblem on it for special occasions. Daryl

Graham headed the Anti-Violence committee. Mary Weaver, a veteran who lost her son Randy to police brutality, became invaluable to the organization keeping us all in line. Earl Williams, Earl Faison's father was another strong member. Henry Shoiket stood strong with his wife, Mary, at many of the protests and Justice Mondays at over one hundred-years-old. He is a hero along with Aminifu Williams, another POP elder. Aminifu met Malcolm X and was part of the first Kwanzaa Celebration in California in 1966 with Maulana Karenga. Shelia Reid, mother of Jerome Reid, who was killed by police and initiated Justice Mondays. Marion Pitts, believed to be the outspoken, no-nonsense, speak-the-truth character in Sister Souljah's book. Dr. Ellyne Culver, at every POP march and rally her feet would allow her to travel along with Jean Lowrie, who would make sure you ate well. Jon Levine, labor advocate, photographer and writer/editor of the *Fire on the Mountain blog*, highlighting many of POP's activities. They are all ancestors now, whispering in our ears along with Frederick Douglass.

And now our warriors include Larry Adams, vice chair with a passion for labor and human rights struggles historically and globally. POP presentations that give historical context to our present-day issues are his forte. His engaging style is in full swing when representing POP at various speaking engagements.

Ingrid Hill, POP's corresponding secretary, is a retired Seton Hall Professor who, like Adams was pulled to POP on Faison's tragic cord. Officially POP meetings are run by Hamm, but unofficially, Adams and Hill keep things rolling. If Larry is coming in late from another speaking engagement or meeting, Adams and Hill start the meeting. If Hamm must leave early to get to another event, Adams and Hill continue with the agenda.

Steve Hatcher heads the Plainfield Branch and faithfully runs the membership drive throughout much of the year on the corner of Broad and Market in Newark. Other members include Zayid Muhammad, New Black Panther/poet/writer/historian/co-founder of the POPcorn Kidz Black history group, and Lisa Davis (Angela Davis fire on social media). Sandra Hayward is the founder of POPcorn Kidz, a Black history group that was meeting monthly at the Irvington Branch more than five years before COVID. The sagacious Willa Cofield's life story is a history lesson stretched back to her days as a schoolteacher in segregated North Carolina. She shares her story through film in her documentary, *Brick School Legacy*—a pioneering boarding institution which provided education for African Americans in segregated North Carolina from 1895 to 1933. Josie Gonsalves is a professor and founder of *Public Square Amplified* an online community news site. Jean Ross Esq is a consummate advocate for prisoners. Many have expressed interest in beginning a prison chapter. Valerie Cobbertt, sister of Guila Dale III, a retired Army Veteran who was shot and killed by Newton, NJ police officers in front of his home on July 4, 2021. There is the always deeply thoughtful educator, Diane Colson. Colson and Cobbertt are in charge of Hamm's scheduling now. Melanie Shane, Lorraine Harris, Bella August, Pat Clark, Sharon Baldwin and Angenetta Robinson compose the Montclair chapter and they host the Table Talk with POP fundraiser every year. Carlos Dufflar and Angel Martinez represent the New York chapter. There are still others on the front lines like Alfreda Daniels; Brenda Edwards; Steve Bernhardt and his wife, Vijay; Atiyah Bey; John Brinkley; Fred Nguyen; Susan Newton-Washington; Shazaliza Williams— all binding their cords together, raising the POP banner while continuing the fight.

Chairman by Annette M. Alston

As you might imagine, getting Larry to sit down long enough to do the many interviews for this book had its own set of challenges. We would usually meet at *Panera's* in Montclair, and he was usually running late due to meetings, demonstrations, interviews, phone calls from people in need, et cetera ... that went longer than expected. I was totally fine with it because it would give me more time to find a relatively quiet, somewhat isolated place in *Panera's* to prepare for the interview by reviewing notes et cetera. There were a couple of times he absolutely surprised me and got there before me, sitting there grinning like he knew he got me.

A few times we met at the POP/NJ Action office on Bloomfield Avenue. That's when I had the opportunity to see all the signs that had been made and collected over the years. It's also where he keeps all the plaques he was awarded because there is no room where he is currently staying.

Panera served us better as a place to meet in spite of the other people in the restaurant because chances were that on the Sunday evenings, we usually managed to schedule a time, he still had not eaten at all during the day. His rooming house did not have an oven or stove to cook in, so he had to eat out every day. The menu at *Panera's* had more variety to accommodate his pescatarian diet and it was healthier than the fast-food mainstays. Larry wasn't much into soups, salads, or tea. He'd order Mediterranean sandwiches and/or mac-and-cheese and then he was set to talk until the place closed. There were moments I felt as though I was speaking to a college professor. His wealth of historical knowledge encouraged me to read more, and I do. But it's still far from adequate. I'd have to read nonstop for two years or more to get half the knowledge Larry has.

Larry retired from NJ Transit two years ago. At the time, I thought NJ Transit was the only thing that kept some sort of guard-railing around his life, preventing him from spending everything within him? I wondered if retirement would just free him to find more reservoirs of sustenance and strength in the form of movement — one in a direction people can see, a course they will want to chart. I'm praying for the latter because, like Moses, everyone deserves to see the Promised Land before they die.

It's December 22, 2019. Larry is standing at the podium in the community room of REFAL on South Ninth Street and Thirteenth Avenue. It is flowering with the same kind of diversity as was seen a few weeks earlier at the Rutgers Dome. There were people from North Jersey, South Jersey, and Middlesex County. There was shades of Jesse's (or should we say Fred Hampton's?) rainbow — all with one purpose. Everyone was waiting for The Announcement. Larry is the state chair of Senator Bernie Sanders' campaign for President. He feels that the Sanders program addresses the needs of the masses of the people in this country. Sanders has consistently agitated for these things for more than 40 years. As part of a strategic plan to enter Sanders' name as part of a line, Larry was asked to run for the U.S. Senator position against Democratic Senator (and later, Democratic Presidential candidate) Senator Cory Booker.

Is that movement I hear and see? Someone is running who is going to set the temperature, not be a political thermostat (something Booker's many critics can claim). Can the United States of America be ready to graduate, evolve? Will it recognize it can be strong enough to embrace the poor, the mournful, meek and those who hunger and thirst after righteousness? Is there enough of a constituency in the United States of America that is ready to support a progressive and radical agenda?

I watched Larry as he stood behind the podium, knowing that he was a hesitant warrior in this campaign. But there was something about the testimonies that were shared in that crowded room. Something about the Facebook post affirmations that whispered something to him that he's known deep in his heart. *It's time.*

"I'm not running to occupy an office. Can't just be about putting people in office but about fundamental transformation. I'm running to build a movement. I've been in the movement for almost fifty years, and I'll be in it for whatever number of years I have left."

"I was kind of running because I wanted to help Bernie out but after I saw all of that stuff on Facebook, I'm running because I want to win. I think we can win this!"

"If we do this, this won't be the beginning of a campaign, but this will be the beginning of something greater than a campaign."

Two days later Larry was on the track at Brookdale Park in Montclair. It was his sixty-sixth birthday and it was time for his annual birthday run. He had to do one more mile than he did the previous year. Last year he jogged six miles. This year it would be seven. His youngest daughter Imani waited patiently on the bench as he made his laps and she kept track. I had just had a total knee replacement surgery almost three weeks before. But I took my walker out there and went around once in solidarity. Of course, he lapped me about four times before I made it around once.

He kept saying, "I'm going to attempt to do seven miles." I knew, barring some injury, he would complete it. His whole life has been a testament to his belief in his ability to do better. We may not be able to keep up with Larry, but hopefully, we can move far enough along to make real progress.

This leg of Larry's journey has been met with deep concern from people in the struggle and who love him. *Why is he doing this? Why is he going against Booker?* The answer is simple: whether he runs alone or with a crowd, leading the pack or behind it, Larry's direction has never changed.

— December 2019/November 2022

POST-SCRIPT: ADHIMU CHANGA, A MAN DEVOTED TO STRUGGLE WITHOUT HATE AND GREATNESS WITHOUT EGO

By Norman Finkelstein

Norman Finkelstein is one of the nation's most prominent anti-Zionists and one of the most significant public intellectuals on the Left today. He knew Hamm during his Princeton days and shared his recollections below.

I don't remember the first time I met Larry Hamm, who we would all come to know not as Larry, but Adhimu Changa. I remember him from the Princeton graduate dorm.

I was active in Left politics at the time. The main manifestations of Left politics back then on Princeton's campus was the People's Front for the Liberation of South Africa, of which Larry was a leader, along with Sharon Kalemkiarian, who's now a California judge and Marsha Bonner, who wrote a book on the Central Park Five case. Here are things that stuck in my mind about him. First of all, Princeton back then — and is still — a very, very white place. And a lot of the students you met, even those on the Left, can be from very entrenched and established ruling elite families.

And for example, I remember one guy who was on the Left, but his father was in the Central Intelligence Agency, a part of government that back then had an uglier representation than the Ku Klux Klan.

* * *

One thing about Larry which has always been remarkable to me is how deeply respected he was by all the white students at Princeton. It wasn't a kind of phony, fake white liberal respect they claim for Barack Obama. (Barack Obama is used by white liberals to prove how cool they are, just like in my day white liberals used to brag about how much they loved jazz. I hate jazz now because of this: white liberals have spoiled it for me. And Obama has replaced jazz in the white liberal mind.) The respect that white people on Princeton's campus had for Adhimu Changa — almost nobody on campus called him Larry Hamm back then — was completely devoid of any patronizing, any white racist condescension.

I really respected him from the beginning, because there was something about his authenticity. There has never been a fake bone in that man's body. This is why I think he could do well as a US Senator because it's impossible to come with any skeletons. He's an open book. Very comfortable in his skin, nothing to hide. And definitely not "radical chic." Larry was consistent to the point that forced you to believe him and believe in him.

I've always considered Larry and [fellow Princeton anti-apartheid protester] Allan Nairn as enigmas because there is nothing to trace how they became who they are. I mean, in Larry's case, I met his mother. I thought he looked like her and I was shocked to find out years later he was adopted. She was an honest Christian woman. *So how did this apple fall from that tree?* I still don't know. And if you see pictures of him from high school, he does not look like a guy who would spend his life protesting, agitating.

We didn't know it then, but initially he struggled academically to keep up at Princeton. He deeply regrets that he hadn't spent a lot more time studying in high school. The fact that he was so honest about it — he's talked publicly about waking up in the mornings at Princeton crying, because he couldn't keep up with the work — shows you a lot of about his character. It's very revealing. He now counsels high school students to study as hard as they can. He struggled not only academically, but with the wealth and class infrastructure. It blew his mind to be in a ruling-class institution. So, I'm saying he earned the real respect of people who were nothing like him. And he did so because he was true to himself and a real person and a real radical. Young people need to hear about how far honesty, maturity and seriousness can carry you. It has carried Larry all his life because he doesn't have a disingenuous bone in his body. That authenticity is so rare.

* * *

Larry was and is a radical. You can't be a radical unless you're really indignant at the state of things — in his case, Black America. You have to be really indignant.

He was able to relate so well and command the respect of everybody; he was never motivated by hate. Amidst all the moral seriousness, there was and is a genuine warmth, kindness, a sweetness; a niceness about Larry. He wasn't the Martin

Luther King type. He deeply identified with the radical militant, armed struggle part of the Left.

I'm friends with Alice Walker. Most of the time when I see her, I'm more interested in the past and the present. And I ask her impression of this person and that person. One time I asked her impression of Stokely Carmichael and she said that he is just too full of hate and anger for her. Larry is indignant, but he's not angry and not full of hate. It was a shock to the white students — *here's this Black guy named Adhimu Changa and he's from inner-city Newark and a leader in the Black Power Movement there, and he doesn't hate me as a white person. In fact, he likes me.* That shocked people. The content did not match the image in Larry's case.

* * *

Larry was, and still is, the great orator of the Movement. Some of his oratory, to this day — I won't say it's a class of its own, but it's certainly in the first-rank. The speech he gave in Ferguson — that is a *speech*. It was just a small little community gathering. The parents of the victims were introduced. And then he spoke. He talked about how Black leaders came and said to turn it down, turn it down. And he said, no, turn it up, turn it up.

He used to carry around a little brown book pad, a book in which he was constantly learning new words. He wanted to improve his vocabulary, not just as a point on a pedantic point of view or trying to be impressive. He wanted to do it because he enjoyed it and it was critical to his oratory. Each time he would learn a new word, he would open this little book and he would enter it. It was quite impressive.

Post-Script

If you take someone like Frederick Douglass whose command of the English language is frankly terrifying, I think we have to remember that Douglass was an orator and a newspaper editor, but not an organizer. As David Blight and other historians have shown, Douglass was on the road constantly because he was constantly being asked to speak. Douglass had a lot of time to read and write because he wasn't doing the organizing. Larry has kept a fulltime job for 40 years and also has been raising children and also organizing, which meant a lot less time to read and develop his mind through books. He paid a price for that. I wish personally he had had more time to study at Princeton. He just couldn't wait to get back to Newark. He made a choice. Wild horses couldn't keep him in Princeton. He wanted to go back to Newark. He wanted to do the nitty gritty work of organizing. He didn't reach the heights he probably could have. But Larry's not part of the Black elite, like Oprah or the Obamas; he's proud to be part of the Black grassroots. Larry's speeches are filled with the torment, anguish and love of his people.

Larry has the power to speak himself out of his own doldrums. He was going through a divorce. He could be in a really depressed state about it, and then he's called upon to give a speech and he just transforms, he just rises to the occasion. I remember to this day his speech mocking the Sullivan Principles, which were a Black capitalist blueprint used to neutralize the South African apartheid divestment movement. I had seen him five minutes before — desolate. And then something within him just turns on that level of self-control, self-discipline.

* * *

One of my memories of Larry has little to do with words. He, Allan and I were in New York Port Authority waiting for the train. We saw some cops surrounding a young Black person. And all of a sudden, we saw this glower in Larry's eyes. Again, I saw the moral seriousness I had remembered from Princeton. This was not theater; this was not for cameras. He was deadly angry at what he was seeing. He retained his fire, kept it within, but the message was in his eyes: *You have no business treating human beings that way. You have no business treating young Black men that way.*

I am known for *not* keeping my fire within. I was on a panel with Larry recently at Princeton. I ripped into a few of the Jewish students. I was very verbally aggressive. I said to one of the people in the audience who boasted about the fact that he was one of the guards along the Gates of Gaza, I said, "You have no shame. That's the problem. You are a concentration camp guard. You have no shame about that. That's what I can't understand. How can a concentration camp guard boast about what he's doing? You're proud of the fact that you're killing children. Boasting about it. In my day, concentration camp guards used to be embarrassed by what they did."

And I was criticized afterwards by some people for it. Afterward, I thought about whether I had done the right thing — you accept when speaking that there are good days and nights, and bad days and nights. And unless you are a complete narcissist and egotist, you have to listen to other people's opinions of your statements and then make a mental note to not repeat any errors the next time. Of course, I attached the highest value to Larry's opinion, so when I talked to him on the phone the next day, I asked him "Do you think I went over the top?" He answered, "No, you didn't. You were you. And what you said was right." As we were speaking, children were being killed by the Israelis in Gaza. My articulated level of anger was, in his mind, perfectly warranted. To his credit, Larry didn't talk about whether this is tactically correct or strategic. I got off the phone and I felt good about him. I felt good about what I did. Sometimes it's not the place to calculate. It's the place to just speak the truth in an unvarnished and undiluted form.

* * *

Much of Larry's life has been taken up with police brutality and its victims. That's why what I saw in his eyes at the Port Authority is so real. It's not about trying to score a point or use the situation or explore the situation for some sort of political gain. It's real humans and real suffering. He knows it because he deals with the families who are grieving what it means to lose your child, what it means to hear or see your child being sent away for no good reason. And on that level, he maintains his authenticity. It's about real human suffering.

— *As Told To Annette M. Alston, December 2019*

A Life in the Struggle

People Don't Think Anything Good Comes Out of Newark.

People Don't Think Anything Good.

People Don't Think.

Dr. Vicky Gholson [1950-2014] (whose study for her doctoral dissertation was conducted in Newark), in 1994 conversation with Annette M. Alston

Afterword:
ADHIMU, ALWAYS LACED UP

by Zayid Muhammad

Zayid Muhammad is a revolutionary, a writer, a poet/spoken word artist, a teacher, and a stalwart member of the People's Organization for Progress. Like Hamm, he is an electrifying speaker and serious grassroots organizer. He became an activist as a young man after reading a copy of The Autobiography of Malcolm X.

Allah and Malcolm forever changed him. A self-described "NY Panther Cub," he has worked with every major Black Liberation Movement in the New York City area for more than thirty-five years. Zayid has known Hamm for at least 40 years.

The importance of us being able to tell our own stories, from that first slave narrative of Equiano to this very backwards-marching moment, is and has been crucial to our very survival. It has also been at the anchor of us amazingly at times being a transcendent presence in this unwelcoming place that built its mindboggling wealth upon, not one, but two genocides.

This story, one of an adopted Black son of working-class parents, not only tells the story of an irrepressible spirit rising from humble origins to become an exemplary bulwark of resistance to oppression. It tells other stories. This memoir tells stories of a 'Chocolate City' that was once as southern as it was northern, a city whose neighborhood expression once reflected the village character of its Black citizens' traditional African past. It captures the story of a city torn apart as it rose up against Gangster Urban Apartheid and ran it out of town. Finally, it reflects the story of a city whose people love it so, despite all its drama, corruption, poverty, and violence that they stayed and lived through the rubble of 1967 and the stigma of violence that stuck to it like mummified tape for five decades! You are chewing on a narrative sandwich that has all of this and more between its breaded covers through the telling of the story of this incredible working-class native son of Newark, New Jersey, that is the unstoppable Lawrence Hamm.

The legendary Harlem writer John Oliver Killens once said that the Black Liberation Movement needed some 'long distance runners'...some people who could live long enough to show us and tell us how to fight through the protracted dimensions of our struggle that we've been engaged in for only 500 years with the clarity and conviction necessary to be a difference over the long haul. * Lawrence Hamm, sincere and humble enough to tell you without any preconditions of his failures and mistakes, is and has been such a runner. You heard him tell you how terrible he was even at running when he first got into the sport. He talked about how he was so bad that he would get lapped by other runners in his early competitions in high school, but he never gave up...Something inside of him said 'don't quit.' He stayed with it and simply ran more and more until he found his now famous stride, until he became a proven world class runner. That substory of this memoir is not to be treated in passing. To be sure, once he found himself in the throes of struggle, it was that same determination that made him a world class runner that also made him a grassroots leader of treasured character, humility, sincerity, compelling passion, and heroic endurance.

He wanted to modestly anchor the story around the vehicle he shaped that became his instrument of political expression since 1983, The People's Organization for Progress.

What is revealed, however, is how he became the anchor of not only that vehicle, but for the eyes and ears and hearts of so many. I'm talking about people who needed someone who was honest and could be relied on to stand up and speak for them in the face of injustice for now going on fifty years. Fifty years with his famous boundless energy, and those stories, like the launching of New Jersey's Divestment Against Apartheid Movement, or the Marathon for Justice that was the case of Earl Faison. They were not at all confined to Newark...

As I write this, he has just run seven miles run for his sixty-sixth Xmas Eve birthday!

Seven miles at 66!

Not only that, he also just announced his insurgent candidacy for the US Senate as a part of a larger strategy to support Democratic Socialist Bernie Sanders' second serious bid for the White House, an announcement that has already created a buzz far beyond all of our immediate expectations!

Incredible, right?

More incredible is that just several years ago as he stepped into his Sixties, he was damned near crushed to death in an auto accident that required him being cut out of his vehicle! Most of us would not have survived that. Not to mention gotten back in running shape in just a matter of months! Back to answering every call for help...back to seizing every moment to stand up for justice, as he somehow did...

It was in the face of this confrontation with death, a perilously close one by all accounts, did I realize how we, myself-included, were on the verge of making the mistake of taking his long-lunged presence for granted. It was in the throes of this ordeal that I realized how much we needed him, how much we loved him and how much we ought to appreciate him.

"We almost lost him," I said chokingly, breaking down trying to open for him in his public reappearance before a church that we packed to honor Sarah Collins Rudolph, the surviving fifth girl of the bombing of the Sixteenth Street Baptist Church back in 1963.

Big badd, ultra-angry, swaggadocious Panther cub Zayid Muhammad...There I was...In a sea of tears, damn near bawlin' like a baby...realizing our folly....my own folly...of making that mistake of taking him for granted, of not appreciating him in the Land of the Living for what his run...his still making circles of dignity and passionate resistance around oppression truly means.

We need him to run as far as his long lungs and irrepressible heart will take him. We need to clear the path so he can continue.

We need to train up as many from within our ranks to take his baton for when that time comes for him to yield it.

Adhimu, Always Laced Up

His is a run through both the darkest and brightest moments of his city's recent history, and of this country's recent history. He is a living people's torchlight, if you will allow my extension of the Olympian metaphor, that shows us all that we can serve humanity and serve for a long time in a strong way *if* we truly love humanity and justice as deeply as humanity needs and deserves to be loved, especially in the face of so much crippling toxicity and injustice that we must now overcome.

This service won't make you wealthy, but it is enriching as only a 'Love for the People,' pardon my Panther language, can be...a love that serves, a love that speaks out loud against injustice and oppression, a love that will dare to go to extraordinary lengths to put that injustice and oppression on blast...marching from Camden to Philadelphia, protesting for 381 days, camping out at Police Headquarters!... A love for humanity that will do things like that to make a difference, a love that inspires commitment in others to try to be about that same kind of love...

May we all stretch and strengthen our lungs, strengthen our legs, expand our hearts and widen our wings and embrace a vision for a better world, one that we are all going to live in together, whether we like it or not, as we run with this story to a better place and space inside our very selves.

Thank you Adhimu... Lawrence Hamm...For showing us that we can...

*The *Black Scholar*, November 1973, John Oliver Killens, "Wanted, Some Long-Distance Runners"...

--December 2019

Pomfret, Maryland: Lawrence Hamm, Imani Hamm, Nia Hamm-Clark, Laini Hamm at Theresa Burton's funeral on June 2, 2023

ABOUT THE AUTHORS

Lawrence Hamm, a candidate in New Jersey's Democratic primary for the U.S. Senate in 2024, has been involved in every major social movement in the state for the last fifty years. As a nineteen-year-old student activist from Arts High School in Newark, he was appointed to the Newark Board of Education in 1971 by Kenneth Gibson, the city's first Black mayor. Hamm was inspired to become a community activist because of the example of internationally known playwright/poet/activist Amiri Baraka. A graduate of Princeton University, he was part of the student leadership cadre that had a major campus anti-apartheid protest in the 1970s, years before the anti-apartheid movement became dominant on American campuses. He founded the People's Organization for Progress (POP) in 1983. POP, an independent, grassroots organization, became a recognized leader in New Jersey's anti-apartheid and Million Man March movements. A proud father of three daughters who are Rutgers graduates, he has been involved in fighting for quality education, employment opportunities and access to health care and against racial profiling and police brutality. POP, joined by Newark Mayor Ras Baraka and other activist organizations, led a successful, nonviolent protest and rally in Newark of more than ten thousand after the 2020 murder of George Floyd.

A Life in the Struggle

Annette M. Alston is an award-winning writer based in Newark, New Jersey. Her book, *Harriet Tubman for Beginners*, has received national recognition. Her three-part series on the twenty-fifth anniversary of the Newark Rebellion was printed in the *New York Amsterdam News* and the *Newark City News* where it won a NNPA Merit Award, among the highest honors for journalism in the Black press. A retired Newark public school teacher in primary and secondary education, she is skilled in nonprofit organizations, event planning, grant writing, literacy, and coaching. She is a former leader of the Newark Education Association union and stalwart member of the People's Organization for Progress and her South Ward-based church, Greater Life Ministries. She has a bachelor's degree in journalism from Rutgers-New Brunswick and a master's degree in social studies Teacher Education from Concordia University-Portland. She worked with Hamm for two years on this book. A cat lover, her first book—Sheri Berry, the Scritch Scratch Cat—is a fictional children's story about her first cat.

ANNETTE ALSTON'S ACKNOWLEDGEMENTS

What appears to be about the life of one person is really an excuse to mention the names of so many others who were vital to the struggle and must be included in any recorded history of the struggle. This book is inspired by high school students, college students and people who make up the People's Organization for Progress; those New Jerseyans who stand ever ready for revolution.

It is a blessing to have real friends that think enough of you to not only support you verbally but also literally in deed. Thank you, Dr. Howard, for writing the forward, Dr. Norman Finkelstein for writing the postscript and Zayid Muhammad for writing the Afterward.

I'd like to thank more great friends, Ingrid Hill for assisting with the pictures and the POP preamble and reading.

This body of work would be impossible to complete without the research and guidance from three libraries and a network of very professional librarians.

I'd like to thank Princeton's Mudd Librarian, April Armstrong; Orange librarians, Alice McMillan, Barbara Fay and Phyllis

Scott; and Newark Public Library's NJ Room librarians and archivists, Greg Guderian, Beth Zak-Cohen, James Amemasor and Vanessa Castaldo.

I'd like to thank my friends and family, Joy, Audrey, Melanie, Andrea, Mother Rose, Mama Whitley, Mrs. Givens, Mrs. Hyman, Talia, Janet and Lance Young; My Greater Life Ministries church family—— Special thanks to Pastor Michael and Maria Westbrook for acting as readers—— and to the rest of my spiritual family the Bacchus, Witter and Edmonds family, fellow author, Antoinette Bennett and my education protégé, Talia Day.

Always thankful to my many aunts and uncles and cousins for their continual support: There are quite a few I want to call by name but that would get me in trouble.

Finally, to my brothers— Louis and Jonathan, for their consistent love and wise counsel, and of course to the living legends of our family—Mom Fannie and Pop Louis, who made sure they grounded us in faith, humor and service. And, finally, my two cats Sparkle and Shadow, who constantly comfort and entertain me.

PEOPLE'S ORGANIZATION FOR PROGRESS PREAMBLE

We, the members of the People's Organization for Progress, have founded this association to work for the fundamental transformation of the society in which we live. It is our desire to build a more just social order. Our primary goal is nothing less than the complete elimination of poverty, all forms of social, racial and economic exploitation, oppression, degradation, human misery, suffering and injustice.

We shall unify and organize working, poor, and progressive people and strive to foster cooperation, self-reliance, and a militant fighting spirit among them. We shall build our organization so that it may become a viable political vehicle for the oppressed and a significant force for progressive politics. We shall work to unite the greater progressive community, increase its ranks and build a broad mass movement at the local level which will be an integral part of the national, and worldwide struggle for social and economic justice.

Our concern is not only for society as a whole but for the individual as well. We seek not only social transformation but the transformation of the individual through involvement in the struggle for human liberation. We believe that in order for the struggle to transform society to succeed it must be carried out and supported by people imbued with revolutionary values. We want to make the individual socially aware and concerned, more responsible and compassionate, committed and active in the struggle for social change.

We support and involve ourselves in advocacy, self-help, and reform efforts to improve the conditions of the people; however, we believe that the major social, economic, and political problems confronting working and poor people cannot be solved unless there is a radical redistribution of power and wealth in our society and a restructuring of our socioeconomic system that will result in the empowerment of the masses over all institutions that effect their lives.

We vow to uphold the legacy of struggle which we have inherited and not to rest until justice, equality, dignity, and peace are a reality for all.

INDEX

Abbott 151, 157
Abbott vs Burke 151
Abdullah, Daniel 160
Abernathy, Ralph 38
abolitionists 243
Abraham, Rose 212, 236
Abu-Jamal, Mumia 23
Abyssinian signaling 222
activism/activist 58, 79, 99
   degree of 99
   electoral politics and 100
   at Princeton 97
   role of 185
   symbolism 63
Adams, Greg 119
Adams, Larry 221–222, 247
Addonizio, Hugh 30, 42, 44, 85
Affordable Care Act 189
African Liberation Day 75, 87
African Liberation movements 57
African Liberation Week 56–57
African National Congress 87
African National Congress (ANC) 87, 142
agitating 236, 240, 244, 255
American Committee on Africa (ACoA) 89
American Indian Movement 39

Amistad 214–215
Anderson, Sam 88
Angola 84, 88
anti-apartheid 76, 87, 90, 93, 97, 111, 127, 132–133, 135, 142, 219, 267
   cultural events 133
   movement 90, 132
anti-capitalist 76, 85
anti-imperialist 76, 85
anti-police brutality work 173
anti-racism 142
anti-Semitic statements 153
anti-violence 174, 247
   committee 247
   sentiment 174
anti-war march 219
Antoine, Max 181
apartheid 76, 85, 87–91, 93, 95, 115, 120, 129, 133–134, 140, 168, 257, 262–263
   clarity and purpose 134
   consciousness about 133
   forums on 133
   on health of children 89–90
   political system 129
   South Africa 168
Appalachian coal mines 90

Arbery, Ahmaud Marquez 220, 222–224, 231, 233
arson 88
Arthur, Mignon Curry 133–134
Artis, Elizabeth 236
Arts High School 10, 13, 20, 22, 28, 101, 267
Ashford, Kashad 182, 196
Atkins, Henry 142
autonomy 231
Ayon, David 94

Baby Boomers 5, 22–23, 235
Baldwin, Sharon 222
Baraka, Amina 70, 107
Baraka, Amiri 2, 30–31, 33–34, 39, 41, 53, 63–64, 70–71, 73–78, 86, 129–130, 166, 196, 236, 267
Baraka, Ras 129, 170, 195, 219, 267
Barber, William 15
Barringer High School 34
beliefs 15
Bell, Charles 41, 65
Bell, Tedock 236
Bernhardt, Steve 229, 248
Bethany Baptist Church 190, 193
Bey, Atiyah 248
Bey, Fredrica 154
biases 49–50
Biden, Joe 228
Big Six 6
Bikila, Abebe 26–27
Biko, Steve 133
Birmingham church bombing 236
Black/Blacks
  communities 1, 42–43, 45, 54, 57, 62, 64, 74–76, 87, 99, 145, 155, 226–227
  cultural and educational meeting 227
  employment for 10
  humanity 157
  identity 61
  intellectual magazines 83
  men, mass movement of 155
  music industry 154
  nationalism 86, 149
  nationalist symbolism 49
  people, socioeconomic conditions of 120
  racist 65–66
  self-determination 85
  students 36, 88, 99
  victims 223
Black Consciousness Movement 56–57
Black Cops Against Police Brutality 170
Black Liberation 63, 84
Black Organization of Students (BOS) 122
Black People's Organization 124
Black Power 26, 32, 44, 64, 69–70
  community control 33
Black Power Conference 22
Black Power Movement 21, 32–33, 65
Blackwell, G. 200
Bland, Sandra 236
Bonner, Marsha 96, 253
Bontempo, Michael A. 68, 74
Booker, Cory 73, 131, 224, 226, 229–230, 252
Boyd, Leroy 236
brainstorming 121
Branch, George 72–73

Index

Brendel, Barry 228
Brodie, Elayne 42
Brooks, Rayshard 236
Brown, Debbie 174
Brown, J. Anderson 93
Brown, Rebecca 236
Buchanon, Norman ôAkiliö 49
Burton, Anthony. *See*
   Hamm, Lawrence
Burton, Theresa 163, 187, 261, 266
Bush, George W. 111, 150
Byfield, Natalie 96

Cabral, Amilcar 81–82, 84, 123
Callaghan, James 30, 44
Cammarieri, Richard 122–123
campaign
   organization 130
   workers and fundraisers 139–140
Campbell, Mary Helen 236
capitalism 95, 167
Carlos, John 26
Carlton, Brad 191
Carmichael, Stokely 82, 256
Carnegie, Joyce 168–169, 171–172, 174
Carpinteri Jr., Paul 176
Carter, Jimmy 111, 148, 212
Castro, Fidel 84
Castro, George 94
cell-based communication network 93
Central High School 52
Central Ward 5–6, 30, 52, 64, 71–73, 209
Cervase, John 42, 46–48, 54, 60–62
Chamberlain, Kenneth 236
Changa, Adhimu. *See*
   Hamm, Lawrence

character assassination 69
Chavis, Ben 88, 131, 135–137, 149
Cheema, Jan 174
Chertoff, Michael 177
Chisolm, Shirley 127
Churchman, Gladys 42–43, 60
citizenship 83
civics
   courses 50
   organizations 224
Civilian Complaint Review Board 195–196
civil rights 32–33, 140–141, 188
   organizations 119
   violations 179, 182
Civil Rights Movement 21, 38, 65, 239
Civil War 27
class-orientation school assembly 22
class struggle 82
Cleary, Robert J. 175
Clemente, Roberto 48
Clinton, Bill 145, 148, 153, 156
coalition 187, 195
Cobb, Claude 7
Cobb, Stella 7
Cofield, Willa 248
Coker, James Malik 169
Coleman, Jerry 134
collective accomplishment 235
Colvin, Claudette 188
commercial advertisements 128
commission 66, 136, 143, 150, 196
Committee for a Unified Newark (CFUN) 53, 64
common ideology 158
communications 228–229

275

Communications Workers of
America (CWA) 181, 226
community 5, 9, 42, 56, 66, 121,
131, 152–153, 171
activists 138
based organizations 132
campaigns 71
control 32
decision-making 122
development 73
institution 234
involvement 46
milies and 153
needs and building 53–54
think-tank 232
youth and segments of 49
concentration camp 257
conformity 17
Congress of African People.
See Committee for a Unified
Newark (CFUN)
Connor, Bull 2
conspiracy 88, 179, 182
constitutional violations 195
consumer safety standards 111
contemporary history 197
Conte, Richard 171–172, 176
contradiction 158–159
convictions 180
co-op. *see* People's Energy
Cooperative (PEC)
corruption 225
Council, Rufus 236
court 3
COVID-19 220, 222
Crew, Stanton 181
crime 2–3, 148, 152–153
criminal justice system 182

Crooms, Richard 15
Cross Pentecostal Church 14
Culver, Ellyne 247
curriculum
revision 52
writers 57
Curtin, Pete 37, 64
Curvin, Bob 31

Daniels, Alfreda 160, 233, 248
Daniels, Danette "Strawberry"
169, 173–174
Daniels, Ron 143
David, Theresa 33, 102, 163, 266
Davis, Angela 43, 88, 248
Davis, DeLacey 170
Davis, Lisa 106, 248
decision-making process 51, 71–72
de-facto announcement 227
Deliverance Church 174
demonstrations 171–173, 181,
187–188, 192
Detroit Alliance for a Rational
Economy (DARE) 116
development, trickling of 121
Dexter Avenue Baptist Church 137
Diallo, Amadu 159–160, 169–170,
173, 178, 188, 223
diaspora 56
Diggs, Charles 94
Dillard, Justin 227
Dilworth, Kevin 176
Dinkins, David 148
disappointment 183
disillusionment 183
disruptive influence 68
distortions 49
divestiture, demands for 93

Index

Donaldson, Vicki 72
Dorsaw, Joann 68
Douglass, Frederick 127, 210, 212, 240, 247, 257
Downtowner Motor Inn 35
drugs 152–153
Du Bois, W.E.B. 82–84, 141, 205
Duffler, Carlos 248

economic growth 112
economic recession 121
education 137
  organizations 71
  system 38
Education Law Center 151–182
Edwards, Brenda 248
egalitarian 141
elementary schools 1, 7, 10, 53, 164–165
emotion 160, 178
Equiano 261
Espichan, Carmen 177–178
ethnic conflict 15
ethnic groups 93
Everett, Terrance 169
Evers, Medgar 236, 244

Faison, Carolyn 183
Faison, Earl 105, 161, 169–177, 179–185
family 19
  emotional 91
  members 177
  permission 171
  and POP 224–225
  responsibilities 114
Farrakhan, Louis 155–156
fascist politics 148

fatal shootings 230
FBI 137, 178, 181
federal agencies 231
federal civil rights investigations 196
First Amendment 78, 195
Fishman, Paul 196
Flomenbaum, Mark 175
Florio, James 151
Floyd, George 219–221, 224, 231–233, 236, 267
Floyd/Taylor/Arbery uprisings 231–232
Foner, Philip 83
forced physical isolation 222
Fortunato, Joe 172
Foster, Kathleen 239
Fraternal Order of Police 196
Freedom Rides of 1961 136
Freedom Ways 83
Front Line Artists 233
Fuller, Howard Fuller. *See also* Sadaukai, Owusu
Fullilove, Helen 41–43, 47, 59–60
funds/fundraising 229–230
  control of 158
  process 227
Fuqua, Darryl DeRose Laqua 182
Furr, William 236

Gainer, Hattie 236
Garfinkle, Neal 134
Garner, Eric 236
Garner, Wayne 141
Garth, Andrew 176, 182
Garvey, Marcus 2–3, 48, 214
Gary Convention in 1972 63, 128
Gaye, Marvin 78

277

gender 49–50
Generation Gap 22–23
Gibson, Kenneth A. 1, 6, 21, 31,
  36–38, 42–43, 61, 64–68, 72–74,
  120–122, 128–131, 134, 140,
  142–143, 174, 204, 267
Gilmer, Raymond 236
Giuliano, Anthony J. 47, 71
Gonsalves, Josie 230, 248
Goodman, Robert 130
Gordon, Spiver 138
Graham, Daryl 152–153, 246–247
Graham, Jahqui 182
Grant, Julie 74
Grant, Ralph T. 130
grass roots organizations 190, 234
Graves, Carol 44, 69
Greadington, Jacqui 197
grief 183–184
Guiliani, Rudy 148
guilty 178

Hackett, Mims 172
Hadi, Saleemah 229
Hall, Charlie 193
Hall, Debi 68
Hamer, Fannie Lou 236, 244
Hamm, Charlene 78,
  97–98, 100–101
Hamm-Clark, Nia 266
Hamm, Imani 109, 114, 165,
  227, 253
Hamm, Laini 105, 109, 168
Hamm, Lawrence 5, 20, 77, 102,
  109, 163–164, 166, 262, 265–266
  Birth Story and Birth Mother
    Discovery 163–166
  Childhood 5–17

Combatting Police
  Brutality 163–185
The Million Man
  March 153–158
Newark Board of Education 1–2,
  35, 37–72
The Newark Rebellion 9, 19–22
The Newark Teachers' Strike
  31–38 40, 43, 51, 55, 66
The Rainbow Coalition
  136, 142–154
The Struggle against Apart-
  heid after Princeton 86–96,
  132–134, 253, 257
United Church of Christ Com-
  mission for Racial Justice
  (CRJ) 135–139
Hamm, Michelle 114
Hammond, David 22, 102
Hampton, Fred 145, 149, 252
Harris, Elder 114
Harris, James 25
Harris, Kelly 239
Harrison, Isaac 236
Hart, Gary 131
Hatcher, Steve 160, 247
Hawk, Raymond 236
Hayward, Sandra 248
Hearns, Radazz 196–197, 244
Hekalu Umoja House of Unity 131
Henry, Toby 6
Hess, Arnold 30, 44, 60
Hightower Brothers 11
Hill, Ingrid 190–191, 244–245,
  247, 269
Hill, Oscar 236
Hispanic community 42
historic homage 191–192

Index

Hobbs, Roosevelt 141, 174, 246
Hogue, Spencer 138
homelessness 184
hope, sense of 150
Howard, M. William 10, 109, 130–131, 190, 269
Howard, R 131
Hudson, Walter 182
Hughes, Jake 8
Hulett, John 137
humanitarianism 66
human rights 188
Hurt, Patricia 176

imminent manpower shortages 176
Imperiale, Anthony 2–3, 47–48, 68, 74
institutional change 197
insurgency 20
integration 188
inter-group dynamics 38
Ismael, Tasha Salaam 152
Italian racism 30

Jackson, George 82
Jackson, Gerald 228
Jackson, Jesse 38, 70, 127
Jackson, Jimmie Lee 236
Jackson, Keith 180
Jackson, Reginald 157
Jacob, Jesse 41–45, 48, 60, 71–72
James, Sharpe 45, 74, 142, 174
Johnson, Andrew 213
Johnson, Angie 118, 121
Johnson, Matthew 227–228
Johnson, Ruben 153
Jones, Aiyana 223, 236
Jones, Arthur 133

Jones, Jessie Mae 236
"Justice Monday" protests 229–230
justice system 198

Kaepernick, Colin 3
Kalemkarian, Sharon 94
Kamako's Blues People 70
Kamal, Abdul Wakil 82, 196, 236
karate 15–16
Karcher, Alan 144
Karenga, Maulana 194, 247
Kawaida Towers 71, 77, 129
Kean, Thomas 134
Kennedy, Joe 112, 194
Kerr, Edward 71
kidnapping 164
Killens, John Oliver 262, 265
King, Coretta Scott 38, 136
King, Martin Luther 2–3, 14, 47–48, 82, 168, 187, 197, 214, 236, 240
King, Rodney 149–150, 155, 159, 173–174
King's 1968 Poor People's Campaign 15
Kinoy, Arthur 140–141
Knight, Curtis 246
Knoll, Gregory 69
Kornegay, Wilbur 173, 246
Ku Klux Klan 149, 254
Kurzynowski, Nikki 228, 230

labor, bankers and exploitation of 120
Last Grave at Dimbaza 89
Lenin, V. 82–83
León, Roger 199, 203, 208
Lewinson, Ed 246
Lewis, Claude 62

279

Lifland, J 179–180, 183
Lincoln, Abraham 208, 210–213
Liuzzo, Viola 137
Lockett, Tyrone 160
Lordi, Joseph P. 69
Louima, Abner 159–160, 169, 173
Lowrie, Jean 247

Machel, Samora 84
Malanga, Thomas 42–43, 48, 60
Malcolm X. Shabazz High School 48–49
Mandela, Nelson 87, 134, 148
Mann, Assatta 228, 230
Marburger, Carl 62
marches 192
Marcus, Jerome 25–26
Martin, Keith 191
Martin, Robert Lee 236
Martin, Trayon 181
Marx, Karl 31–32, 75, 82–83, 119–120
Mascia, Emil E. 69
Mason, Barry 26, 28–29, 178, 195, 208
Mayse, Tasha 150, 152, 223
McClain, Elijah 236
McCormick, Lisa 225
McMillan, Gladys (Ayo) 145, 154
McNair, Denise 138–139
media 195
Menendez, Bob 225
Mersier, Jr., Albert 236
Mfalme 81
Miller, Michelle. *See* Michelle Hamm
Million Man March 154–155, 157–158

Million Man Montclair 181
Mitchell, Mike 99
Mnumzana, Neo 142
mobilization skills 173–174
Mondale, Walter 131
Montgomery Bus Boycott 190
Moore, Lenny 28
Moran, Michael 236
Morheuser, Marilyn 151–152
Moss, Eddie 236
Mosselle, James 67, 69
movement on Princeton 96
Muhammad, Khadir 153
Muhammad, Muneer 197
Muhammad, Zayid 248, 261, 269
Munnerlyn, Charlotte 145, 154
murder 223
  definition of 175
Murray, Cornelius 236

Nader, Ralph 111
Nairn, Allan 94, 111, 254
Nance, Jim 74
National 25, 57, 62, 83, 133, 149, 190–191
National Association of Colored People (NAACP) 25, 57, 62, 149
National Awareness Alliance 182
National Black Political Convention in Gary 64
National Negro Liberty Party 127
National School Board Convention in San Francisco 43
negotiated agreement 55
neighborhoods
  destruction of 21
  health centers 74
Nesbitt, Prexy 89

Index

Neto, Agostinho 84
Newark City Council 45, 196
Newark Coalition for
    Neighborhoods 122–123
Newark Federation of High School
    Student Councils 34, 36
Newark public schools 50
Newark's Black Power
    Movement 128–129
New Ark Student Federation
    52–53, 58, 86, 96, 103
Newark Teachers Union (NTU) 32,
    36, 42, 44, 69, 191
New Black Panther Party 181, 191
New Jersey 25, 27, 30, 32, 64, 73, 86
    Association of Black
        Educators 25
    Jericho Movement 191
    Million Man March 158
    Rainbow Coalition 143
Newton, Huey 77
Nkrumah, Kwame 76, 82, 84, 86
Noble, Gil 142
non-violence 33
Nonviolent Coordinating
    Committee 53
NOW-New Jersey Branch 191
Nyerere, Julius 76, 84

Obama, Barack 189–190, 254
Operation Breadbasket/Operation
    PUSH 70, 128–129
oppression 3
optimism 150
Orange City Council 176
Orange Police Headquarters 171
Oregon Cascade Mountains 26
Organization of Negro
    Educators 45
Outward Bound Program 26–27
Owens, Jesse 13

Pan-Africanism 75, 86
Pan-African organization 3
Pannell, Phillip 140, 150, 152, 159,
    169, 245–246
Parker, Wilbur 30, 44
Parks, Rosa 38, 48, 57, 107, 188
Payne, Bill 214
Payne, Donald 128
Payton, Tyrone 176, 182
People's Energy Cooperative
    (PEC) 112–114, 116, 119, 135
People's Organization for Progress
    (POP) 21, 99, 116, 118, 120–
    121, 124, 130, 149, 159, 166,
    180, 187, 223, 261, 263, 267–269
    creation and maintenance of 100
    family and 224–225
    power of 231
    program 194
    Rainbow Coalition to 145
People United for Better Schools
    Coalition (PUBS) 122
Perdue, B. 135
Petti, Michael 42–43, 47, 65
physical scars 160
Pitts, Marion 173–174, 247
police 3, 169, 177–178
    aggression 170
    career 170
    departments 220
    militarism 223
    shooting 223–224
police brutality 30, 150, 159–161,
    171, 174, 181–182, 189, 233, 259
    continuation of 240
    demonstrations 169

pattern of 224
victims of 181, 222–223
political
  activity 115, 233
  capital 48
  education curriculum 54
  endorsements 125
  leadership 117–118, 142–143
  movement 64, 113, 124
  organization 116, 124, 139–140
  struggle 115
  theory 84–85
  violence 220
Ponder, Erwin 240
POPcorn Kidz 248
"post-pandemic" 2022 230
poverty 30, 137
Powell, Adam Clayton 14
practice making 193
Princeton graduate school 101
prison for embezzlement 44
Pritchett, Forrest 240
protesting 159, 184, 219, 240, 255
public aftermath 176
public criticism 48
public high schools 30
Public Interest Research Groups (PIRGs) 111
public policy 60
public schools 1, 52, 57, 61–62, 151, 199
public secondary schools 50, 52
Pugh, Michael 235

Quality in Education Act (QEA) 151

race/racial/racists 10, 13, 28, 68–69, 76, 87, 127, 150, 189
  analysis 119
  condescension 254
  economic underpinnings of 85
  groups 93
  ideas and practices 54
  Italian 30
  victims of 222–223
  violence 143
radical/radicalism 75
  expression 230
  groups 192
  segregation 85
Rainbow Coalition 142, 144, 149, 152
Ramsey, Nello 173–174
Reagan, Ronald 114–115, 125, 127, 129, 131, 135, 137, 150
rebellions 20–21
Redden, John 64
Reid, Jerame 182, 196–197, 247
Reid, Shelia 182, 197, 247
relationship 8
religious/religion 15
  conflict 15
  contradictions 158
  groups 190
revolution 81
Rice, Tamir 236
Richardson, George C 61
Riley, George 94, 111
Riley, Joyce 114, 135
Ringold, Brad 160
riot 20
Rippey, Brandon 192
Roaring Valley Track and Field Camping 27
Robeson, Paul 82–83, 161, 190
Rodino, Peter W. 230
Rodney, Walter 82

Index

Rosenstein, Hettie 236
Rountree, L. 200, 207
Rudolph, Sarah Collins 264
Russell, Timothy 224
Rutherford, Wiliam 133
Rutledge, James 236
Ryerson 13, 22

sacrifices 199
Sadaukai, Owusu 75–76
Sanders, Bernie 225–226, 228, 252, 263
Sanders campaign 225–226, 228
Sanders, Henry "Hook" 138
Sanders, James 236
Saunders, Don 114
scholarship 72
schools 13
  communities 57
  curriculum 49–50
  system 32
Schwartz, Patty 176
Scott, Leslie 229
self-reliance 234
sensationalism 58
sense of satisfaction 55–56
sentencing 179–180
Service Employees International Union 181
Sharpton, Al 128
Shelby vs Holder 137
Sherman, W. 212
Shoiket, Henry 219, 247
Shoiket, Mary 192
Simadiris, Marcella 160, 248
Simmons, Allen 229
Simms, James 160
Sistah Souljah 138, 149, 153. *See also* Lisa, Williamson

Smith, Brian 18, 76
Smith, John 20
Smith, Thomas 182
Smith, Tommie 26
Smith, Victor Louis 236
social change 83, 139–140
  desire and design for 116
socialism 86, 226
social justice 100
social media 228–229
social movements 57, 86
social system 55
social transformation 116
socio-economic system 84
Sokudela, Nomazizi 133
Soul music 11
South Africa 148
  apartheid 115
Southern Christian Leadership Conference 38
Spath, Gary 149
speech 256
Spellman, Eloise 236
Stanley, Craig 214
starting-line blues 28
Steed, Connie 120
Steed, Ed 116, 118
Stevens, Thaddeus 210, 212
Stewart, Judith 200
St. Michael's Chapel 142
St. Michael's Hospital 10
Stone, Chuck 52
structural change 119, 198
Student Nonviolent Coordinating Committee 39
students 67, 95, 253–254
  civil rights movement 91
  demands 51–52, 61
suburban school districts 151

Sullivan Principles 257
symbolism 49
system of governance 167

Taliaferro, Richard 236
Taylor, Breonna 220, 223, 236
Taylor, George Edwin 127
Taylor, Richard 132
Taylor, Stanley 71
teachers 11–12, 49, 52
Tema, Elia 130
testimonies 177
Thomas, Glenn 59–61
Thompson, Eugene 130
Thoreau, H. 32
Till, Emmett 183, 188
Titus, Franklin 59, 203
Tortorella, Anthony 181
Toto, Frederick 236
Touré, Sékou 84
transformative movement 189
Treat, Robert 48, 206, 214
Troutman, Darlene 223
Trump, Donald 106–107, 214–215, 225, 234
Tse-Tung, Mao 83
Tubman, Harriet 48, 210, 214, 268
Tucker, Donald 143, 160
Tucker, Doug 192
Turco, Louis M. 47, 65, 68
Ture, Kwame 82
Turner, Albert 138
Turner, Evelyn 138
Tutu, Desmond 133

United Community Corporation 59
Universal Negro Improvement Association (UNIA) 2–3

Vailsburg High School 34, 67, 69
Valentin, Rafael 176
victimization 50
Vietnam War 19, 32–33
Villani, Ralph 71
violence 19, 152–153, 155–157
    drug- and gang-oriented 145
vocational technical schools 53
volunteer organizations 231
Voting Rights Act 136–138
voting rights demonstration 138

Washington, Harold 128
WBAI 173
WBAI-FM 173
Weaver, Mary 247
Weaver, Randy 247
Weequahic High School 28
Westbrooks, Dennis 52, 63, 70, 73–74
West, Cornel 109, 149
West Kinney Junior High School 22
Westmoreland, William 90
West Side Park 23
white administrators 47
White, Jimmy 60
Whitman, Christine 157
Wilkins, Roy 62
Williams, Aminifu 160
Williams, Earl 105
Williams, Hosea 38
Williams, Junius 78, 122
Williams, Malissa 224
Williams, Nat 160
Williamson, Lisa 133, 156. *See also* Sistah Souljah
Williams, Sagirah 183
Wilmington 10 88, 135

Index

Wilson, Leroy III 240
Women in Support of the Million Man March (WISOMMM, Inc) 159
Woodson, Carter G. 212
Woodson, Condell 169
Working for Councilman Westbrooks 70
Wright, Fred 177
Wright, Nathan 62

X, Malcolm 14, 31, 48, 55–56, 70, 75–76, 85, 122, 163, 168, 194, 214, 236, 244, 246, 261

Young, Andrew 38–39
Young Communist League 192

Zambrana, Fernando 41–42, 47–48, 60
Zangari, James 140